WINDOWS 98

Second edition

Bernard Frala

CASSELL&CO

First published, revised and adapted, in the United Kingdom in 2000 by Hachette UK

English translation by Prose Unlimited
Concept and editorial direction: Ghéorghïi Vladimirovitch Grigorieff
Additional research and editorial assistance: Stuart Bell, Derek Atkins, Jane Eady, Johan Rinchard and John Cardinal.

A CIP catalogue for this book is available from the British Library

ISBN 1 84202 039 0

Designed by Graph'M
Layout by Bernard Fabrot and Chouka
Typeset in Humanist 521
Printed and bound by Graficas Estella, Spain

Hachette UK
Cassell & Co
The Orion Publishing Group
Wellington House
London
WC2R 0BB

Web site: www.marabout.com/Cassell

Contents

How to use this book ?

Welcome to this visual guide. It explains how to carry out some one hundred or so operations, ranging from the simple to the more complex, in a clear and methodical manner. The book is divided into thematic chapters, which are in turn divided into sections. Each section deals with a separate topic and explains its many facets and uses, as well as detailing all related commands.

The orange 'Checklist' bookmarks that appear throughout the book contain lists of the procedures you must follow in order to complete a given task successfully. The accompanying screen shots have arrows pointing to certain parts of the screen. When the points in the checklists are numbered, they correspond directly with these numbered green arrows. When the points in the bookmarks bear letters they do not relate directly to the arrows, but simply provide additional useful information. When the arrows pointing to the screen are orange they give information on a particular feature, whilst the red arrows alert you of a possible danger, such as a button to avoid pressing at all costs!

In addition to illustrations of relevant screen shots as they should appear if instructions have been followed correctly, the Screen Shots series also features 'Tips' boxes and 'light-bulb' features that will help you get the most out of Windows 98. There are often two ways of doing things in Windows and shortcut keys are useful ways of saving time for frequently used commands. The 'Tips' boxes give these handy time-saving hints, while the light-bulb features provide additional information by presenting an associated command, option or a particular type of use for the command. Finally, to reassure you that you are on the right path, flow charts summarising the screens through which you have just worked, appear at intervals throughout the book.

Happy reading

Windows 98 and Windows 98 second edition

This book deals with both Windows 98 and the later version called Windows 98 second edition, though in most instances we simply refer to it as Windows 98. Windows 98 is the updated version of Microsoft's Windows 95 operating system. An operating system is the most important piece of software, or program, installed in your computer. It controls the other programs and therefore enables you to tell the computer what to do. You therefore need to become familiar with the operating system commands that let you use your computer: launching a program, copying files, shutting down the computer, installing new programs and so on.

Before Windows came on the scene, the only way to make a microcomputer's operating system work was by entering a series of commands using a precise syntax: a lot of people were put off by this very user-unfriendly approach. However, now, everything has changed and we have a very visual user interface (the link between you and the computer) which is very easy to use.

You make Windows 98 work by using a mouse to click on an icon (a pictorial symbol) or window. To get rid of a file, you just drag its icon to the *Recycle Bin*! No more commands to type in to start a program: a double-click (two quick clicks in succession) with the mouse does it all.

As you'll find from this book, running and using an operating system like Windows 98 means that you'll never (well, hardly ever) have to key in long, hard-to-remember command lines. Also, Windows 98 handles your entire system, including all the peripherals (additional devices) you connect to it. As soon as you power-up, Windows 98 will detect any new devices (monitor, modem, video card) and install the right programs (drivers) to run them. All you have to do is actually plug them into your computer. As you'll see, Windows 98 is packed with new tools, wizards and features to speed up your work and make it as straightforward as possible.

What's new in Windows 98 second edition ?

The second edition of Windows 98 is virtual identical to the previous version. The changes in this version are important nonetheless as they have fixed bugs and Y2K problems. This edition moreover includes new versions of additional programs for the Internet, games and multimedia files (including the famous MP3). More specifically:

Internet Explorer 5
The Web browser is now faster, more reliable and features a button for listening to radio stations throughout the world.

Outlook Express 5
The e-mail and newsgroup software is now fully customisable and includes a button for direct connection to Hotmail.

NetMeeting 3
The audio and tele-(video)conferencing software.

DirectX 6.1
The multimedia system foundation for Windows that packs more power for games.

Media Player 6.4
The multimedia player not only for Web multimedia files but for files from different sources.

Furthermore, Windows 98 makes it easy to create a local area network at home using one or more old computers, with a single Internet connection and a single modem, to surf from multiple computers.

Finally, as with every new edition, Windows contains dozens (indeed hundreds) of new drivers. They essentially include the new USB (for modems) and FireWire drivers (for digital video and still cameras). And this version uses the full capabilities of the Pentium III processor.

Chapter 1

Getting started

Starting up Windows 98

We described Windows 98 as an operating system; you can see the truth of that statement as soon as you switch on your computer. Following a quick check for defective components performed by the program resident in the computer's **ROM** memory (the **BIOS**), Windows 98 takes over and displays the *Starting Windows 98* screen. It begins by loading a few startup files which the computer needs to run properly. Then it checks that all devices — keyboard, screen, printer, modem — are properly connected. While all this is going on, your screen will display the logo and name of the operating system. This may seem to take a long time, but Windows 98 is actually very busy searching for the various hardware devices and getting them operational for you to use. After this first sequence, you'll see command lines from the startup files *Config.sys* and *Autoexec.bat* scroll down the screen. These are still there to let you run MS-DOS applications. Windows 98 finishes off by loading in a series of other files — drivers and managers — that you need to run the connected devices properly. Once you see the mouse pointer, a few icons scattered around your desktop and a bar running along the bottom of the screen, you can breathe a sigh of relief. It means Windows 98 has loaded with no problems and you're ready to start work.

HOW TO

When Windows first starts up, it displays a Welcome to Windows dialogue box. To close it and have your desktop looking something like the figure below (the background picture and the positions of the icons may vary), click on the close button marked with an X in the top right corner of the dialogue box. Windows 98 will ask if you want to show this box again the next time you start up. Click on the Yes box if you do, or No if you don't.

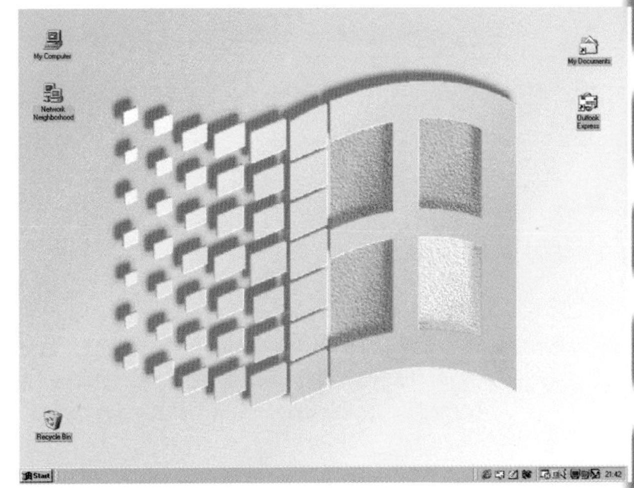

TIP

Don't touch the keyboard while the computer is starting up. Some of the keys (F8 in particular) will call up a special startup menu in text mode starting with the title Microsoft Windows 98 Startup Menu. If you do see this, just press the "1" key to select normal startup, then press the Return key to restart the bootup procedure.

Starting up Windows 98 for the first time

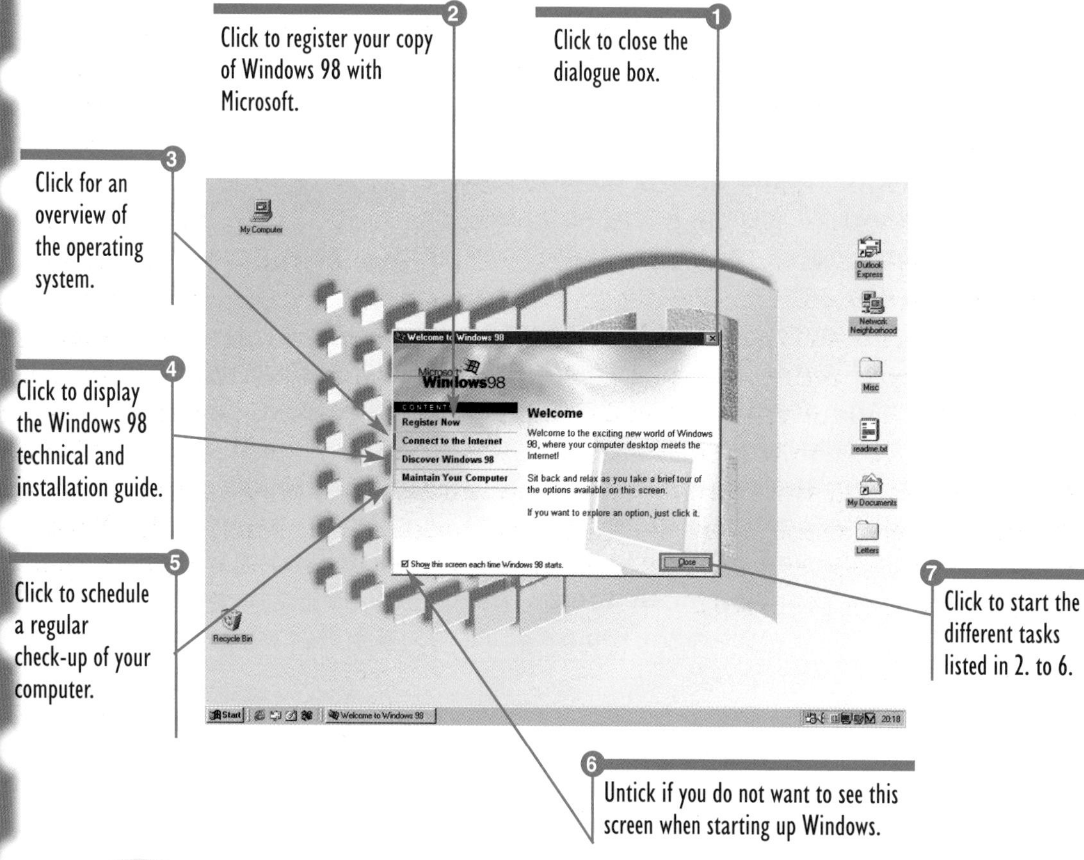

A Click on the X button. Windows 98 asks if you want to show this dialogue box next time you start up. Click on *Yes* or *No* depending on whether you want to see this box next time you turn on your computer.

B Click on one of the titles for a tour of the features, or click *Close*.

During startup, the screen will display the Microsoft logo and the program name. This file is called Logo.sys and is in the root directory. You can use a drafting package to edit it and alter the contents or replace it with a different image. Make sure you keep a copy of the original file and give the new file the name Logo.sys. The shutdown screens are in files named Logos.sys and Logow.sys. You can change them or substitute new images too.

The Windows 98 desktop

Every time you start up your computer, you'll see the Windows 98 desktop on your screen. It is a workspace on which you'll see a series of little pictures (or icons) and a horizontal bar with a button marked *Start* on it. We call the desktop a workspace because you can get to all your programs from it. You can also put documents on it — a letter, fax to send, image or memo. You can change the colour and appearance of your desktop (see *Control Panel*); Windows 98 comes with a set of patterns that you can use as the background of your workspace. You might have more or fewer icons on your desktop depending on the options you chose when installing Windows. Some of them are essential and will always be there. The *My Computer* icon gives you quick access to all your system's disk drives, the programs to personalise it (*Control panel*), and your printers. You use *Inbox* to send and receive messages over a local area network or on-line service. The *Recycle Bin*, as its name suggests, is the 'wastepaper basket' where you dump files you no longer want. You cannot remove the *Recycle Bin* or any of the other icons mentioned from your Desktop; all you can do is shift them around. A horizontal bar, called the *Taskbar*, contains a button labelled *Start*. This lets you start up different programs installed on your computer's hard disk. Click on it to display a main menu with at least nine headings or commands. These commands let you carry out all routine tasks. Windows 98 also gives you a toolbar where you can put icons which are shortcuts to frequently used programs.

TIP

Over time, your desktop may well get cluttered up with windows and dialogue boxes. Some windows may hide your desktop altogether so you cannot see it any more. You can use a keyboard shortcut to minimise all your open windows quickly and see your entire desktop: press the Windows and D keys together. The Windows key is the one with the Windows logo on it.

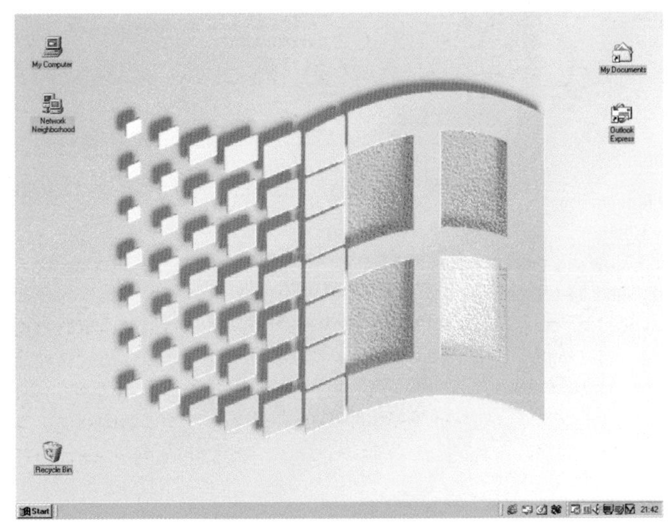

Windows 98 desktop

The icons on the desktop when Windows 98 starts up. A rapid double-click on any icon opens a new window.

1 My Computer is open. This is a window displaying, among other things, icons which represent all the disk drives on your system. To close this window, click on the X button in the top right corner.

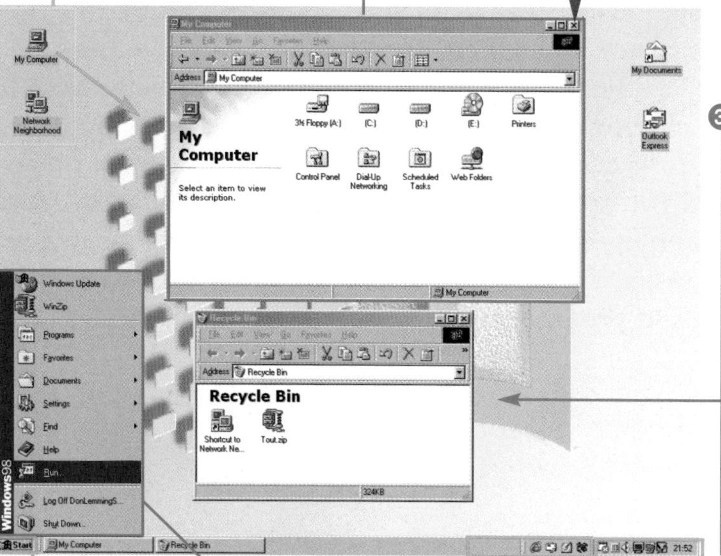

3 The Recycle Bin contains all the files you don't want any more and have deleted. The contents of the Recycle Bin are also displayed in a window, which you can close by clicking on the X button.

The Windows 98 taskbar and its Start button. Clicking on the button displays a menu of at least nine commands.

2 From the Start button, you can run all routine tasks. To hide the menu, click once on any blank part of the desktop, avoiding all icons.

You can personalise the taskbar to give you access to your most frequently-used programs.

Windows 98 displays the time on the taskbar. The other symbols show all the programs loaded into memory when Windows 98 starts up.

A A double mouse-click (two clicks in quick succession) opens the window of *My Computer* or *Recycle Bin*, as appropriate.

B Click once on the *Start* button to display the menu of commands.

C Click once on the *X* button to close an open window.

D Click on the desktop (away from the menu and any other object) or press *Esc* to close the *Start* menu.

••••• ***Hint*** •••••

You can change the appearance and colour of the desktop to suit you. To do that, go to Control Panel (see Chapter 04) and click on Display.

The taskbar

By default, Windows 98 puts the taskbar across the bottom edge of your screen. Keep it in sight — you'll find it's very important. It has the *Start* button which, if you click it, brings up a menu with nine or more commands. You'll notice a black arrow to the right of the first five commands. This means that clicking on it will display a submenu. The *Programs* command gives you access to all the programs installed on your computer, and any new ones you put on. Click on *Programs* to bring up the first submenu. Drag the mouse pointer onto *Accessories* to bring up a new submenu. Finish by clicking on *Notepad* to bring up the mini word processor that comes free with Windows 98. The other *Start* menu commands work the same way, apart from *Help, Run, Log Off* and *Shut Down,* where one mouse click will run the *Windows 98 help program* or display a dialogue box. The taskbar also has a series of buttons showing all the programs loaded into memory (open programs). We'll see in the next chapter how you can run several programs at a time under Windows 98. You can call them up or clear them from the screen one after the other from the taskbar just by clicking on the button for the program you want to use.

HOW TO

You can put the taskbar on the bottom, top, left or right of the screen. To move it to the top of the screen, for example: click on the bar (avoiding all of the buttons) and hold the mouse button down. Drag the mouse pointer to the top of the screen, keeping the mouse button held down; you'll see a horizontal line following the pointer. When that line is placed horizontally on the top of the screen, let go of the mouse button to see the taskbar displayed in its new place.

TIP

As well as the Start button, the taskbar contains buttons showing all the applications loaded into RAM. Here, Paint Shop Pro, the music CD player, My Computer, and Recycle Bin are all running. But only My Computer is visible on the screen. Windows 98 tells you this by showing its button recessed on the taskbar. The other applications are minimised to buttons on the taskbar.

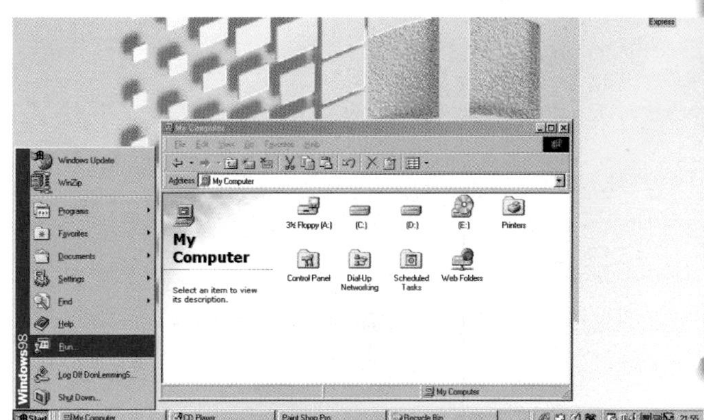

Within *Start*:

The *Windows Update* menu runs Internet Explorer and connects to the Microsoft website to automatically update the operating system.

The *Programs* menu lets you run any of the applications installed on your computer's disk drives.

The *Favorites* menu contains short cuts that let you easily reach websites that you have found interesting.

The *Documents* menu lists recently opened documents.

The *Settings* menu brings up a submenu from which you can get to the *Control Panel*, printers or the taskbar.

The *Find* menu gives you various options, including searching for files on your hard disk.

The *Help* menu runs the Windows 98 help program.

The *Run* menu brings up a dialogue box that lets you run certain programs.

The *Shut Down* menu displays a dialogue box to shut down the computer properly.

The taskbar

The *Log Off* menu is used to end a session for a user connected to a network. You will only see this menu if your computer is networked with other computers.

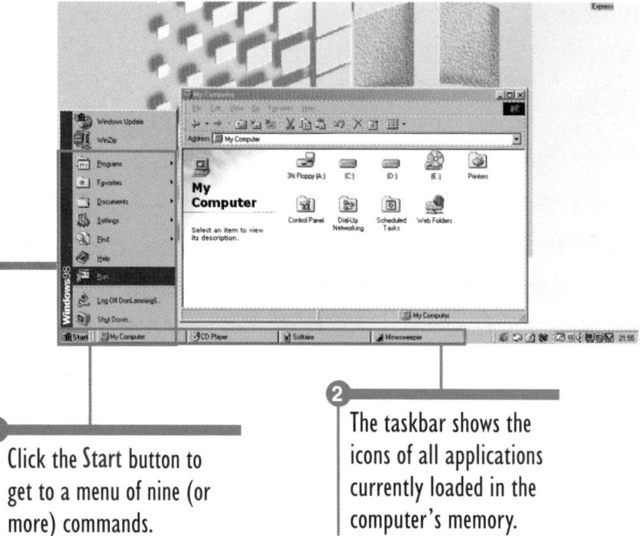

1 Click the Start button to get to a menu of nine (or more) commands.

2 The taskbar shows the icons of all applications currently loaded in the computer's memory.

You can change the taskbar properties by right-clicking (clicking with the mouse's right-hand button) on a blank area of the bar to bring up a context (or pop-up) menu. Drag the mouse pointer onto the Properties command for Windows 98 to highlight the name. Click to bring up a Taskbar Properties dialogue box. Another way is to click the Start button, then Settings, and finally Taskbar and the Start menu.

Checklist

1 The **Start** button menus have a black arrow alongside.

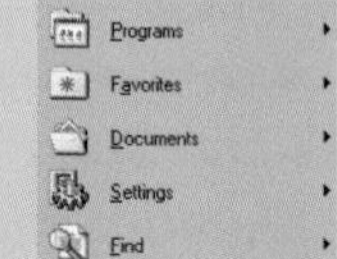

Clicking on an arrow brings up a submenu with new commands. Commands without a black arrow (like ***Help*** and ***Run***) will run immediately you click them: the former loads a help program while the latter brings up a dialogue box on screen.

2 The buttons housed on the taskbar show which programs are currently running. To display a program, simply click on its button. The recessed button is always the program that is currently open — the one your cursor is on. To hide the window, simply click on the same button again.

Starting or closing a program

The point of a computer is to run software applications: a word processor to write letters, a DTP package to lay out the pages of a book, a spreadsheet to compile statistics, etc. Windows 98 is there to help you run all your applications as quickly and painlessly as possible.

Step 1: when you install an application under Windows 98, a folder name and application name are automatically placed in the *Start* menu. You can see this with the *Notepad* application (a simple word processor), which Windows 98 has installed in the *Accessories* folder with the unsurprising name of *Notepad*.

Step 2: Windows 98 gives you access to all your applications via the *Start* menu and the *Programs* command. You can check that by clicking on the taskbar button, then on *Programs*. You'll see a list of folder names and the names of the various applications installed.

Step 3: Windows 98 brings up a dialogue box in which you can enter the command line which will run the application. This is the same line you would have entered when working under MS-DOS. Obviously, if you don't know exactly where the application is located, it will be far easier to use the submenu in the *Programs* command. However, to install new software, you can quickly type in *A:install* or *A:setup* in the dialogue box and then confirm by clicking on the *OK* button.

HOW TO

You can run software installation procedures via the Run dialogue box. In most cases the procedure will be called Install or Setup, and will run from the floppy disk drive (usually A:) or the CD-Rom drive (usually D:). For software on diskettes, type in A:install or A:setup. For software on CD-Roms, type in D:install or D:setup.

TIP

Windows 98 lets you introduce paths to all your programs in a Quick Launch toolbar. To display it in the taskbar, right-click and select the Toolbars/Quick Launch command in the pop-up menu. To run an application quickly, simply click on its icon in the toolbar.

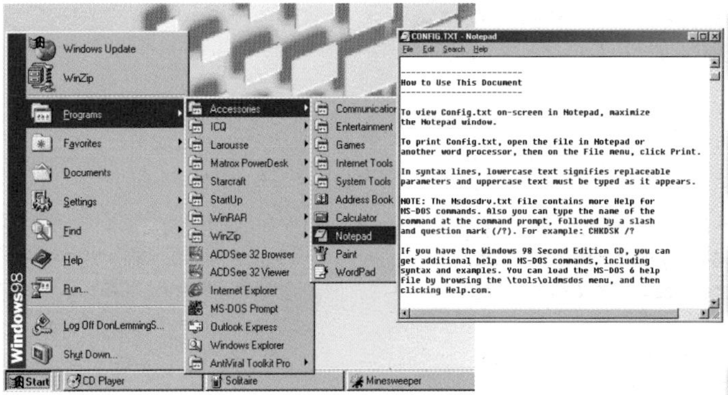

Running Notepad

Start/Programs/Accessories/Notepad

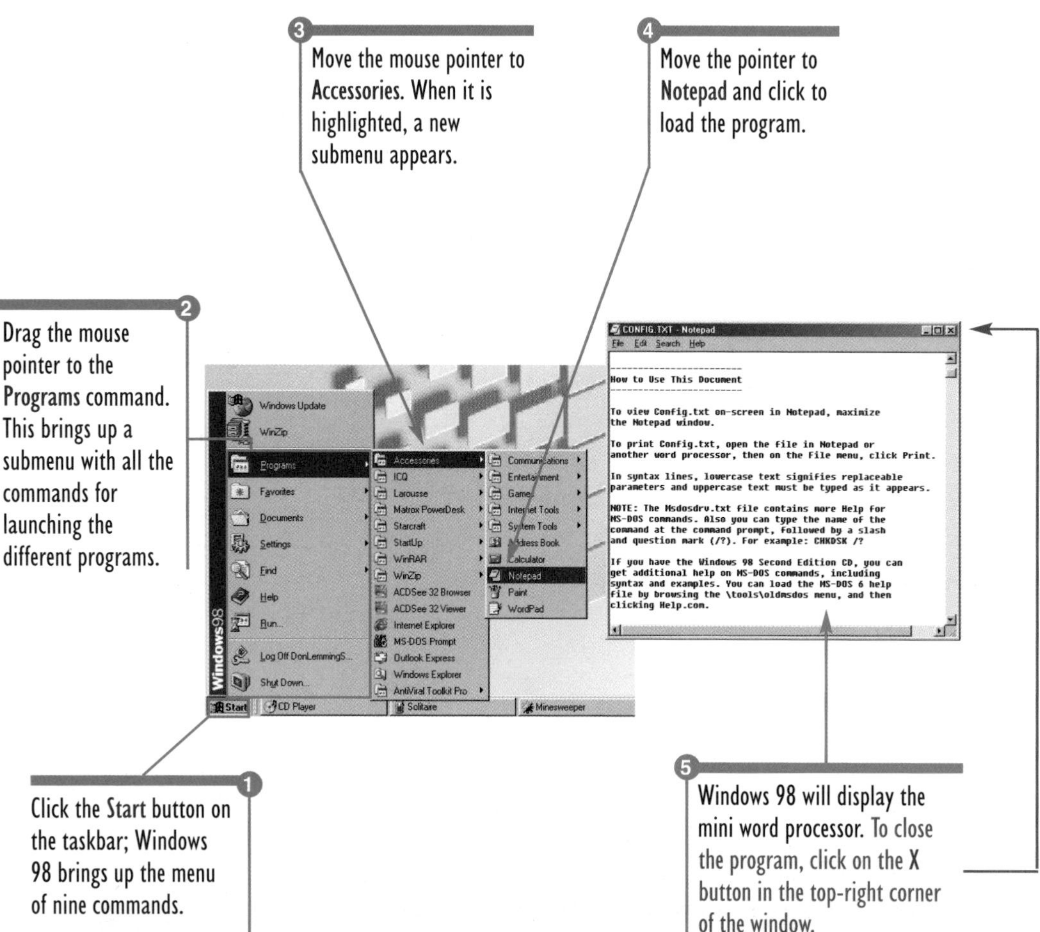

1 Click the Start button on the taskbar; Windows 98 brings up the menu of nine commands.
2 Drag the mouse pointer to the Programs command. This brings up a submenu with all the commands for launching the different programs.
3 Move the mouse pointer to Accessories. When it is highlighted, a new submenu appears.
4 Move the pointer to Notepad and click to load the program.
5 Windows 98 will display the mini word processor. To close the program, click on the X button in the top-right corner of the window.

Programs are often grouped together in folders. The Notepad word processing program is part of the Accessories folder. To run it from the Start button, you must go through the Programs command, then the Accessories folder. Once in the Accessories submenu, a single click on Notepad will start the program.

••••• ***Note*** •••••

A folder is like a drawer in which you can store documents or entire programs. In this particular case, the folder is a group of different programs, one of which is Notepad.

Running a program

Start/Run

The Run dialogue box lets you enter the command line needed to run a program. Notepad's application file, for example, is Notepad.exe, which you'll find in the Windows 98 installation folder (usually just called Windows), so you can enter the command string *\Windows\Notepad* in the Open text box.

Click on the OK button to run the command and load Notepad.

The Quick Launch toolbar houses short cuts to all your most-used programs. A simple click on the icon representing the program will start it. To display the Quick Launch toolbar, right-click on the taskbar and select the Toolbars/Quick Launch command.

2 Drag the mouse pointer to the Run command and click when the word is highlighted. This displays the Run dialogue box on the screen.

3 Windows 98's default is to put the cursor in the Open text box. If you can't see it, simply click with the mouse pointer in this box. Type in the name of the file which runs the program.

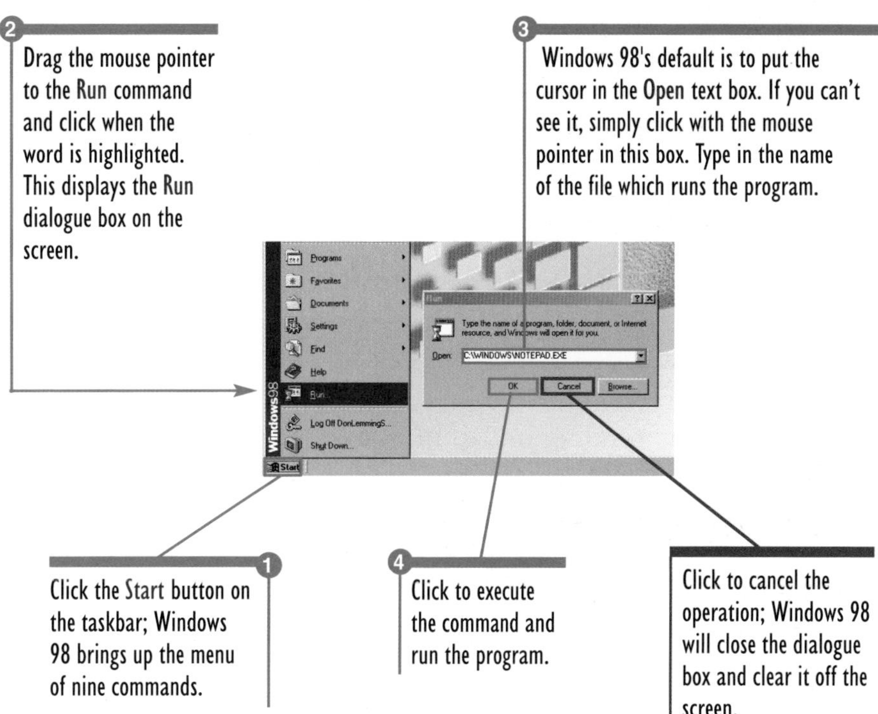

1 Click the Start button on the taskbar; Windows 98 brings up the menu of nine commands.

4 Click to execute the command and run the program.

Click to cancel the operation; Windows 98 will close the dialogue box and clear it off the screen.

Windows 98 keeps the last command strings entered in the dialogue box text area. To get back to them easily and save having to re-enter them, click on the downwards arrow at the far right of the box. Windows 98 displays a list of command lines, so all you need do is click on the line you want to see displayed in the Open box.

Quitting Windows 98

Under the **MS-DOS** operating system, once you had closed a program and returned to the C:> prompt, you could turn off the computer. You can't really do that with Windows 98; you must tell the system that you want to stop using the computer. Why? Remember, when it starts up, Windows 98 has to check all the peripherals connected to the system, referring to the registry (the heart of Windows 98). It makes the same checks when it shuts down. So if you turn off the power suddenly, you could well damage the registry information, and some devices might not be recognised when you start up again, or Windows 98 might simply refuse to load. If the system is brought to a sudden halt, the *ScanDisk* program will automatically run the first time you restart after the crash. It runs tests which can detect problems or damage to your hard disk.

You shut down a computer running under Windows 98 by clicking the *Start* button then selecting the *Shut Down* command. The operating system displays a *Shut Down Windows* dialogue box with the *Shut down* box selected. If it isn't already selected, all you have to do is click on it. This type of button (see window below) is called a radio button. To finish shutting down, click the *OK* button. Windows 98 will ask you to wait while it carries out all its checks, and then display a message telling you it is safe to turn off your computer. Some of the newest computers power themselves off once Windows shuts down.

TIP

The other options in the *Shut Down Windows* dialogue box do not shut down the computer; you can use them to restart the computer, or to work in DOS mode (with the C: prompt).

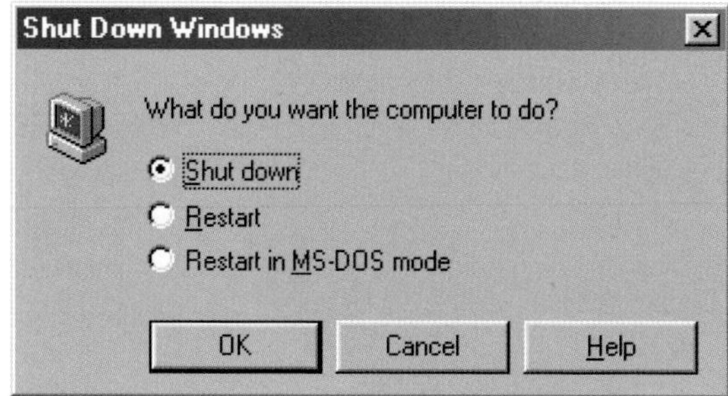

Quitting Windows 98

Start/Shut Down/Shut Down

A You must always shut down your computer by the proper procedure: Start/Shut Down and the Shut Down Windows dialogue box.

B Wait for two messages to be displayed. The first asks you to wait; the second is the one you are waiting for: it's now safe to turn off your computer.

Hint

These two messages are in files called Logow.sys and Logos.sys. You can use a drawing package to edit and personalise them, or replace them with different images. Make sure to keep a copy of the original files. Both files are in the *\Windows* folder in the operating system.

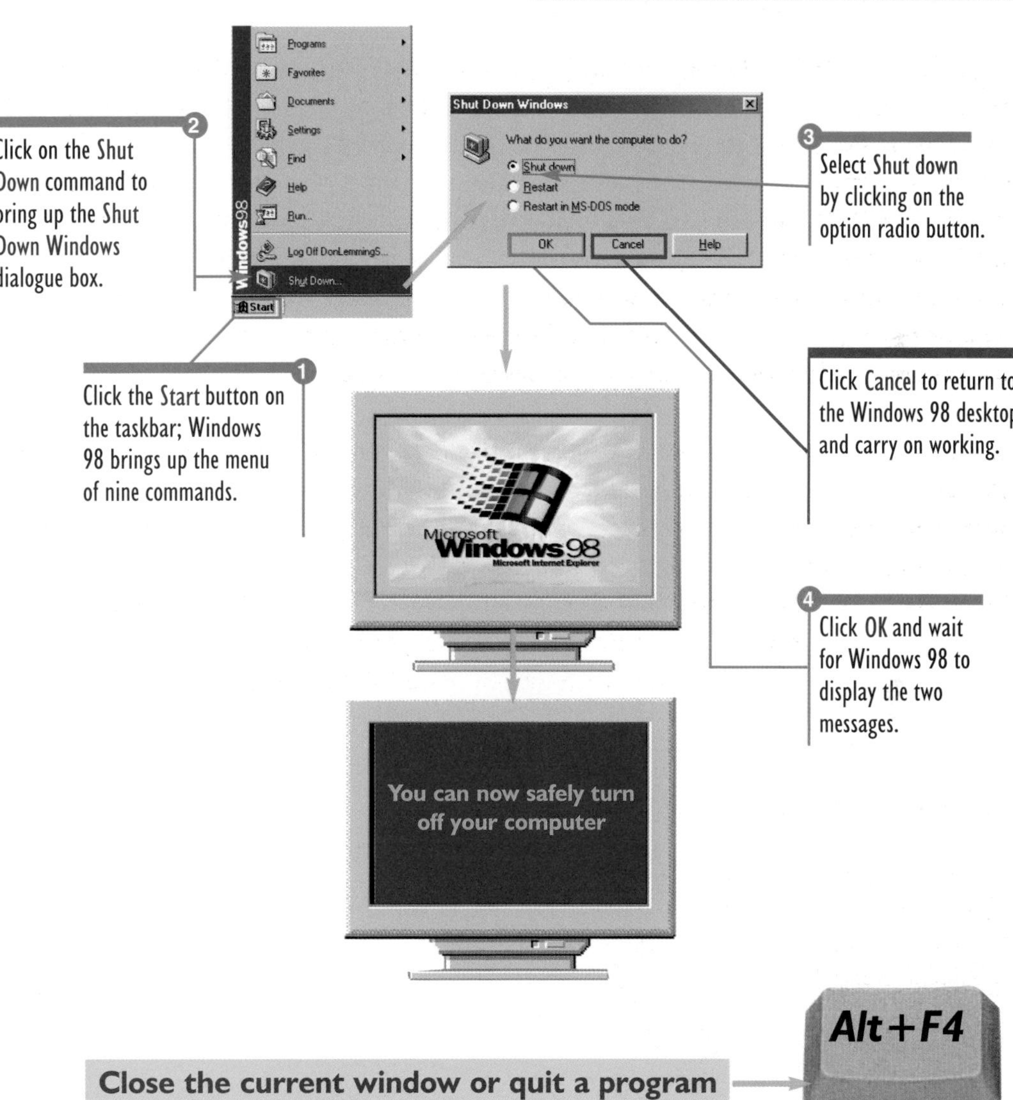

1 Click the Start button on the taskbar; Windows 98 brings up the menu of nine commands.

2 Click on the Shut Down command to bring up the Shut Down Windows dialogue box.

3 Select Shut down by clicking on the option radio button.

Click Cancel to return to the Windows 98 desktop and carry on working.

4 Click OK and wait for Windows 98 to display the two messages.

Close the current window or quit a program → **Alt+F4**

Chapter 2

Working with Windows 98

Icons, Shortcuts and Folders

Windows 98 uses a graphical interface and icons to make objects easier to handle. Icons are little pictures with properties, often with a name attached (the name of the file or object they stand for). You can move or delete them, and they run a task when you click on them with your mouse. There are different types of icon, according to how they look and what they do when you click on them. Every time you create a document in your favourite word processor, Windows 98 creates an icon to represent it. If you decide to create a new folder, Windows 98 displays an icon to stand for that. Folder icons look like miniature yellow office folders and represent directories in which you can store information such as other folders (which we call subfolders) or files. Double-clicking on a folder's icon opens a window. Programs are represented by the logo of the company that produced the software: double-clicking on it will run the program and bring it up on screen. Document icons stand for files: they can be text, sounds, images, or tables. These icons are generally what you have produced using a program. Double-clicking on a document icon usually displays the document's contents on screen. Program shortcut icons are the same as the program icon itself, except that Windows 98 puts an arrow in the bottom left corner. A program shortcut is a quick way of starting a program from a place where it is not located.

HOW TO

This is how you create any of the icons mentioned on the Windows 98 desktop:

Right-click and select the New/Folder command to create a folder icon.

Right-click and select the New/Shortcut command to create a program shortcut.

Right-click and select the **New/<file type>** command to create a document icon.

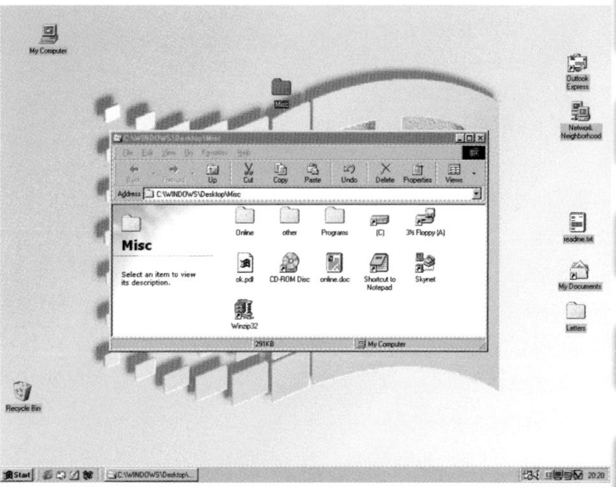

TIP

You can create an icon that stands for a file or other object elsewhere than on the desktop. You do that with the File/New command of the menu displayed in the folder or Windows Explorer.

Right-clicking brings up a context menu. Use the New command to create new icons.

Use the New/Folder command to create a new folder.

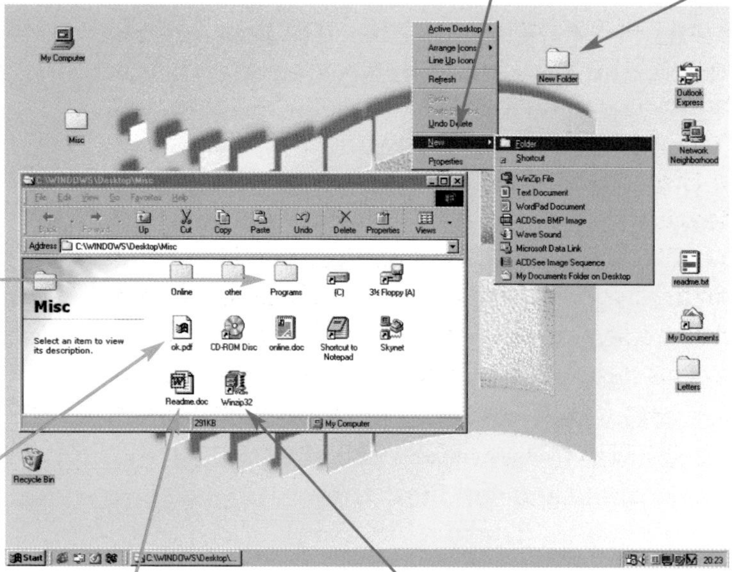

Icon for a folder contained in the Miscellaneous Programs folder.

A document icon; this one was created with the word processor, Word.

The Microsoft Word icon shows that the word processor is active. For the moment, it is minimised to its simplest form: its icon.

Shortcut to a file compression (zip) program.

Right-clicking on an icon brings up a context menu. With this, you can copy, move, rename, delete, print it or display its properties.

Working with the windows

Apart from the desktop, Windows 98 displays objects in windows. Double-clicking on the *My Computer* icon brings up a window containing other icons. Double-clicking on a program icon displays a window showing the contents of the program you have just loaded. Generally, whatever you do in Windows 98, you will be working in a window. To make things easy for users, all windows look the same and have a series of buttons. You can move windows around the desktop, make them bigger, reduce them to a taskbar button or close them. A window has several main features. The title bar identifies the program it represents and always has three buttons: to minimise, maximise and close it. Horizontal and vertical scroll bars let you scroll through the contents of the window and see any other objects which it is too small to show. A status bar gives you handy information, like the number of objects in the window or the size of the file selected. A toolbar houses different buttons which are shortcuts to the control menu commands.

HOW TO

It's easy to open a window:

Double-click on a folder icon; Windows 98 displays its contents in a window.

Double-click on a program icon; Windows 98 displays the application in a window.

Double-click on the Recycle Bin icon on the desktop; Windows 98 displays its contents in a window.

TIP

You can have multiple windows open on the desktop. With too many open, it might get cluttered, so you can reduce them or organise them using the context menu commands on the taskbar. Right-click on a blank area of the taskbar and select either Cascade, Tile or Minimise All Windows.

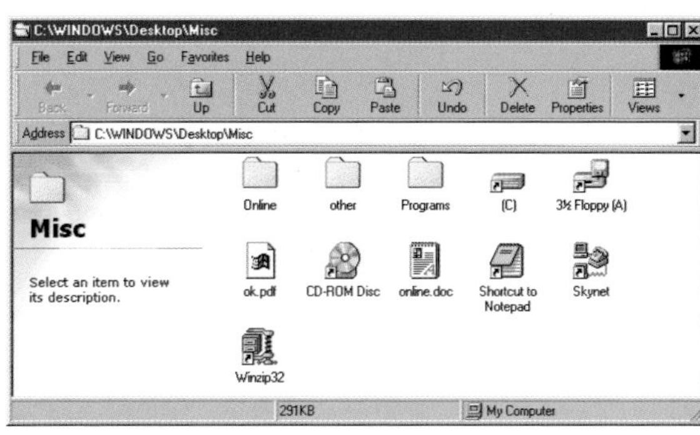

A typical window

The control menu button (sometimes called the system button) contains the commands for doing things with the window: moving, resizing, restoring, maximising and closing it.

The title bar contains the name of the program or folder.

The minimise button reduces the window to an icon sitting on the taskbar.

The maximise/restore button enlarges the window to completely fill the screen. This completely covers up the desktop. If the window is already full-size, it restores the window to its original size.

The menu bar contains different commands according to what application you are in. All windows specific to Windows 98 contain the same commands.

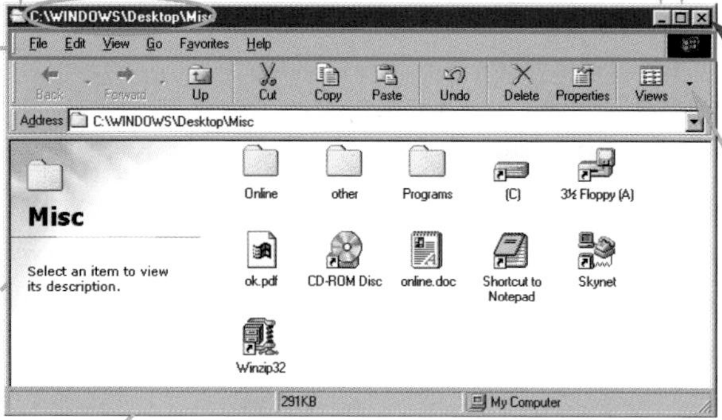

The close button will close the folder or the program. Windows 98 will remove it from the computer's memory.

What the window contains: icons, folders, an application, etc.

The toolbar houses a series of shortcuts to the control menu commands. They will differ with the type of application you are in. All windows specific to Windows 98 contain the same toolbar.

The status bar displays information about the window's contents (for folders) or the application displayed.

The status bar and toolbar might not be shown in a folder window. You can display them with the commands View/Toolbar/Standard buttons and View/Status bar.

Moving a window

You use the mouse to move a window. Left-click on the window's title bar. Move the mouse, keeping the left mouse button held down. When you let go of the mouse button, the outline box displayed by Windows 98 shows the window's new position.

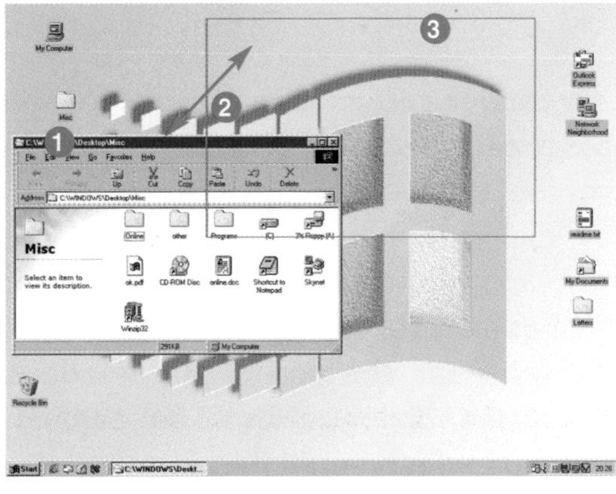

Checklist

1. Click on the window's title bar with the left mouse button, and keep it held down.
2. Still keeping the left button held down, move the mouse pointer to where you want the window to be. You'll see an outline box moving with the mouse pointer.
3. When the outline box is where you want it, take your finger of the mouse button to see the window reappear.

Resizing a window

Depending on whether you put the mouse pointer on a corner or the borders of the window, the cursor will turn into a diagonal or horizontal/vertical two-headed arrow.

You can change the height of the window by putting the pointer on the top or bottom border, and its width by putting the pointer on the left or right border.

Checklist

1. Put the mouse pointer on the top right corner of the window. Windows 98 changes the pointer into a diagonal, two-headed arrow. 

   Click on the left mouse button and hold it down.
2. Move the mouse, keeping the button held down. The outline will get bigger or smaller as you move the mouse.
3. When the box is the size you want it, let go of the mouse button and the window will be resized.

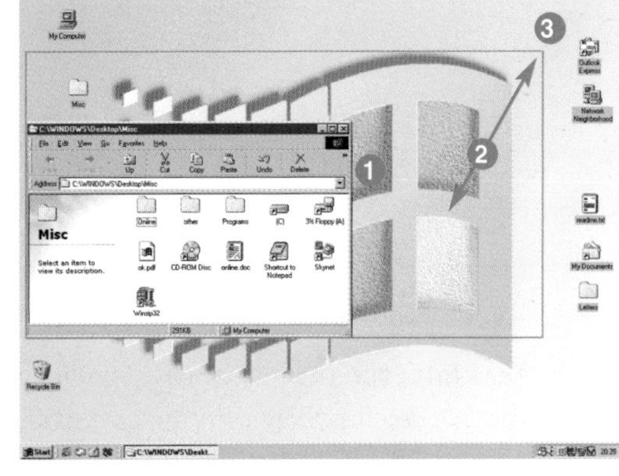

Dialogue boxes

The dialogue boxes shown on screen let you choose options, properties or settings for a particular object or aspect. Most dialogue boxes have tabs which considerably increase the number of options you can have within a single box. The *Display* dialogue box alone lets you set the properties for aspects such as the background, screen saver, appearance, various visual effects and the settings of your video card. To get to the options, just click on the relevant tab near the top of the window, and Windows 98 displays them in the same dialogue box. To confirm the options chosen, just click the *OK* button which you'll find in most dialogue boxes. Clicking the *Cancel* button lets you quit the box without making any of the changes you chose.

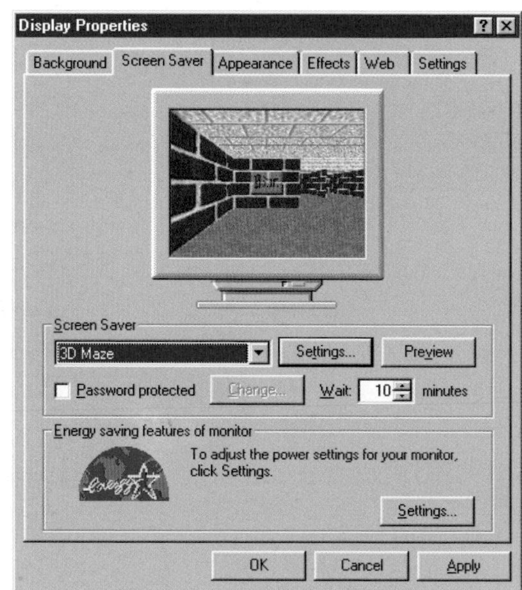

TIP

You can also close any dialogue box that has a Cancel button without making any changes by pressing the Esc key.

Dialogue boxes

Checklist

A To change the settings available in the box: click on the radio (option) buttons, click a check box, select options from lists, or type entries in a text box.

B Click on the *Apply* button to confirm the new settings and keep the dialogue box open on screen.

C Click the *OK* button to confirm the new settings and close the box.

D Click the *Cancel* button to cancel your selections and close the box. Windows 98 will keep the settings as they were before.

Click on the tab to view the options for an aspect in the dialogue box.

Windows 98 gives you a preview of the properties selected.

Click the arrow on the far right of the text box to scroll down the list. Select an option from the list to display it in the text box.

Click the button to display a new dialogue box associated with the selected item.

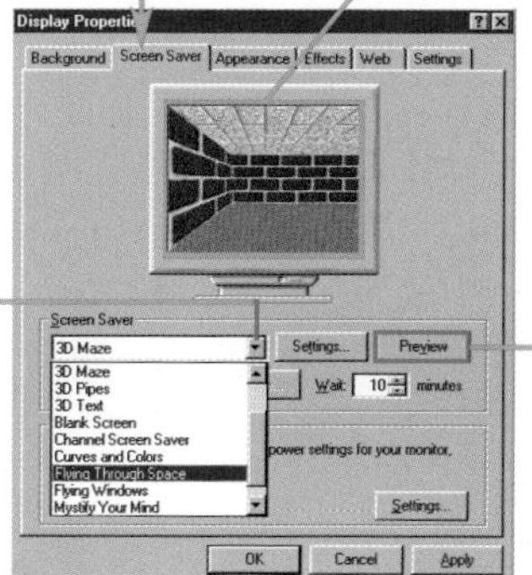

Click a radio button to select the option.

Click the box to activate the option.

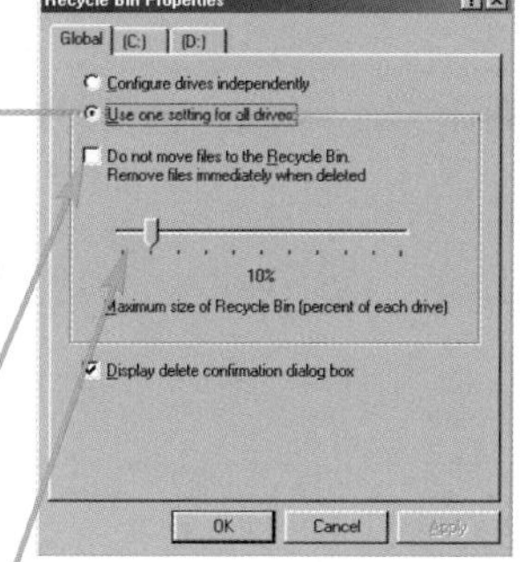

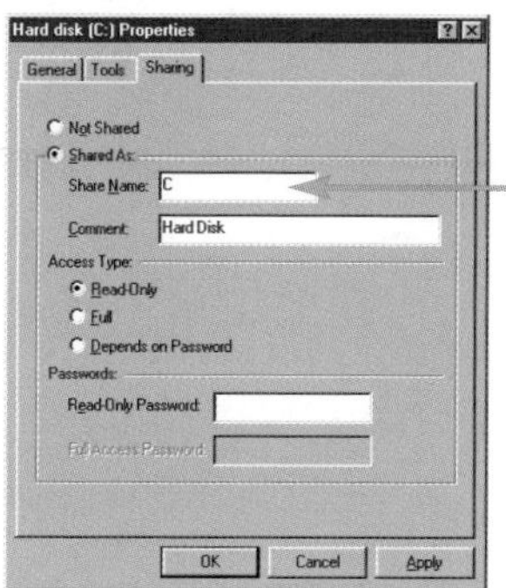

Type a value in the text box.

Click on the slider with the left mouse button; hold it down and drag to the left or right to change the option value.

All dialogue boxes have two buttons:

? gives instant information about the option selected.

X closes the dialogue box without making any of the changes selected.

Examples of dialogue box elements

List boxes

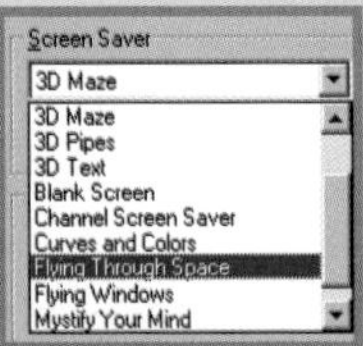

List boxes let you select an option from a preset list. Click on the arrow at the far right of the text box to scroll down a list of different items. When you select an item, Windows 98 automatically puts it in the text box and activates it. Windows 98 only takes account of the option displayed in the text box.

Radio buttons

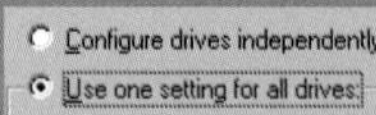

There are always two or more radio buttons; they let you choose between a set of options. Clicking on a button selects that option from the group. You can never activate two buttons in the same group.

Command buttons

Apart from the **OK**, **Cancel** and **Apply** buttons, other command buttons bring up a new dialogue box for the item named on the button.

Tabs

These display a set of options for the tab name in the same dialogue box. Actually, they simply let more options be fitted into the same dialogue box. To display the options for the tab heading, just click on the tab.

Background | Screen Saver | Appearance | Effects | Web | Settings

Slider

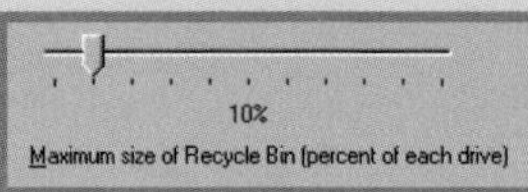

This changes values marked on a graduated scale beneath (or above). To move the sliding control and change the value, click the left button, hold the mouse button down and drag it left or right. The value will change as the control moves. When you reach the value you want, let go of the mouse button.

Text box

A text box lets you enter a numerical value or a string of characters.

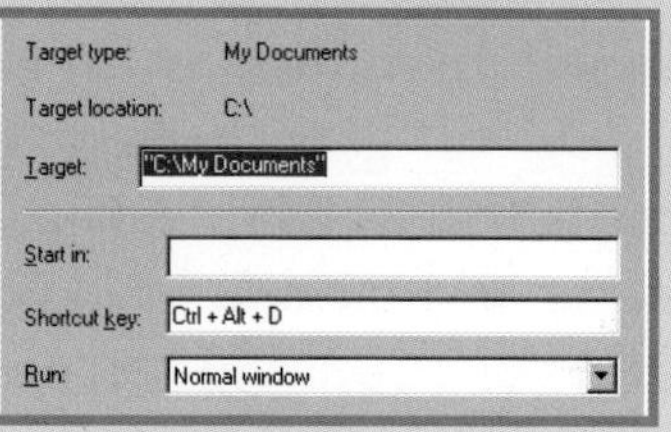

Preview

A preview gives you an idea of how the properties selected will appear without quitting the box. It saves you having to flip back and forth between the object and its dialogue box.

Checkboxes

A tick in a check box means that option is activated. To choose an option, click on the box once. Clicking on the same box again will deselect the option.

You don't need to use a mouse to activate these options. You can use keyboard combinations:

Alt + the underlined letter (see page 36's TIP): activates/deactivates the option.

Tab or Shift + Tab: scrolls through the options.

Up and Down arrow keys: selects a radio button in a group.

Space: to tick a check box or activate a command button.

F4: scrolls down a list of preset options.

Ctrl + Tab or Ctrl + Shift + Tab: scrolls through the tabs of a dialogue box.

Enter: to confirm options and close the box.

Esc: to cancel the changes made and close the box.

Command menus

Command menus are everywhere — thank goodness. They are what you use to give orders to Windows 98. The first menu you encounter is that hidden in the *Start* button. It contains nine commands that bring up a submenu or dialogue box, or run a program. All windows and applications running under Windows 98 contain a menu bar. So as not to confuse users, the operating system and software developers have tried to standardise these menus as much as possible by putting commands into related groups. So the first group on the menu is always the *File* group, containing all the file management commands (*Open*, *Close*, *Save*, *Print*). There are other types of menus, too: context menus. As their name suggests, these menus contain commands specific to the object selected. A context menu doesn't contain the names of menus, just a list of commands. The number of commands in the list varies with the object selected. Context menus are really just shortcuts to save you having to move the mouse pointer to the top of the window (which is where the menu bar usually is). The *Start* menu is a special menu, displayed when you click on the *Start* button housed on the taskbar.

TIP

All commands and menu names have at least one letter underlined. This lets you use the keyboard to run the command. All you do is press the Alt key and, at the same time, the underlined letter in the menu you want. Windows 98 exposes a drop-down list of the commands in that menu. Then press the key for the underlined letter to perform the chosen command.

HOW TO

To run a command in a menu bar:

Click on the menu name to expose a drop-down list of commands.

Drag the mouse pointer down until the command you want is highlighted.

Left-click to perform the command.

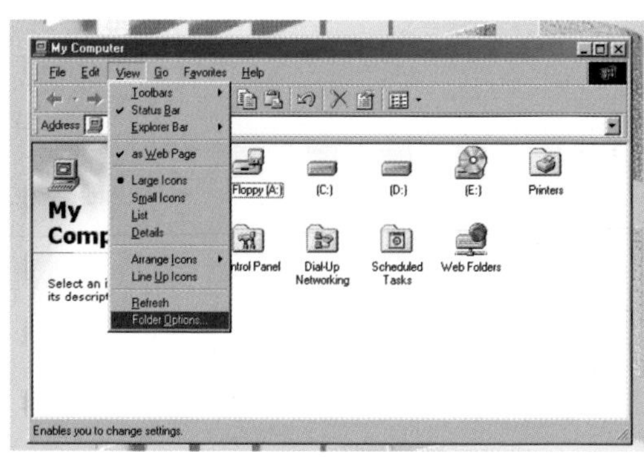

The different types of menu

A Click on the menu name that contains the command you want.

B Drag the mouse pointer to the name of the command. Windows 98 highlights it.

C Click to perform the command.

••••• ***Hint*** •••••

To get rid of a menu's command list, click on an area of the folder or desktop with no other objects on it. Even simpler: use the *Esc* key.

2 The menu bar of a folder. Click on the menu name to show a list of commands.

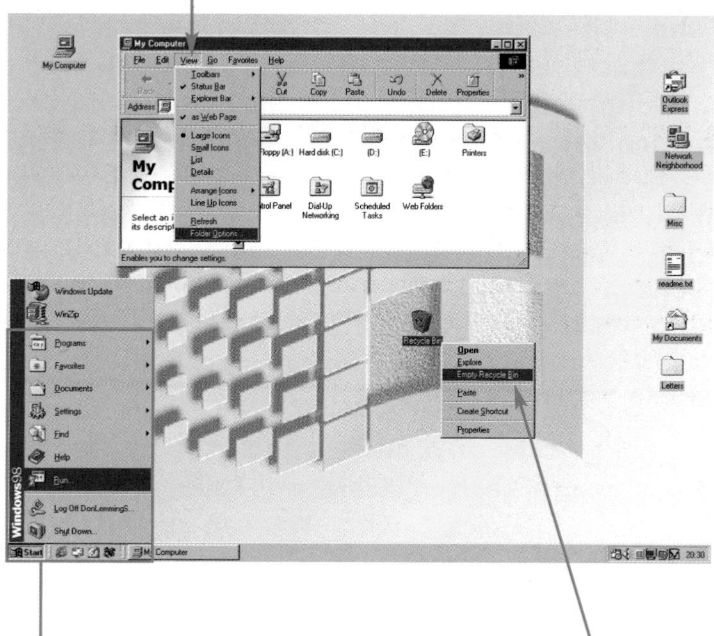

1 The Start menu pops up when you click the Start button on the taskbar.

3 The context menu for the Recycle Bin. To display it, right-click on the object. To perform a command, move the pointer to the name and click.

Toolbars

Windows 98 gives you a quick route to certain commands through toolbars. Each icon stands for a particular command on a menu. Clicking on the icon does exactly the same thing as putting the pointer on the menu name, clicking and selecting the command. Every folder and applications window has a toolbar. Obviously, not every program has the same number of icons. The default for some windows is not to display the bar, but a command like *View/Toolbar/Standard* buttons will immediately display it under the menu bar. While icons give you a fair idea of what they stand for and do, Windows 98 gives you extra assistance in the form of a help box giving a short explanation of what tasks it performs. To display it on screen, place the mouse pointer on the icon and leave it; after a few seconds, the information will pop up on-screen. Windows 98 offers two other types of toolbar: addresses and links. The address bar lets you navigate quickly to different folders or disk drives. You can also type the address of a website into it if you have an Internet connection. The links bar lets you store shortcuts to different sites, so that just clicking on an icon immediately displays the site's home page; this saves you having to type in the address.

You can also put different toolbars on the taskbar: Desktop, Links, Addresses and a toolbar called *Quick Launch*. To bring them up, just right-click on a blank area of the taskbar and select the command *Toolbars/Addresses*, *Links*, *Desktop* or *Quick Launch*. You can customise the Quick Launch toolbar by putting shortcuts to your most-used programs on it for quick access from the taskbar.

TIP

Get into the habit of using the toolbar; it's often easier to click on an icon than to click on a menu and select a command. To have the names of icons permanently displayed in the toolbar, use the command View/Toolbars/Text labels.

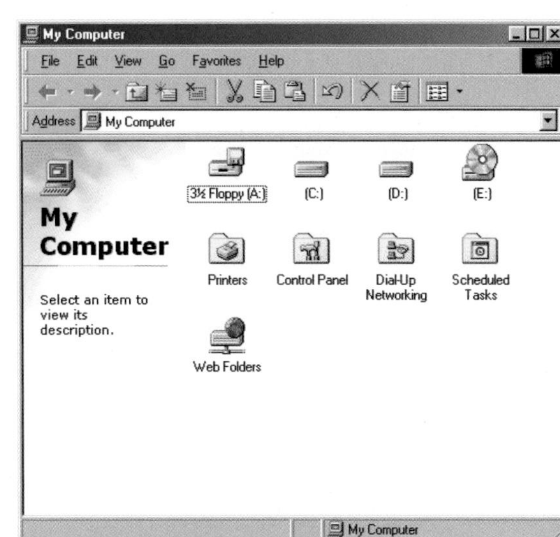

Window toolbars

A If the standard toolbar is not displayed below the menu bar, use the command *View/Toolbar/Standard buttons* — and there it is.

B Click on an icon to perform a menu command.

C Use the command *View/Toolbar/Standard buttons* again to hide the toolbar.

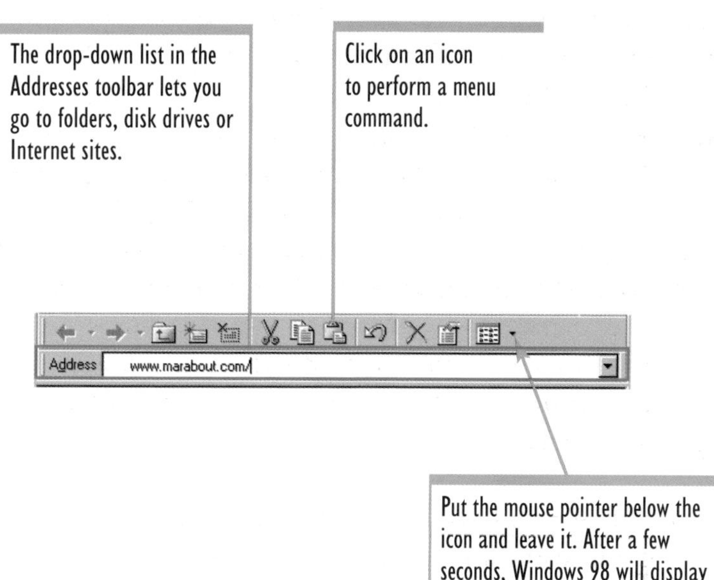

The drop-down list in the Addresses toolbar lets you go to folders, disk drives or Internet sites.
Click on an icon to perform a menu command.
Address
www.marabout.com/
Put the mouse pointer below the icon and leave it. After a few seconds, Windows 98 will display a help box telling you what function it performs.

Taskbar Quick Launch toolbar

Click on a program icon to launch it immediately from the Quick Launch toolbar.

Toolbar icons

www.marabout.com/

F4

The drop-down list in the *Address* toolbar is a very quick route to the different folders on a hard disk. Click on the arrow on the far right of the text box to display a list of your system's drives and the current folder. Select a different drive name and Windows 98 will display its folders in a window. You can also enter an Internet address in this text box, confirm it by pressing Enter and Windows 98 will take you directly to the Internet site.

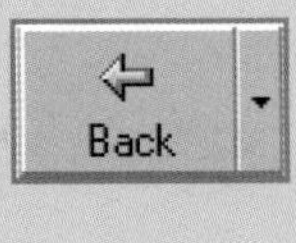

Click on this icon to display the folder or page of an Internet site previously displayed. This is an easy way to navigate between the different pages of a site.

Click on this icon to display the next folder or page of a displayed Internet site. This is an easy way to navigate between the different pages of a site.

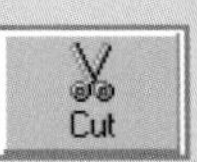

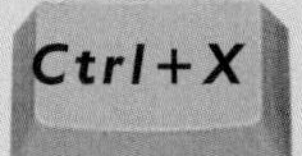

If you have selected an item, clicking on this icon moves it to the clipboard. You can then copy it to another folder or the desktop.

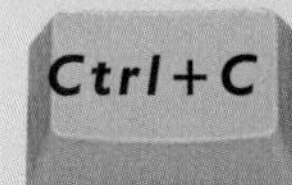

If you have selected an item, clicking on this icon copies it to the clipboard. You can then copy it to another folder or the desktop.

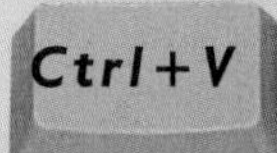

Clicking on this icon copies to the desired place whatever has been moved to the clipboard using *Copy* or *Cut*.

Clicking on this icon displays the contents of the folder one level up. You can use this to navigate through your disk's contents right back up to the desktop.

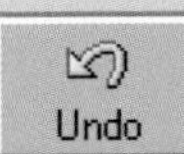

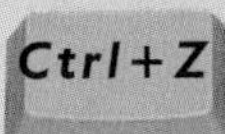

This icon undoes the last operation you performed. If you deleted something by mistake, click on the icon immediately to restore it.

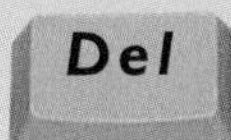

Clicking on this icon deletes a selected item, but doesn't move it to the clipboard. You can always restore it with the *Undo* button.

Windows 98 keeps track of all the operations you perform, so if you rename and then delete a file, you can always recover it by clicking first on the Undo icon, and then restore its previous name by clicking again on the same icon.

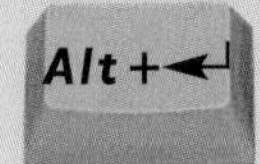

This calls up the *Properties* dialogue box for the selected item. You can then change the attributes of the object.

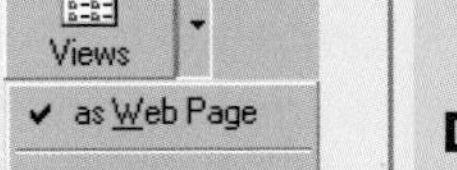

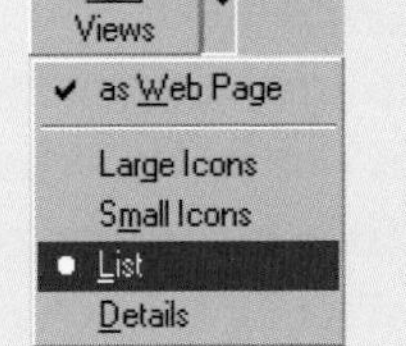

Large icons command

Displays all the files in the window with big icons.

Small icons command

Displays all the files in the window with small icons. This lets you display more files in the same amount of window space.

List command

Displays the files contained in the window in a vertical list, which lets you display more files in the same amount of window space.

Details command

Displays the files contained in the window in a vertical list, but with additional information about each one: type, total size, free space, date modified. The Details icon maximises the information that can be displayed in the window space.

My Computer

My Computer is the real information hub of Windows 98. From this window you have a bird's eye view of all the drives connected to your system: floppy drives, hard drives, CD-Rom drives, removable drives, etc. You can get to all the information stored in your computer from *My Computer*, but *My Computer* also contains four key folders: *Control Panel* (to configure Windows 98 and all the peripherals connected to your system), *Printers* (to identify and store the settings for your printers), *Dial-up Networking* (information on the settings for connecting to on-line services) and *Scheduled Tasks* (to run programs automatically at specified times). You can move easily from folder to folder and view their contents using the shortcuts offered by Windows 98. From *My Computer*, you can copy, move, rename or delete files or entire folders. You'll see later that you can also do all these things in another program that comes with Windows 98: Explorer.

TIP

To get to My Computer: minimise all the windows on your screen and double click on the My Computer icon situated on the desktop. You can also create a shortcut on the taskbar Quick Launch toolbar. To do that, click on the My Computer icon and hold the mouse button down. Move it onto the toolbar and release the button; Windows 98 will automatically put a My Computer icon on the Quick Launch toolbar. Now, you will be able to get to the My Computer window without having to close all the other windows open on your screen just by clicking on the toolbar icon.

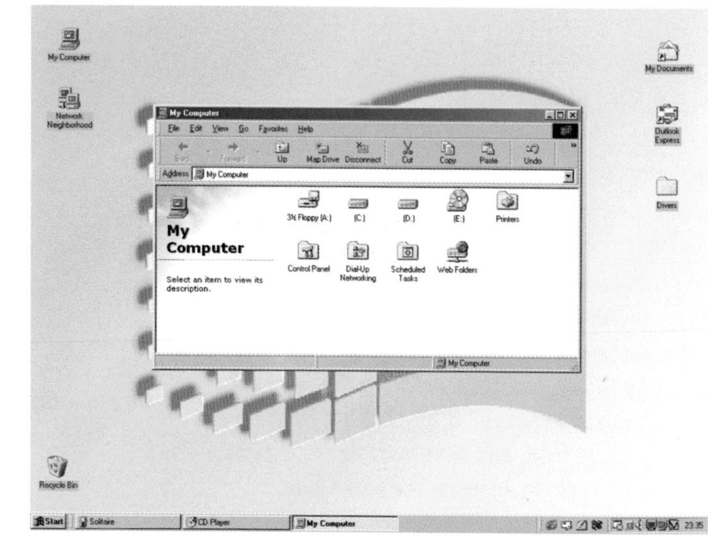
My Computer
Select an item to view its description.

What's in My Computer

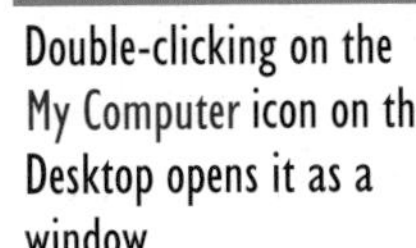

Double-clicking on the My Computer icon on the Desktop opens it as a window.

My Computer displays the names of all the drives, hard disks, removable drives, CD-Roms and shared (network) drives. Double-click on the drive name to display its contents.

The menu bar is identical to that found in a folder.

The toolbar has the same icons as you'll find in a folder.

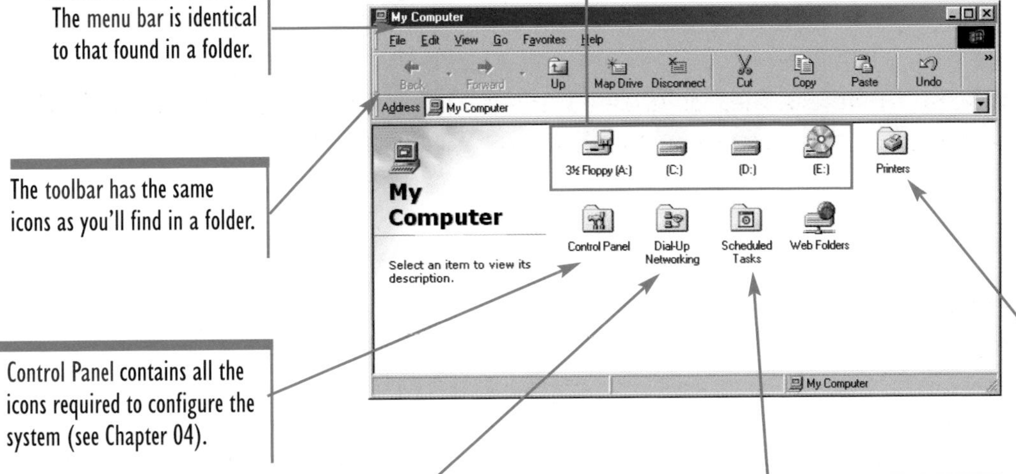

Control Panel contains all the icons required to configure the system (see Chapter 04).

The Printers folder lets you configure the settings of printers connected to the computer (see Chapter 04).

Dial-up Networking contains the settings for connecting to on-line services (Internet, CompuServe,...).

The Scheduled Tasks folder lets you schedule tasks for the operating system to perform automatically at regular intervals. These are the computer's maintenance operations.

You cannot move the icon for a drive out of the My Computer window. But you can still create a shortcut to it from the desktop of the Quick Launch toolbar. Click and drag the mouse outside the My Computer window or onto the Quick Launch toolbar. Now, you need never have to open My Computer again to access the contents of a disk.

Moving around from My Computer

1 Open the **My Computer** window by double-clicking its icon on the desktop.

2 Double-click on the C: drive.

3 Windows 98 opens a new window containing all the folders and files on the disk.

4 Double-click on the **Derive** folder (for example) to view its contents.

5 Windows 98 opens a new window containing all the folders and files in the **Derive** folder.

6 Double-click on **Math** to move down the folder tree-structure.

7 Windows 98 opens a new window displaying the contents of the **Math** folder stored in the **Derive** folder on drive C.

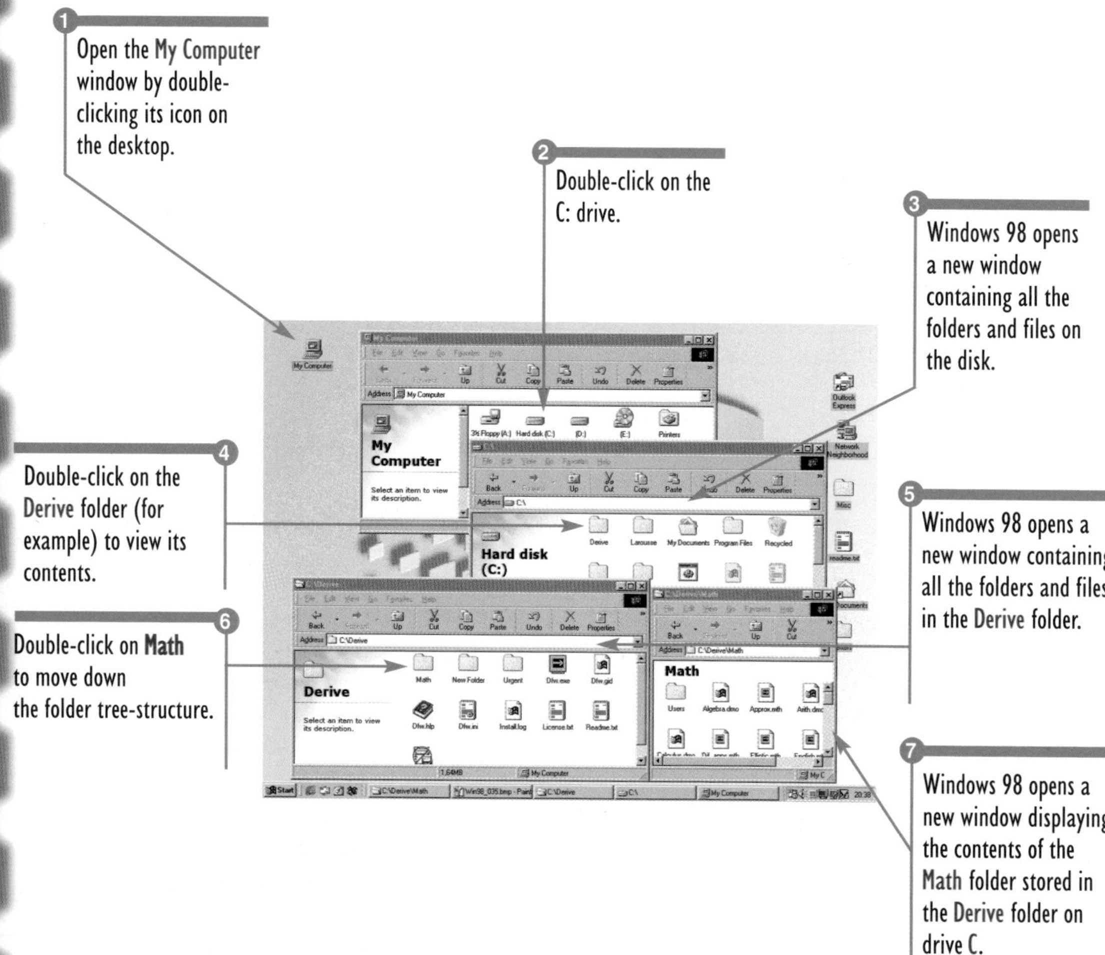

A To view the different folders on a disk drive, simply double-click its icon.

B To go up one level in the tree structure, click on the *Up* icon on the toolbar, or press the *Back/Delete* key.

Hint

To clear all the windows from your screen in one go, hold down the *Shift* key and click on the close button of the last screen displayed.

Viewing windows

View/Folder Options/General Tab/Settings button

If you don't want your desktop to get cluttered up quickly, you'd do well to select the option **Open each folder in the same window.**

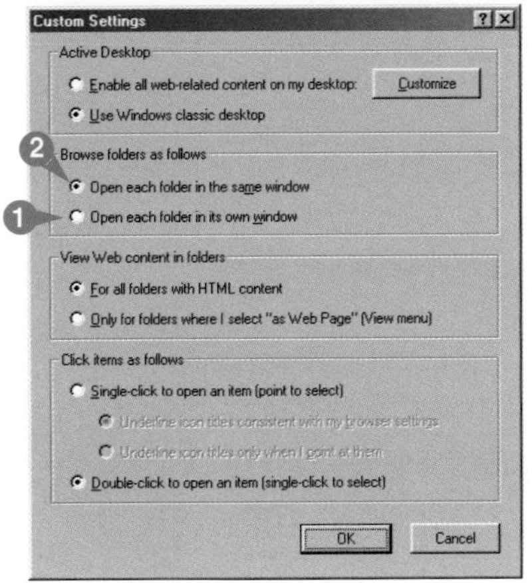

Checklist

1. Click on this option to get Windows 98 to open a new window each time you double-click on a folder to view its contents (see example on previous page).
2. Click this if you want Windows 98 to open each folder you view in the same window.

Checklist

1. Click this option to show all types of files.
2. Click this box not to have hidden and system files displayed.
3. Click this option to have Windows 98 display the full path (e.g., *C:\Derive\Math*) in the title bar of each folder window.
4. Click this if you don't want Windows 98 to display file extensions in windows.

View/Folder Options/View Tab

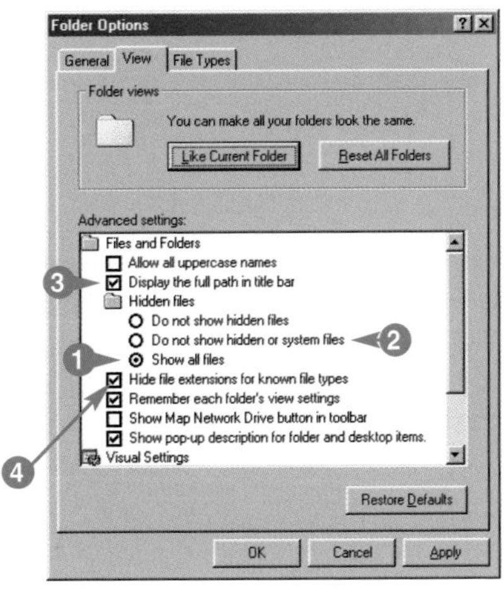

Hidden and system files are essential for Windows 98 and other applications to run properly. Hiding them can be a good way of ensuring that nothing untoward happens to them.

Moving information

1 Open My Computer and double-click on drive C:.

2 Double-click on the source and destination folders in turn. You can resize them to display them alongside each other.

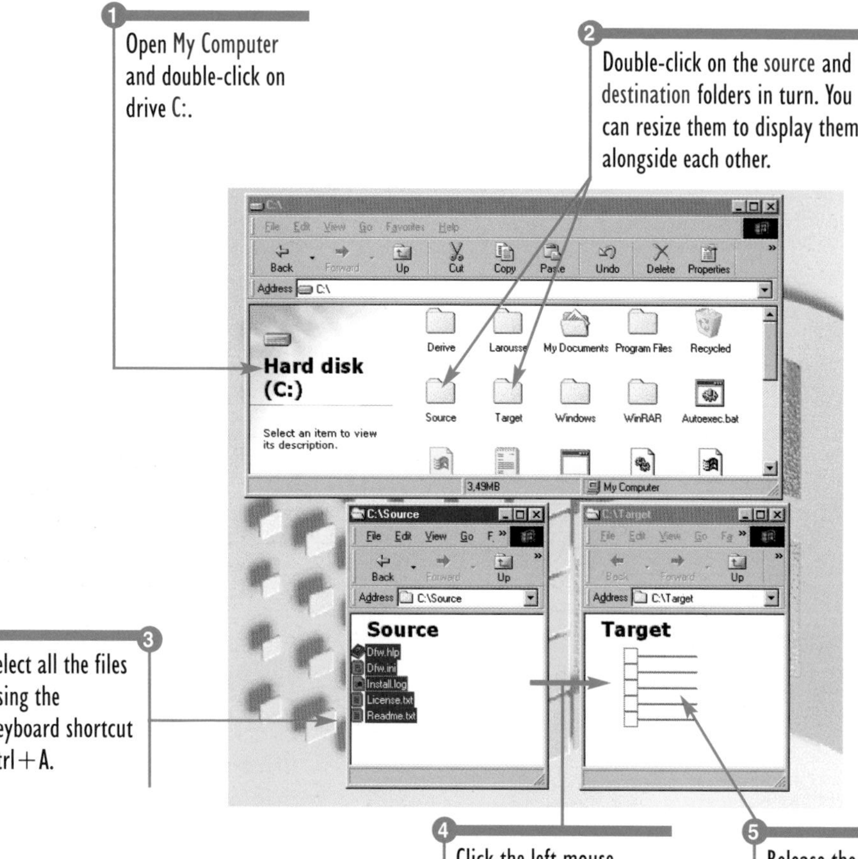

3 Select all the files using the keyboard shortcut Ctrl+A.

4 Click the left mouse button, hold it down and move the pointer onto the destination folder.

5 Release the mouse button and the files will appear in the destination folder. Moving them automatically removes them from the source folder.

In two words

A Select the files to be moved in the folder which contains them (the source folder).

B Click the mouse button and hold it down.

C Keeping the button held down, move the pointer onto the folder where you want the files to be (the destination folder).

D With the pointer on a blank area of the destination folder, release the mouse button and the files will appear. If the file sizes are big, Windows 98 will display a dialogue box telling you how the transfer is progressing.

Hint

You cannot use this drag-and-drop technique to move files from one drive (say *C:*) to another (say *D:*). In this case, Windows 98 will just copy the files, leaving the original ones intact in the source location.

Moving information between disk drives

Ⓐ Select the files to be moved.

Ⓑ Right-click and drag the mouse pointer to the destination file.

Ⓒ Release the mouse button for a context menu to pop up.

Ⓓ Select the *Move here* command to move the file.

••••• **Note** •••••

To change your mind, simply select the *Cancel* command.

1 Open My Computer and double-click on both disk drives.

2 Open the destination folder in drive D: and the source folder in drive C:.

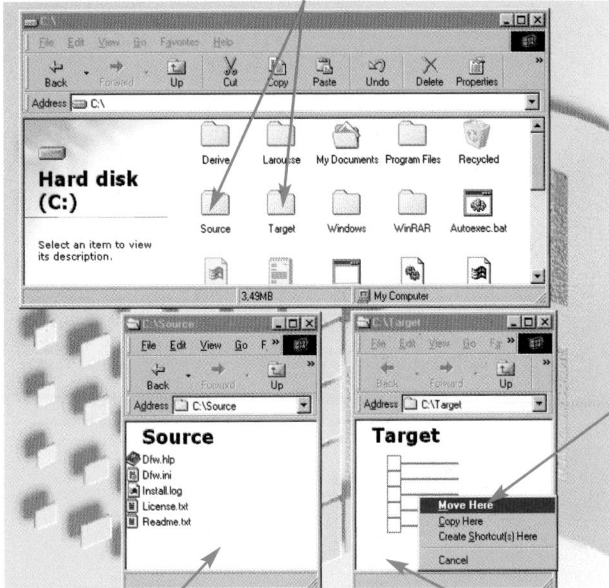

3 Select the files to be moved, right-click on the selection and drag the pointer onto the destination folder in drive D:.

4 Release the mouse button on a blank area of the destination folder. A context menu will pop up.

5 Select the Move here command to move the files. The files will show up in the destination folder, and disappear from the original folder.

Copying information

1 Open My Computer and double-click on drive C:.

2 Double-click on the source and destination folders in turn. You can resize them to display them alongside each other.

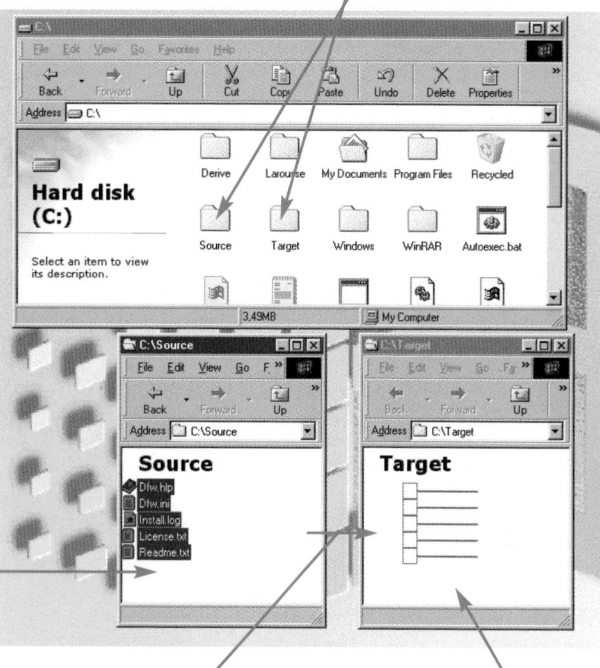

3 Select all the files using the keyboard short-cut Ctrl+A.

4 Press the Ctrl key, click on the selected group, hold the left mouse button down and drag the pointer onto the destination folder.

5 Release the mouse button and the files will appear in the destination folder. The files will still be displayed in the source folder.

A Select the files to be copied.

B Press the *Ctrl* key and click on the selected files.

C Keeping the mouse button held down, drag the pointer onto the destination folder.

D With the pointer on a blank area of the destination folder, release the mouse button and the files will appear. If the file sizes are big, Windows 98 will display a dialogue box telling you approximately how long the transfer will take.

••••• ***Note*** •••••

When you copy files, Windows 98 puts a square with a plus sign in it (+) below the mouse pointer.

Checklist

1. Select the file to be deleted. To select more than one file, press the *Shift* or *Ctrl* keys.
2. Choose *File/Delete* or use the *Delete* shortcut.
3. Click on the *Yes* button in the *Confirm File Delete* dialogue box.

Note

Never use the *Edit/Cut* command to delete a file. Windows 98 will store it in the clipboard, but will not remove it from the folder.

Deleting files

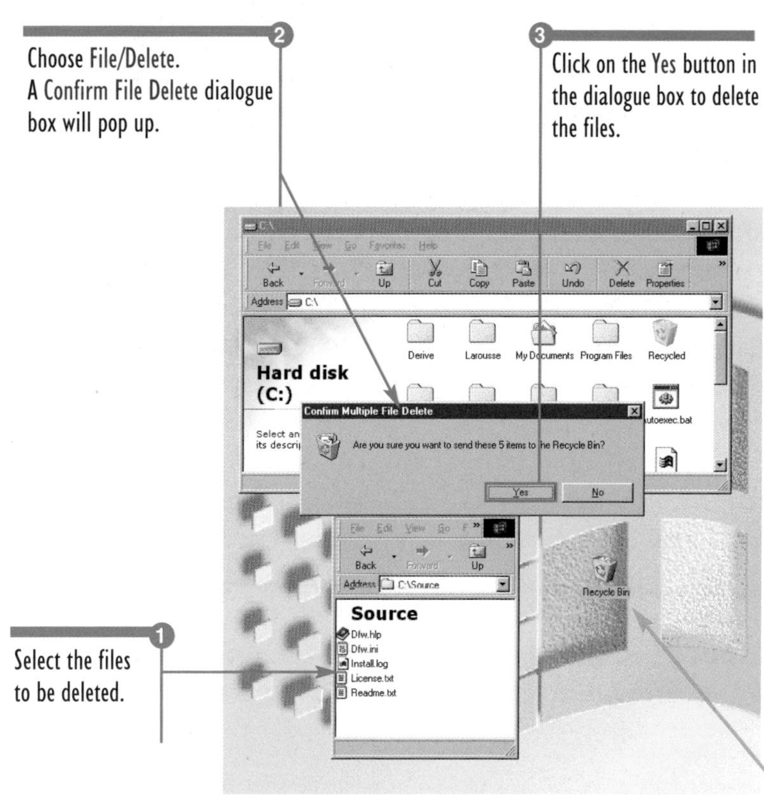

1. Select the files to be deleted.

2. Choose File/Delete. A Confirm File Delete dialogue box will pop up.

3. Click on the Yes button in the dialogue box to delete the files.

Windows 98 moves the files out of their original folder and into the Recycle Bin.

Properties

Disk drive - Folder - File - Shortcuts

All objects present in the operating system have properties which differentiate them from other objects. All the properties of an object are stored in a single dialogue box which pops up onto the screen when you right-click on the object and select the Properties command from the context menu. The dialogue box will have one or more tabs depending on the object you have selected. The first tab is general information: the name of the object, the dates when it was created and last modified, its position on the disk, size in bytes and kilobytes and its attributes. You can change these easily by simply clicking on the corresponding box. To prevent a file being modified, for example, you can tick the Read-only box. If the object selected is a disk drive, the Properties box will also have a Tools tab. You click on this tab to carry out all the maintenance operations on the drive: checking for errors on the disk with ScanDisk, backing up files with Backup and defragmenting your disk with Disk Defragmenter. All these programs are utilities supplied with Windows 98; they are described in Chapter 05 System Tools.

HOW TO

To bring up the Properties dialogue box for an object:

Click on the object and choose File/Properties if you are in a folder or Explorer.

Right-click on the object to bring up its context menu and choose Properties.

TIP

You won't find a Properties command for the Control Panel, Dial-up Networking, Scheduled Tasks and Printers folders in My Computer. That's because these four objects are special folders used to configure the system or perform maintenance operations.

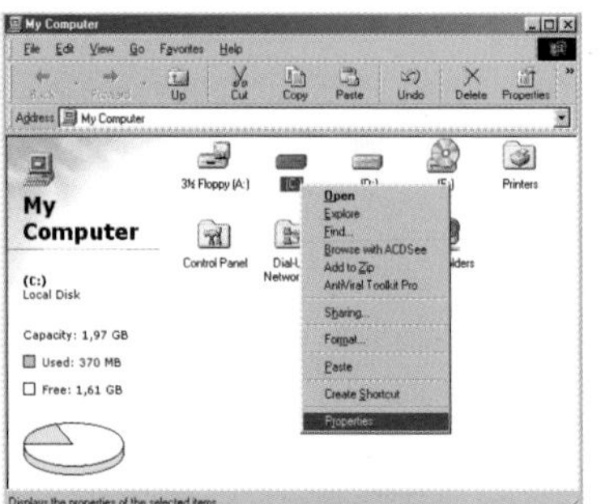

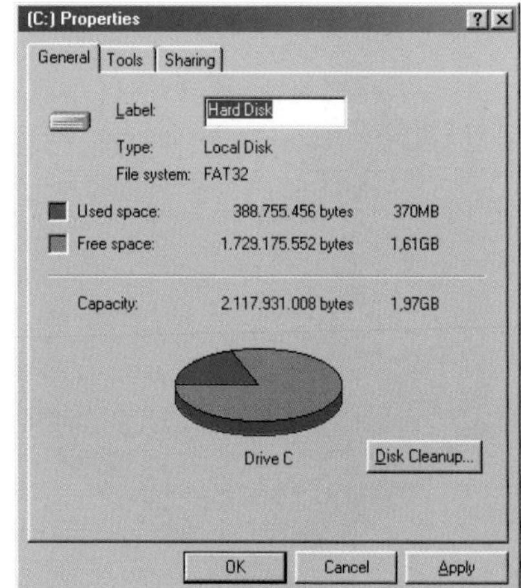

Viewing the properties of an object

Properties/Disk

As well as its name and total capacity/free space, this dialogue box shows the type of drive selected: Local disk — Removable disk — Network connection (for remote disk drives) — SCSI drive — CD-ROM drive — 3-inch-floppy — 5-inch-floppy.

••••• ***Note*** •••••

Windows 98 uses a new hard-disk management technique known as FAT 32 (FAT stands for File Allocation Table). It optimises the management of high-capacity disks by minimising the space used to store data. If the File system under *Type* shows the letters FAT, the disk is using the old-style file allocation table. If it shows FAT 32, on the other hand, the disk has been formatted using Windows 98, which automatically uses the new technique.

Name given to the disk when it was formatted.

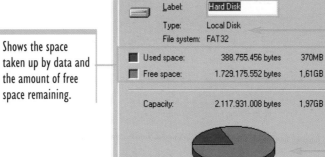

Shows the space taken up by data and the amount of free space remaining.

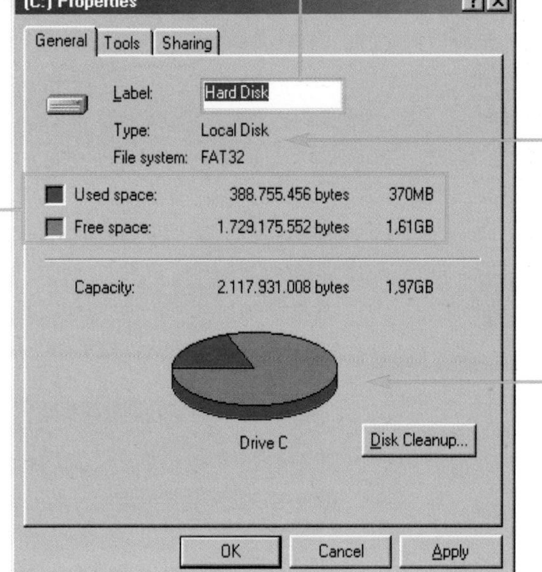

Type of disk and file allocation table used.

A pie chart of the disk space.

Alt+Return

ScanDisk checks the integrity of the data on your disk and corrects any errors. Run it if you have damaged files which you can no longer read.

Backup will backup your files to disk or tape streamers. Click the *Backup now* button to copy the data on your disk.

Disk Defragmenter puts all the bits of files scattered around the disk back into one block. It can speed up your hard disk: use it regularly!

Tools tab

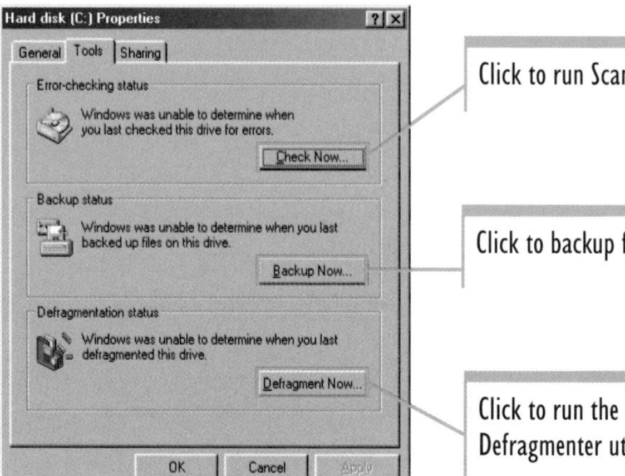

Click to run ScanDisk.

Click to backup files.

Click to run the Disk Defragmenter utility.

You cannot use these tools on a remote network drive or CD-ROM drive.

Sharing tab

Enter a comment that can be viewed on all other computers by selecting Details.

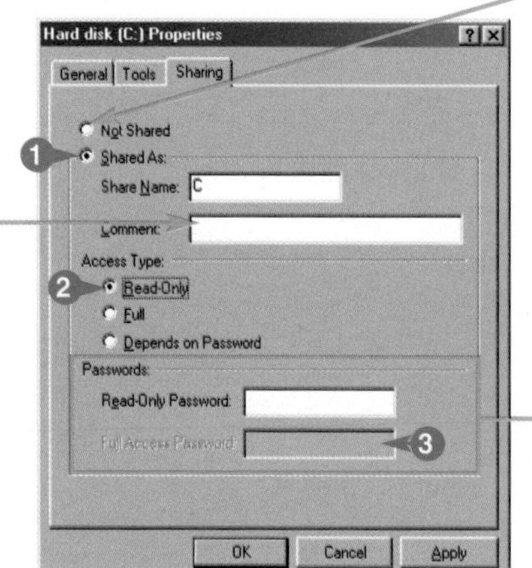

Click to indicate that the disk is not to be shared in a network and cannot be accessed by a remote computer.

Enter a password to allow data to be read, and another to allow the user to write to the disk.

You'll find the Share Name in My Computer below the icon which stands for the networked disk. It tells you the host computer name and the drive letter in the accessing computer.

Checklist

1. To share a disk over a network and give other users access to it, select the *Shared As* option.
2. Then select a type of data access. Click on *Read-Only* to prevent users from being able to change data. They will still be able to read it.
3. Click the *Depends on Password* option to make data accessible only with a password.

Properties/Folder

To find out how much disk space all the subfolders and files in a folder are taking up, don't try and add up all the file sizes. Simply click on the parent folder and press Alt+Enter. Size tells you the total size of all files in the folder and any subfolders.

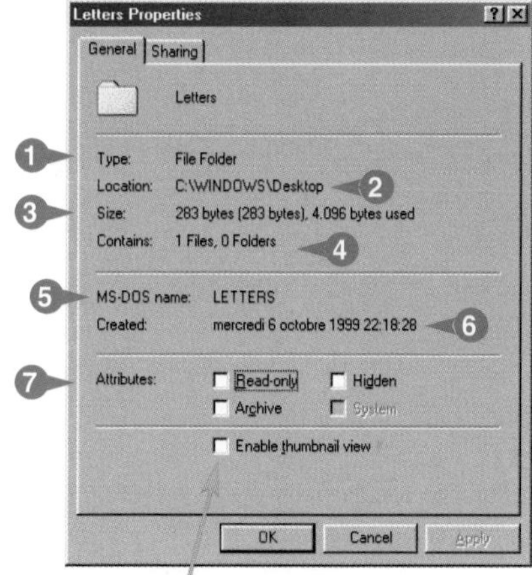

Gives you a thumbnail view of the file in the window.

Checklist

1. The type of object: here, a folder.
2. The name of the drive in which it is located.
3. The size of the folder: Windows 98 shows the disk space used by all the files stored in the folder.
4. The number of files and subfolders in the folder.
5. The full MS-DOS name of the folder. Names with more than 8 characters are truncated and end with ~ followed by a number.
6. The date and time the folder was created.
7. The folder's attributes. Ticking one of the boxes has no effect on a folder.

Properties/File

To modify the attributes of a file, simply click on the relevant check box. If you don't want the file to be visible in the folder, tick the *Hidden* box. But there is no point doing this unless you also activate the *Do not show hidden files* option in the *Folder Options* dialogue box (*View/ Folder Options/ View tab* command).

Type of object: it may be a document file, help file, application or specific type of image.

Shows the folder or name of the drive in which the file is located.

Date when the file was last modified.

Date when the file was last accessed.

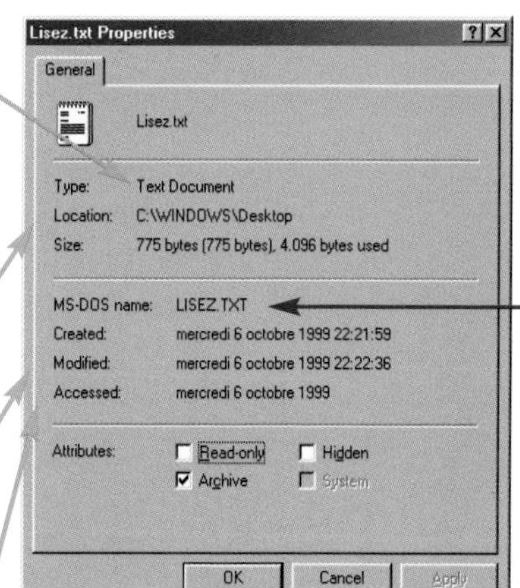

Full MS-DOS name of the file

MS-DOS will not accept file names with more than 8 characters. If you give it a longer name, it will only take the first six characters, then add the symbol ~ and a number (1, 2, 3, etc.). The MS-DOS name is thus different from the name you give it under Windows 98 if it has more than 8 characters.

Properties/Shortcut/General tab

The general properties displayed for a shortcut are the same as for a file. You modify the attributes of a shortcut in the same way.

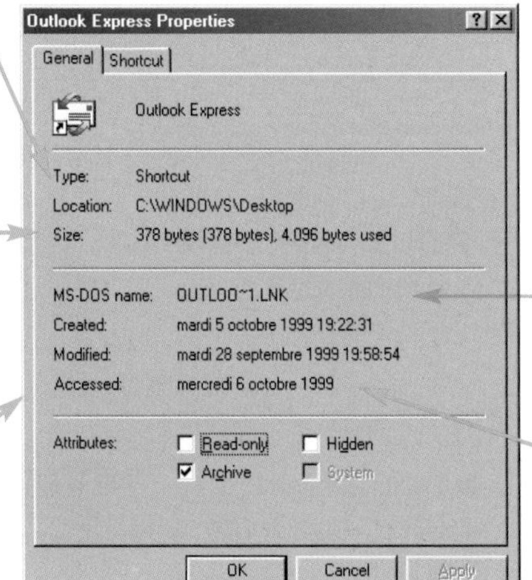

Type of object: a shortcut.

File size. Usually the files are quite small, because they only contain the path to the actual file itself.

The file attributes.

The full MS-DOS name of the shortcut. If you haven't modified the Windows 98 default name, the MS-DOS name will always be SHORTC~#.LNK (where # is a single-digit number higher than 0).

Date the shortcut was last accessed. Windows 98 always displays the current date.

Checklist

1. In the *Target* text box, enter the disk location of the file to which the shortcut refers. Always start with the name of the drive followed by the \ symbol and the names of each nested folder divided by the \. Remember to put the file name (and its extension) right at the end. Put quotes around the whole text string if there are any spaces in it.
2. Some programs use linked files located in a different folder. You need to enter the full path to that folder in the *Start in:* box so that the application can find them and run properly.
3. By assigning a keyboard shortcut in the *Shortcut key* box, you can run an application or open a document very quickly. The best way is to assign *Ctrl* or *Alt* and a letter or number.
4. Click *OK* to confirm the new shortcut or any changes that you have made to it.

Properties/Shortcut/ Shortcut tab

The type of file to which the shortcut refers. If you create a shortcut to the program Word, Windows 98 will display the word Application.

1 Enter the path (drive name and folder names separated by the \ symbol) of the file to which the shortcut refers.

2 Specify the path to the folder which contains the file.

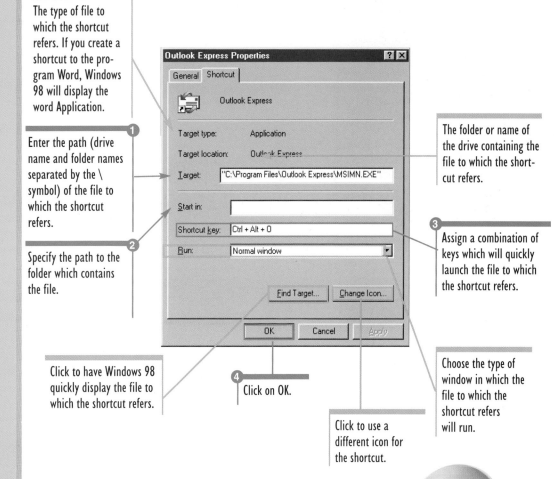

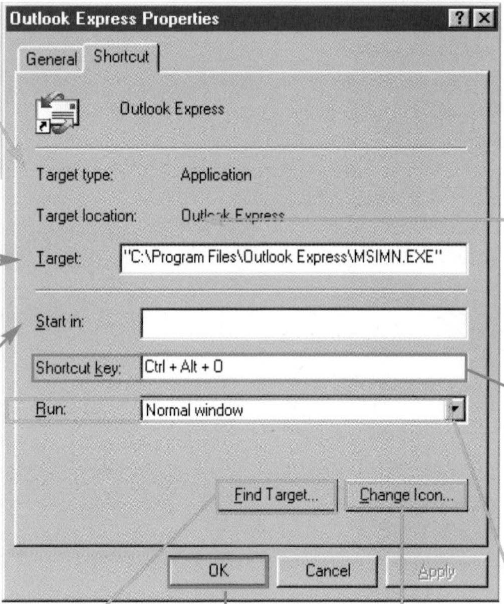

Outlook Express Properties

General | Shortcut

Outlook Express

Target type: Application

Target location: Outlook Express

Target: "C:\Program Files\Outlook Express\MSIMN.EXE"

Start in:

Shortcut key: Ctrl + Alt + O

Run: Normal window

Find Target... | Change Icon...

OK | Cancel | Apply

The folder or name of the drive containing the file to which the shortcut refers.

3 Assign a combination of keys which will quickly launch the file to which the shortcut refers.

Click to have Windows 98 quickly display the file to which the shortcut refers.

4 Click on OK.

Click to use a different icon for the shortcut.

Choose the type of window in which the file to which the shortcut refers will run.

Always having to run your programs from the Start button can be a slow and tedious job. That's why shortcuts to your most used programs are a good idea. Put them separately on the desktop, or group them in a desktop folder. If you create a keyboard shortcut too, you can launch an application just by pressing Ctrl + Alt + a key of choice.

Flow chart of the Shortcut Properties dialogue box

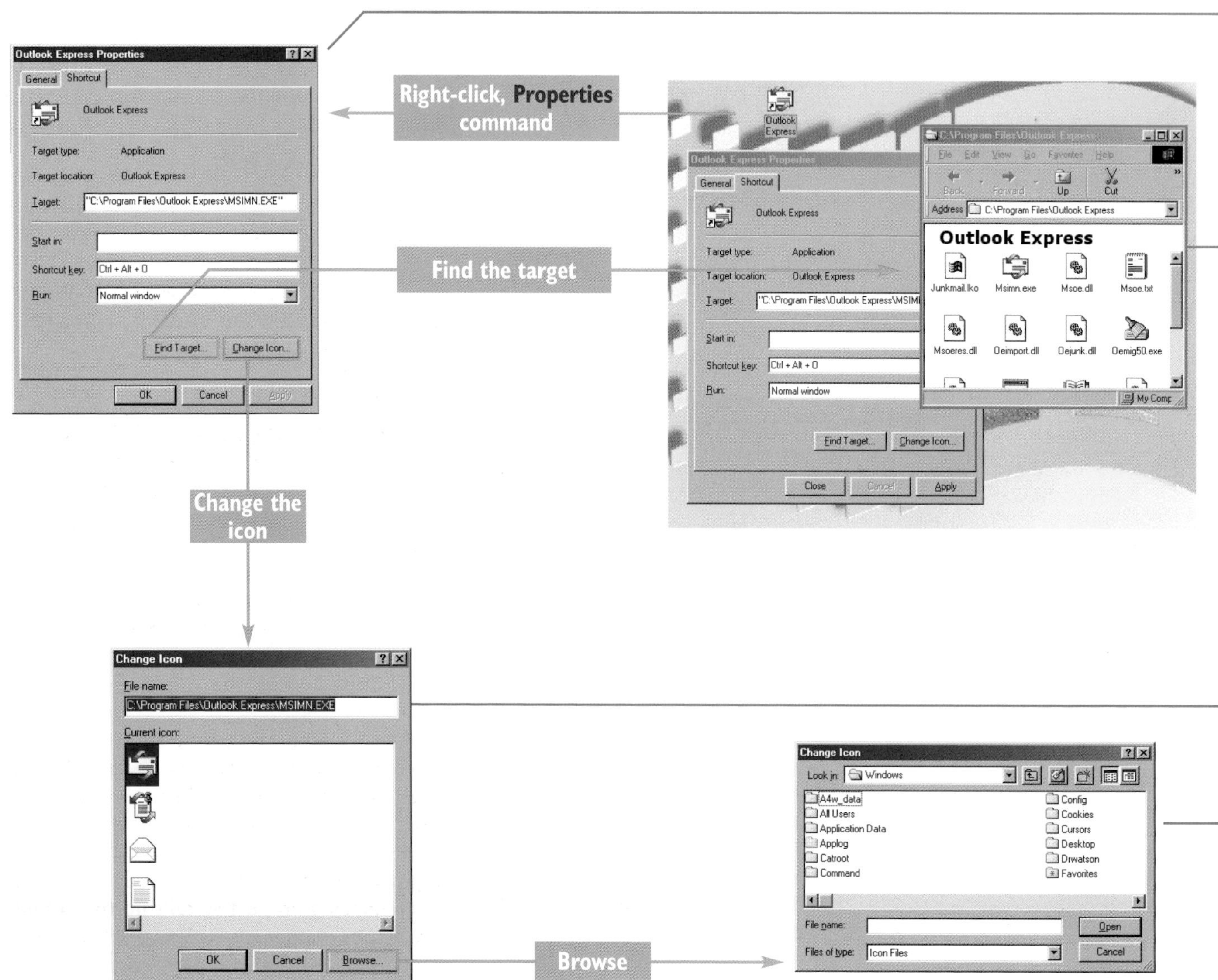

Displays useful information to link the shortcut to the file it refers to.

Displays in a window the name of the file to which the shortcut refers.

Lets you choose a different icon for the shortcut. Windows 98 will suggest a list using special files included in its installation directory.

Lets you specify a different file that contains icons to link to your shortcut.

Accessing the Properties dialogue box

You can view the properties of some desktop objects in different ways. You can right-click on the object and use the *Properties* command in its pop-up context menu, or you can click on the *Control Panel* icons.

The *Properties* command for *My Computer* calls up the *System Properties* dialogue box. You can bring up the same box by opening the *Control Panel* (Start/Settings/Control Panel) and double-clicking the *System* icon. You'll find more details on this and the following boxes in Chapter 04.

The *Network* dialogue box called up via the *Properties* command on the *Network Neighbourhood* icon on the desktop is the same as the one you get by double-clicking on the *Network* icon in *Control Panel*.

Double-clicking on the *Mail* icon in the control panel gives you the same *Properties MS Exchange Settings* dialogue box as the *Properties* command from the *Inbox* icon on the desktop.

Right-clicking on a blank area of the taskbar and choosing *Properties* calls up the *Taskbar Properties* dialogue box. The settings in this box are looked at in more detail in the next section.

Right-clicking on a blank area of the desktop and choosing *Properties* calls up the *Display Properties* dialogue box. You get the same result by double-clicking the *Display* icon in *Control Panel*.

Taskbar properties

The taskbar also has its own *Properties* dialogue box. You can use it to change how the taskbar looks, whether it is always shown on-screen, or, to make more room, ask Windows 98 to show it only when you position the mouse pointer at the bottom of the screen (*Auto hide* option). When you start accumulating too many programs, you can avoid having the *Start* menu taking up all the screen by ticking the *Show small icons in Start menu* box. The other tab in the box lets you customise the program listing in the *Start* menu. When you install a new program, the default is for it to create an entry in the *Start* menu — called a folder — and include a program group in which you'll find the one that runs the application. All the program groups stored in each created folder stand for program shortcuts. Using the *Add*, *Remove* and *Advanced* buttons, you can manage folders and program groups to give yourself a streamlined, user-friendly *Start* menu. You can also manage the different access paths to *Start* menu programs by right-clicking on the *Start* button and selecting the *Open* command from the context menu. Windows 98 brings up a window containing an icon named *Programs*; this corresponds to the *Start* menu command of the same name. Double-clicking on this icon will call up all the folders corresponding to *Start* menu entries.

HOW TO

To get to the taskbar Properties dialogue box:

Click on Start/Settings/Taskbar & Start menu.

Right-click on a blank area of the taskbar to call up a context menu and select the Properties command.

TIP

The taskbar is (virtually) the only way to get to all the applications on your computer. Think carefully about its settings. Properly arranged folders and program groups will speed up access to your most-used programs.

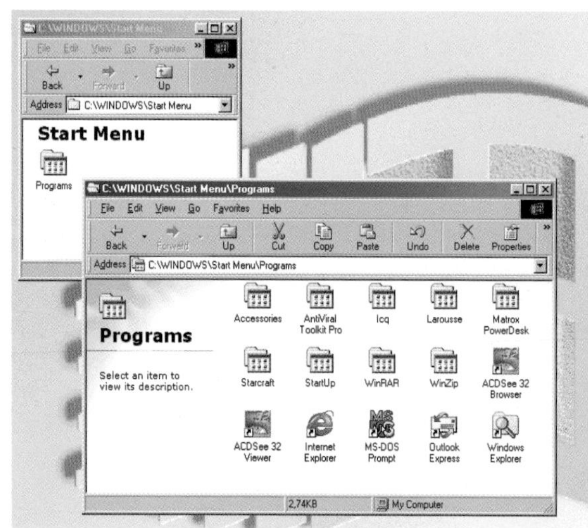

Taskbar properties

Start / Settings / Taskbar & Start menu

Tick the boxes to customise. If you don't want to clutter the screen with the taskbar, tick *Auto hide*. If your *Start* menu is getting crowded with programs, you'd be well-advised to tick the *Show small icons* box *in* the *Start menu*.

••••• ***Hint*** •••••

The dialogue box preview of the taskbar and *Start* menu change as you change settings: keep an eye on them!

Check the position of the taskbar and Start menu commands; they change as you change the settings.

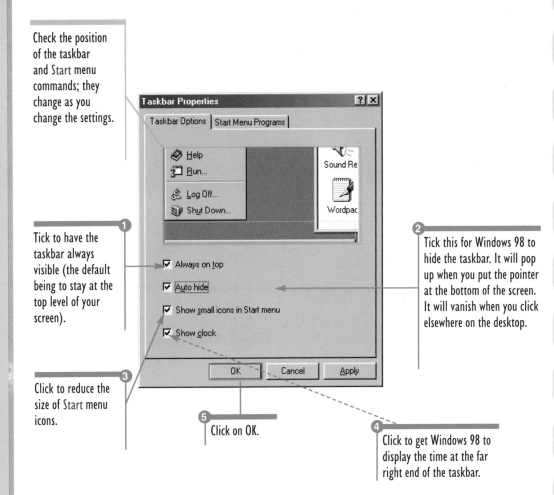

1. Tick to have the taskbar always visible (the default being to stay at the top level of your screen).

2. Tick this for Windows 98 to hide the taskbar. It will pop up when you put the pointer at the bottom of the screen. It will vanish when you click elsewhere on the desktop.

3. Click to reduce the size of Start menu icons.

4. Click to get Windows 98 to display the time at the far right end of the taskbar.

5. Click on OK.

The Start Menu Programs tab is covered on page 64

Flow chart of how to create Start menu shortcuts

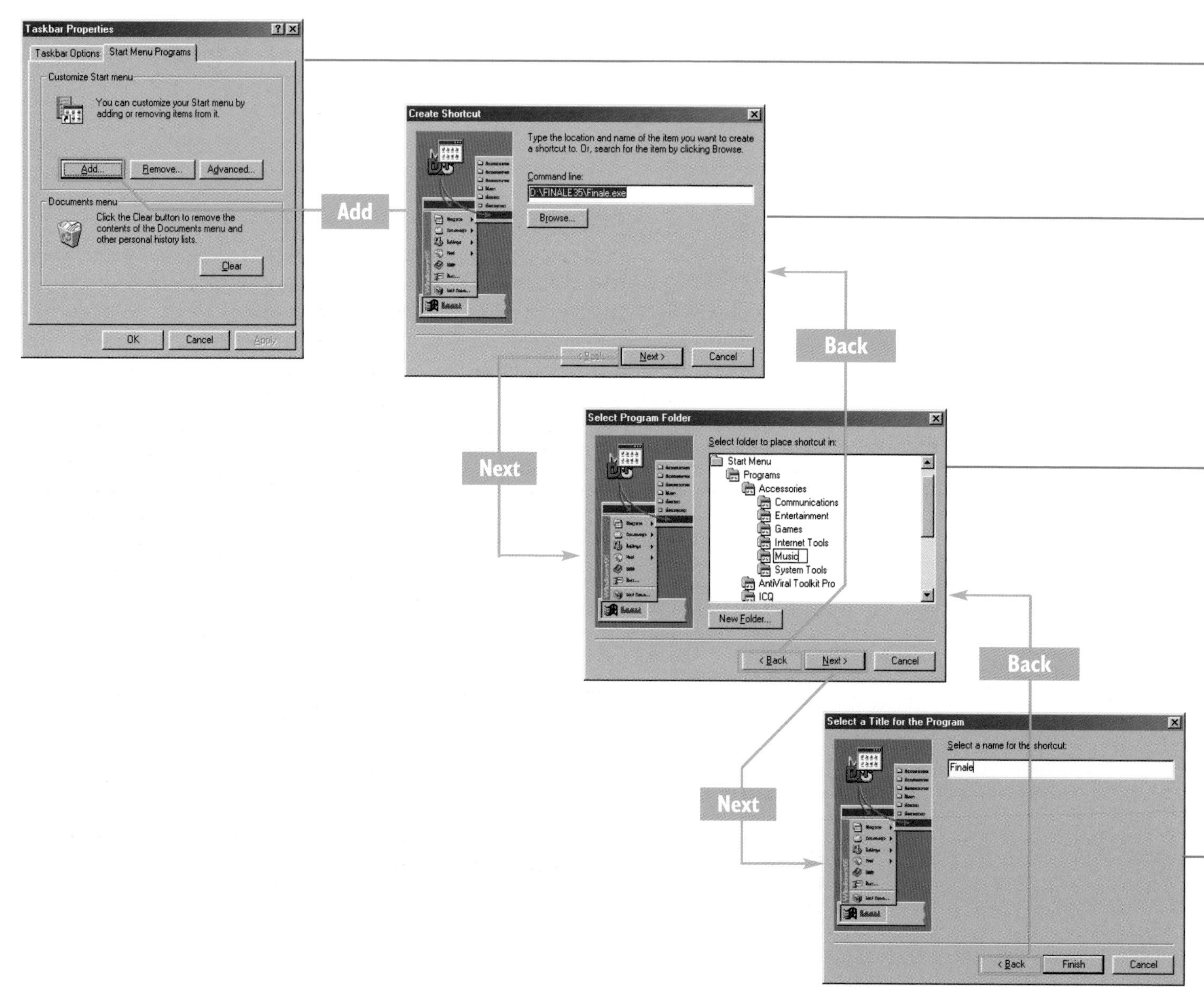

To customise *Start* menu folders and program groups

Enter the path to the new program you want to include in the *Start* menu.

Specify a folder (or create a new one with the *New folder* button) in which Windows 98 should store the new program.

Finish by giving the program a meaningful name: this is how it will be named in the *Start* menu.

In theory

Submenus containing program groups correspond to folders which contain links to application executable files. To create a new path to a program in the *Start* menu, begin by clicking the *Add* button and let Windows 98 walk you through it.

The first thing to do is type in the name of the executable file for the application in the *Command line* text box. You must enter the full path to the file (the letter of the drive and the names of the folders in which it is stored). Remember to enter the \ symbol between folders. Click the *Next>* button, select the folder (i.e., submenu) in which you want the program path to be stored. If you want to create a new folder for the path, click the *New folder* button and enter a name. Click *Next>* to finish, giving a name by which to launch the program; choose something meaningful connected with the program. Click *Finish* for Windows 98 to add a new submenu and new program path in the *Start* menu.

You can see the result immediately by scrolling through the names in the *Start* menu and *Programs* command.

You can also include a path to a program in the *Start* menu above the *Programs* command simply by dragging and dropping a shortcut to the program concerned onto the *Start* button. Windows 98 will automatically add the path to the menu.

Flow chart of how to remove Start menu items

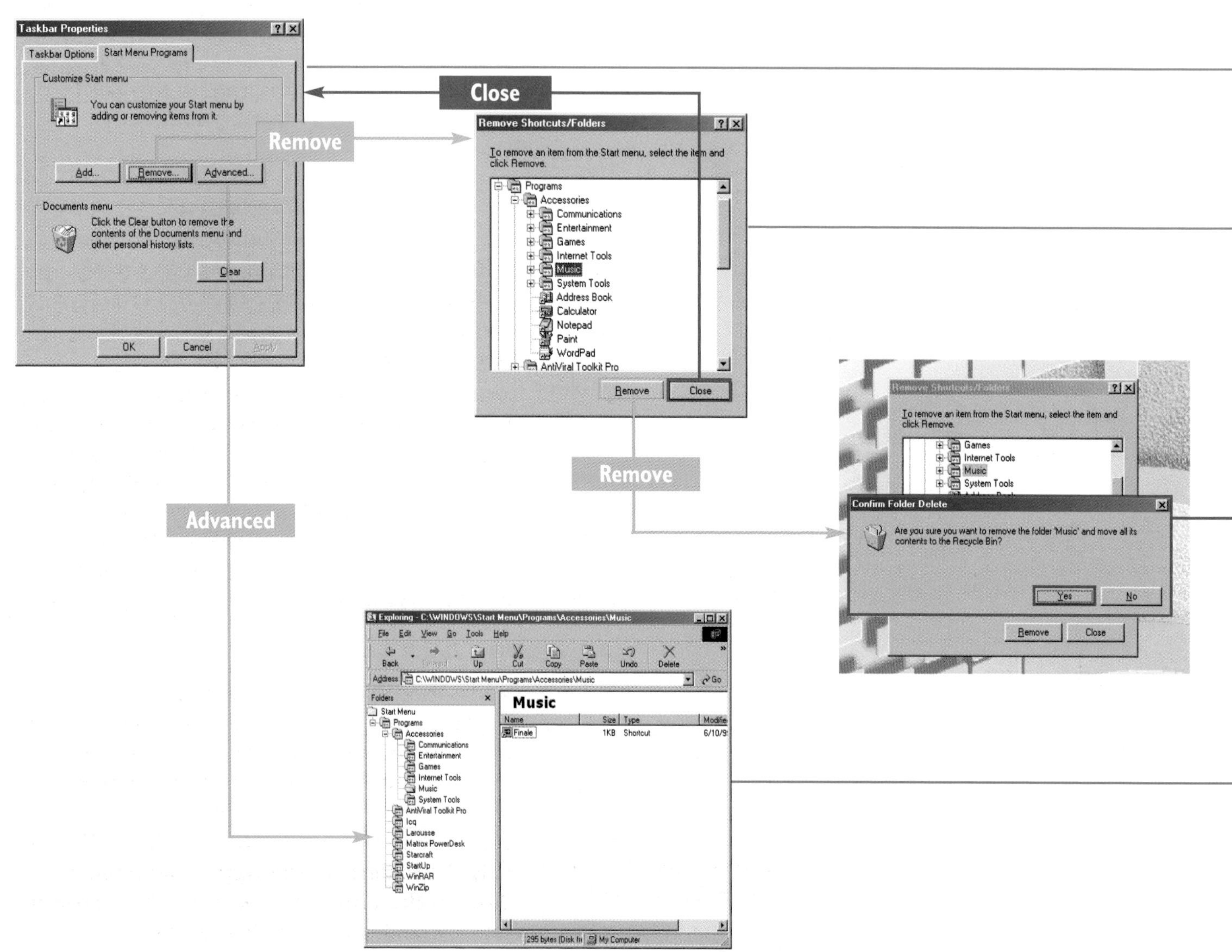

To customise *Start* menu folders and program groups

Windows 98 displays the tree of folders stored in the *Start* menu.

Tells Windows 98 that you have selected a folder and clicked *Remove*. Windows is just awaiting confirmation to delete it.

The *Start* menu program names stand for shortcuts which you can rename or remove as you wish. Windows 98 lets you do that through Explorer, which you can call up through the *Advanced* button.

In theory

Whenever you remove a program, the uninstall procedure should also remove the program path from the *Start* menu. In theory, at least. Often, the procedure fails to update the menu. These unwanted program groups clutter up the *Start* menu and slow down access to working programs.

You delete a folder by clicking on the *Remove* button. Windows 98 brings up a dialogue box containing all the folders in the *Start* menu. Click once on the little (+) sign to display all the sub-folders and shortcuts stored in a folder. Any folder which does not have a sign next to the name only has shortcuts in it, no subfolders. To remove a shortcut, simply click on it to select it. To remove an entire folder, do not open it, but click on its name. Confirm the removal by clicking *Remove*; Windows 98 will bring up a *Confirm Delete* dialogue box. Click on *Yes* to delete the folder and all the program paths.

You can do the same thing through the Explorer window that pops up when you click the *Advanced* button. Browse through the different folders, clicking on the (+) sign to open them, or on the (-) sign to close them. In the left-hand window pane, Windows 98 shows only the folders. In the right-hand pane, it displays the program shortcuts. To remove one, select it and press the *Delete* key.

The Start Menu Programs tab

Whenever you want to customise the *Start* menu, use the *Start Menu Programs* tab in the *Properties* dialogue box and the three *Add*, *Remove* and *Advanced* command buttons.

Click to add a new program to the Start menu.

Click to remove a folder and its associated program group.

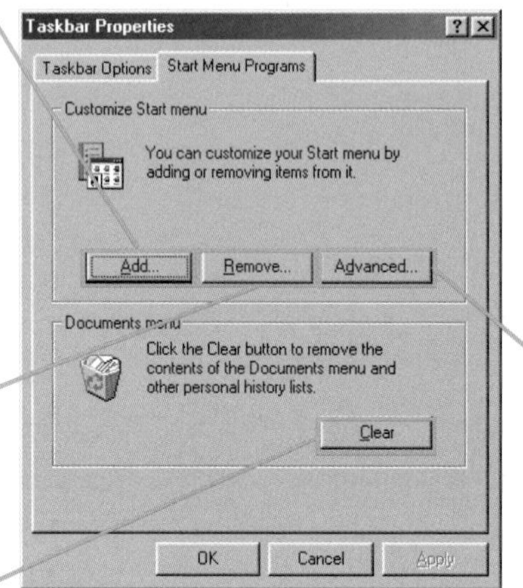

Click to show the folders corresponding to the submenus in the Start menu. Windows 98 uses the same interface as Explorer.

The Advanced button displays the Start menu folders in an Explorer window. You can use this to modify an existing program group. You can also add a new group or remove one this way, but if you use the Add and Remove buttons, Windows 98 will walk you through the process.

Clear button

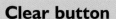

1. The Documents submenu contains the names of recently opened files.

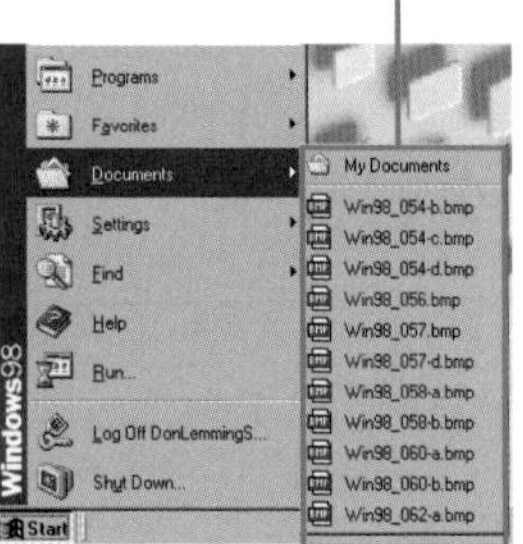

2. Click Clear to remove all files in the Documents command on the Start menu.

Documents menu

Click the Clear button to remove the contents of the Documents menu and other personal history lists.

Clear

3. After you perform the command, the submenu will contain only a path to the My Documents folder.

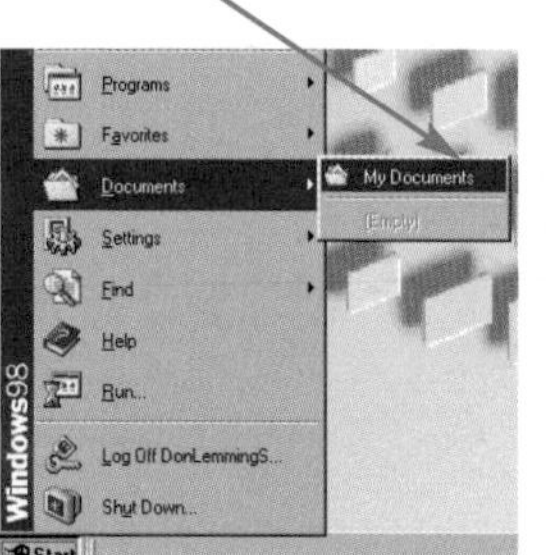

The *Documents* command submenu contains all the files which have recently been opened. This means you can use this submenu to reopen the file quickly and bring it up on screen. Just clicking on the name runs the application and displays the file.

All the files displayed are actually shortcuts that you can find in the folder \Windows\Recent.

Recycle Bin

PC users have been waiting for years for Recycle Bin. Why? Because they're closet Mac wannabees? No, the Windows 98 Recycle Bin is just incredibly practical. As its name suggests, its somewhere to hold deleted files before getting rid of them. Whenever you press the *Delete* key and confirm, the file is moved directly to the *Recycle Bin*, which is actually an area of the hard disk 'ring-fenced' by the system. By definition, it is limited, and when the size of files in it exceeds that limit, the older files are physically purged from the disk and irretrievably lost. You can open the *Recycle Bin* at any time; double-click on the desktop icon (a wastebasket, of course) to bring up a standard window in which you'll find all the files you have recently deleted. The great thing about *Recycle Bin* is that it also stores all the information about files, which makes it easy to put the file back exactly where it was, as if it had never been deleted (one command does it).

HOW TO

To delete a file: click and drag it to the Recycle Bin; it will 'swallow' it automatically. Or, even easier, click on the icon and press the Del key. Confirm the deletion by clicking on the Yes button.

To show the contents of the Recycle Bin: double-click on the desktop icon.

To bring up the Recycle Bin Properties dialogue box: right-click and select the Properties command from the context menu.

To empty the Recycle Bin and purge all the files stored in it from your disk: right-click on the icon and select the Empty Recycle Bin command.

TIP

You can delete a file without putting it in the Recycle Bin by selecting it and pressing the Shift+ Delete keys. If you do that, and confirm it, of course, you won't be able to recover it later unless you have a special utility suite.

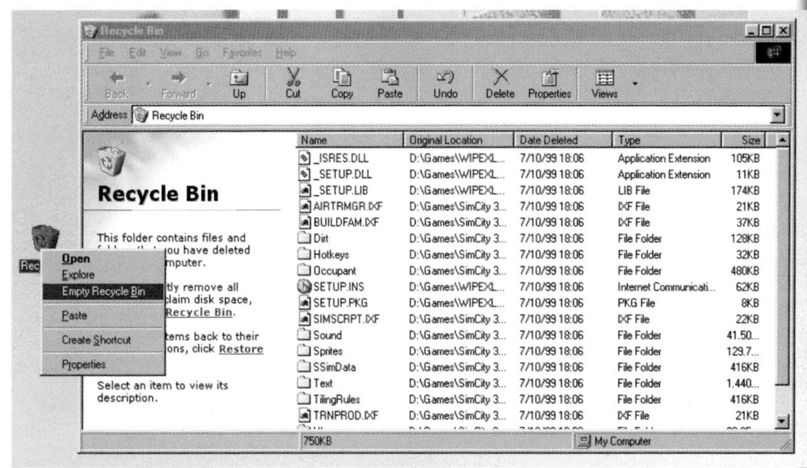

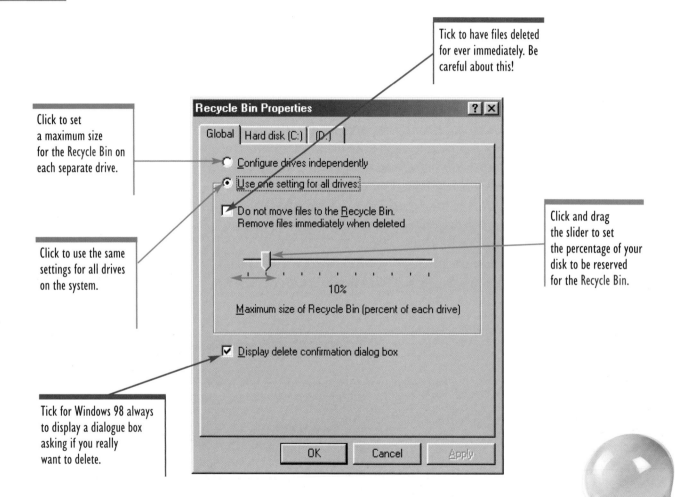

Recycle Bin properties

Tick to have files deleted for ever immediately. Be careful about this!

Click to set a maximum size for the Recycle Bin on each separate drive.

Click and drag the slider to set the percentage of your disk to be reserved for the Recycle Bin.

Click to use the same settings for all drives on the system.

Tick for Windows 98 always to display a dialogue box asking if you really want to delete.

Do not tick the Do not move files to the Recycle Bin box. Instead, use the Shift+Del shortcut (mentioned above) to purge occasional files.

Hard disk tab

The options on this tab will be greyed out if the *Use one setting for all drives* button on the *Global* tab has been activated.

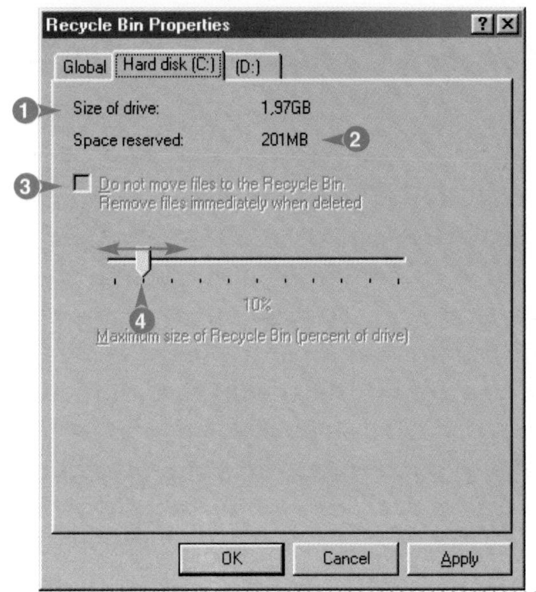

Recycle Bin Properties
Global
Hard disk (C:)
(D:)
Size of drive: 1,97GB
Space reserved: 201MB
Do not move files to the Recycle Bin. Remove files immediately when deleted
10%
Maximum size of Recycle Bin (percent of drive)
OK
Cancel
Apply

Checklist

1. Size of drive.
2. Space reserved by Windows 98 to store deleted files.
3. Tick to have files purged immediately from your disk whenever you delete them. They will not go through the Recycle Bin and will be lost.
4. Drag the slider to set the percentage of your drive reserved for the Recycle Bin.

Checklist

To recover a file, click on the name and choose *File/Restore*.

To purge a file, select it and choose *File/Delete*.

To empty the *Recycle Bin* and purge all files, choose *File/Empty Recycle Bin*.

Note

The items displayed in the Recycle Bin window are like any other Windows 98 object. You can right-click on any of them.

Recycle Bin window

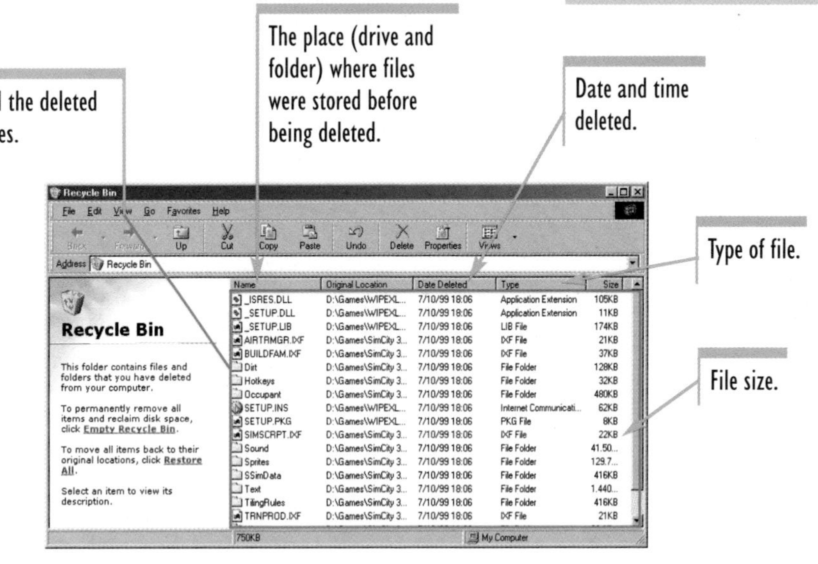

All the deleted files.
The place (drive and folder) where files were stored before being deleted.
Date and time deleted.
Type of file.
File size.
Recycle Bin
This folder contains files and folders that you have deleted from your computer.
To permanently remove all items and reclaim disk space, click Empty Recycle Bin.
To move all items back to their original locations, click Restore All.
Select an item to view its description.

Formatting a disk

When you format a floppy or hard disk, you prepare it so that the computer can store data on it. What you are doing is putting tracks and sectors on it where information can be stored. Windows 98 detects what disk drives you have on your computer and displays them in *My Computer.* To format a disk, simply right-click on the icon that stands for the drive and choose the *Format* command. Windows 98 will not let you format a disk on which files are in use, so you cannot format your *C:* drive if you have Windows 98 installed on it. Nor can you format a floppy disk if there is an *A:* drive window open on your screen. To perform a proper format, putting tracks and sectors on the disk, click the *Full* option in the *Format type* box. Neither of the other two options does this! Whatever you choose, tick the *Display summary when finished* box to see a summary when formatting is complete. It gives you useful information on disk errors, the amount of usable space in bytes, and the space used by system files.

HOW TO

To bring up the Format dialogue box: right-click on the icon that stands for the drive and choose the Format command.

TIP

Formatting erases all the information already on a hard or floppy disk. Before doing it, make sure you have backed up all important data from it.

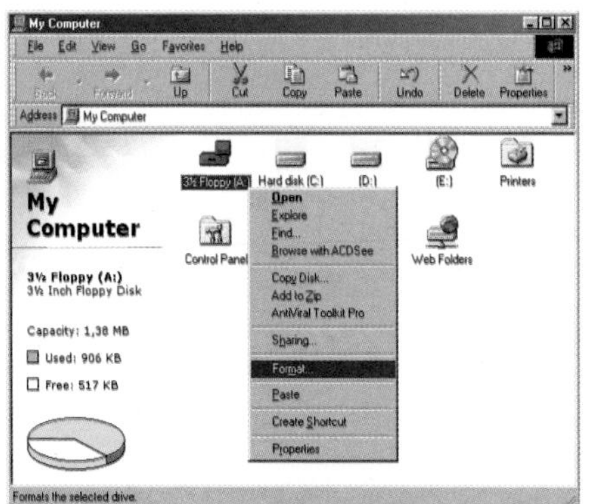

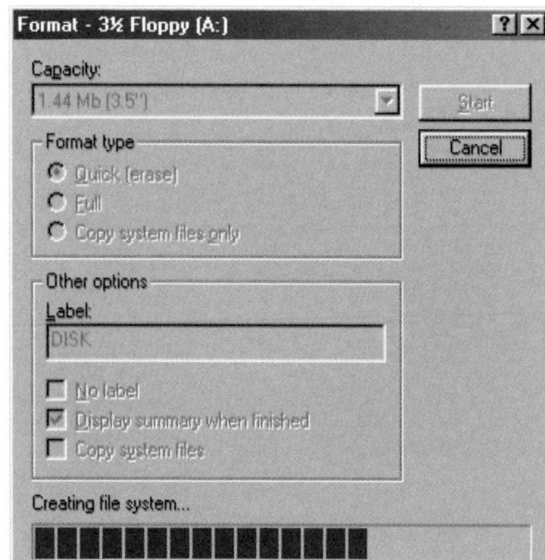

Formatting

Checklist

1. Insert the floppy disk to format in the drive.
2. Check that there is no window open on the desktop showing the contents of the drive.
3. Choose *Full* for a proper format.
4. Tick the *Display summary when finished* box.
5. Click *Start*.
6. After a few minutes, Windows 98 will display the summary; click the *Close* button.
7. Click the *Close* button to clear the *Format* dialogue box.

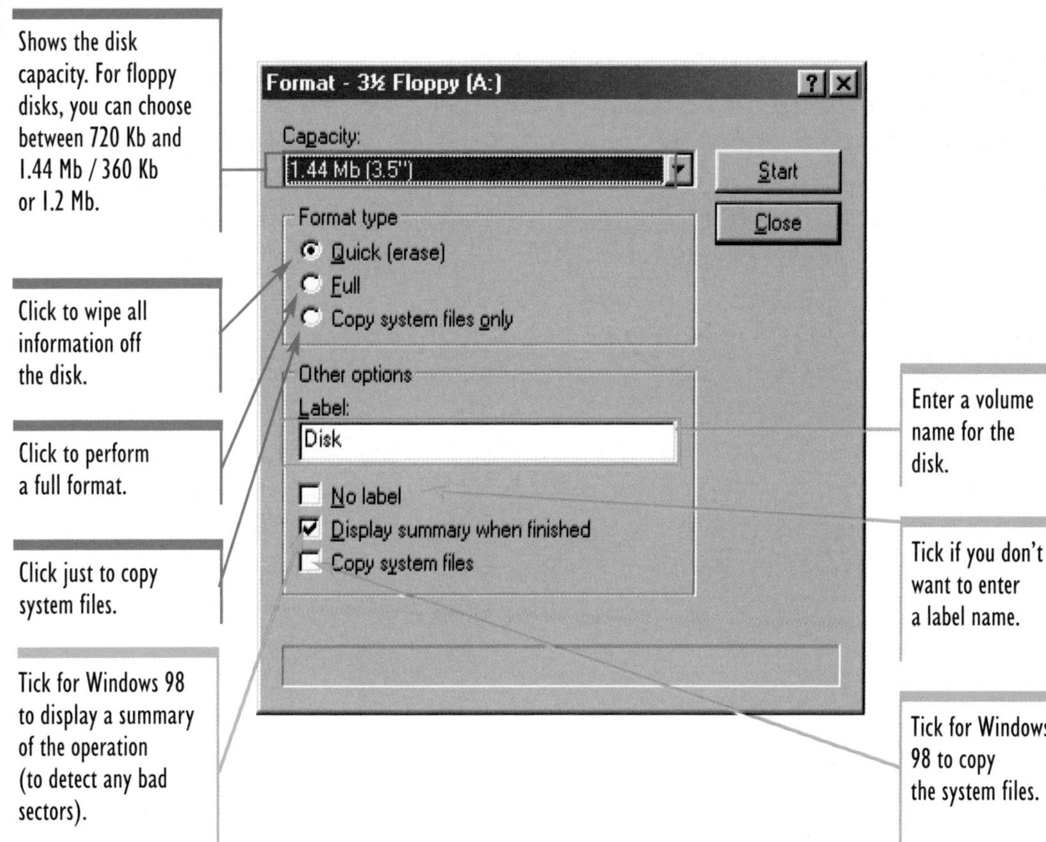

Shows the disk capacity. For floppy disks, you can choose between 720 Kb and 1.44 Mb / 360 Kb or 1.2 Mb.
Click to wipe all information off the disk.
Click to perform a full format.
Click just to copy system files.
Tick for Windows 98 to display a summary of the operation (to detect any bad sectors).
Format - 3½ Floppy (A:)
Capacity:
1.44 Mb (3.5")
Start
Close
Format type
Quick (erase)
Full
Copy system files only
Other options
Label:
Disk
No label
Display summary when finished
Copy system files
Enter a volume name for the disk.
Tick if you don't want to enter a label name.
Tick for Windows 98 to copy the system files.

You cannot format disks for backup or removable drives like Zip drives via the Format dialogue box. If you bring up the context menu for the drive, you will see that the manufacturer's own formatting command has been added to it.

Chapter 3

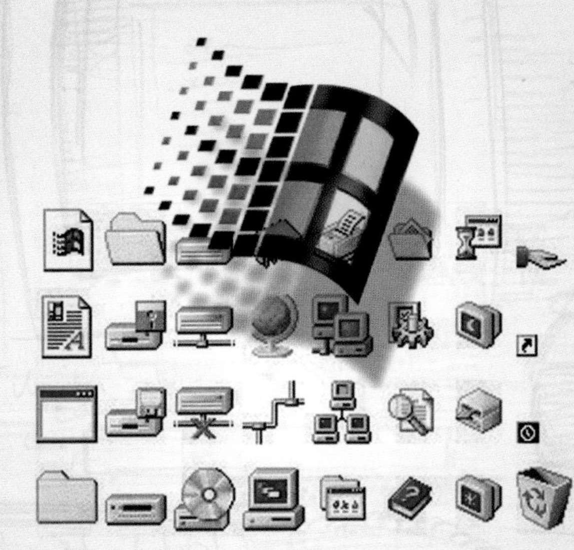

Explorer

Programs / Windows Explorer

Explorer is the perfect way to look at the contents of a folder or disk drive, or display all the items on the desktop. You use Explorer to move through the different folders and subfolders on the computer's hard drive, copy files between folders or to a floppy drive, view the details of a file or run a program. Explorer displays two 'window panes' by default. The left one shows the tree-like structure of the disk contents from the desktop down. When you select a 'branch' of the 'tree' in the left pane, Explorer displays all the subfolders and files in it in the right pane. Explorer offers different ways of viewing the contents of a folder. You can have them displayed as large icons, small icons, or showing detailed information on the date of creation, size and type of files. In the left pane, the tree structure uses the + and - symbols to show that folders are nested. To show subfolders within a folder, click the + sign. To hide the secondary tree structure, click the - sign; that also lets you view more items in the left pane.

HOW TO

There are four different ways to call up Windows Explorer:

Click in turn on Start, Programs, then Windows Explorer.

Right-click on a folder or disk drive icon to bring up a context menu. Choose the Explore command to load Explorer and show it on-screen.

Hold down the Shift key and double-click on the folder or icon standing for the disk to explore: Explorer will appear immediately on your screen.

Go into the \Windows operating system installation folder and double-click on the Explorer.exe icon.

TIP

The best way to call up Explorer quickly is to create a shortcut on the desktop or Quick Launch toolbar housed on the taskbar (copy and paste by right-clicking the Explorer.exe icon and choosing the Create Shortcut(s) Here command from the context menu). Even quicker: assign a keyboard shortcut in the Windows Explorer Properties dialogue box (Shortcut tab).

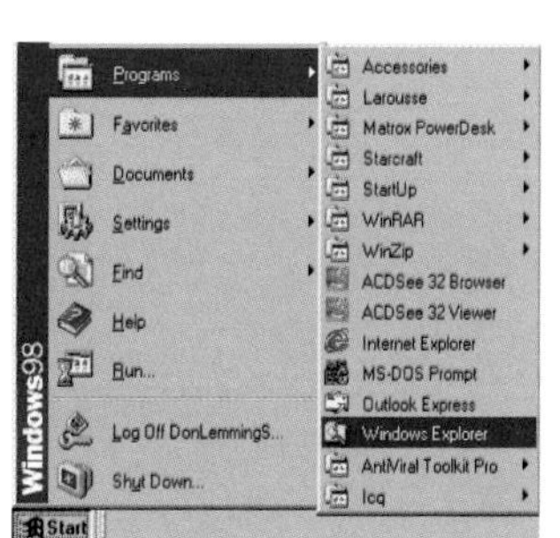

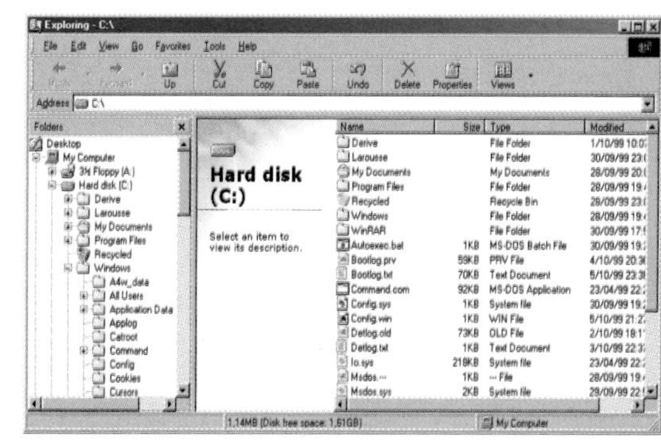

Windows Explorer

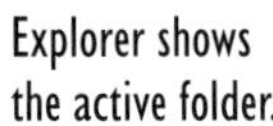

Explorer shows the active folder.

Click to go up one level. The top level is the desktop.

The files contained in the selected folder.

Windows 98 desktop is the highest level.

The + sign indicates that there is a sublevel. Click on the symbol to show the subfolders.

The - sign indicates that the entire subcontents are displayed. Click on the symbol to hide the subfolders.

Select the folder with a single mouse-click; Explorer shows its contents in the right pane.

The total disk space occupied by the files in the folder, and the free space on the drive where the folder is stored.

Click to close Explorer.

You move around in Explorer by clicking on folders or items displayed in the left pane. To expand and view the folders on a disk drive, just click on the + sign to the left of its name or double-click directly on the folder name. To open a folder and view its contents in the right pane, click on its name.

••••• **Hint** •••••

Keyboard shortcuts

F5: refreshes the display.

F6: moves the cursor between panes.

Ctrl+A: selects all objects.

Back/Delete: selects the folder up one level.

+ (numeric keypad): expands a folder.

- (numeric keypad): collapses a folder.

Ctrl+Down arrow: Moves the selector down.

Ctrl+Up arrow: Moves the selector up.

Looking into files

Large icons

You get the same result with the Large Icons, Small icons, List and Details commands on the View menu.

Click to view the left pane of Explorer as a Web page: Windows 98 shows the name of the folder and information about the selected file.

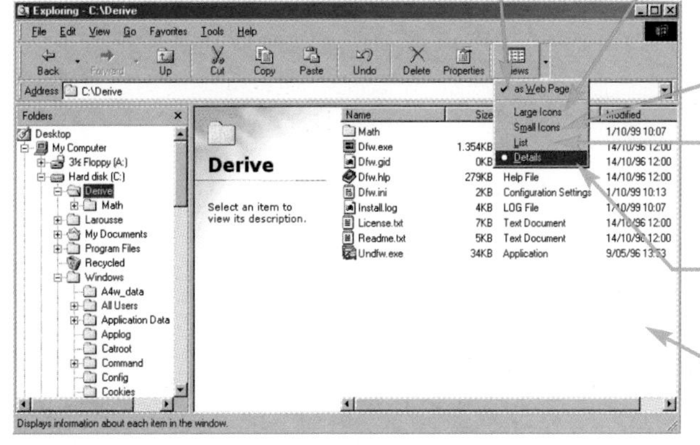

Click to view the files and folders in the right pane as large icons.

Click to view more icons in the right pane.

Click for a list of file and folder names.

Click to display file and folder names with their size, type and date created/modified.

Explorer changes the display according to the mode selected.

Checklist

1. For more information about a selected file or folder, select it by clicking once on its name in the right pane (for files) or left pane (for folders).
2. Click on the *Properties* icon on the toolbar.
3. Click *OK* to close the *Properties* dialog box.

Explorer properties

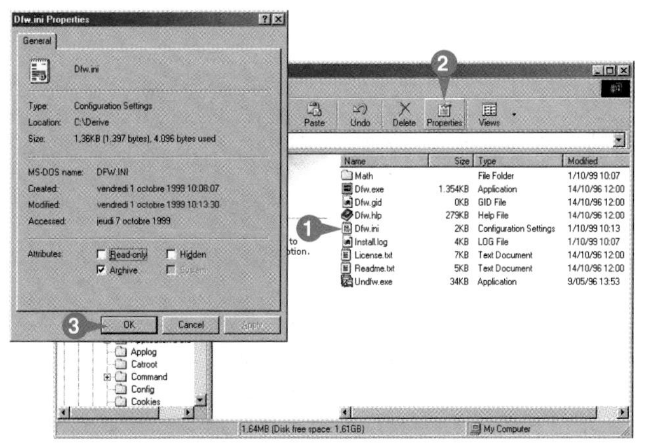

The Properties dialog box also pops up when you select the file or folder and choose File/Properties from the context menu.

Checklist

1. Call up the *Address* toolbar with the *View/Toolbars/Address* bar command.
2. Enter the name of the folder you wish to go to in the text box.
3. Press the *Enter* key to confirm.
4. Explorer opens the relevant folder and displays its contents in the right pane.

Getting to an item

Address toolbar

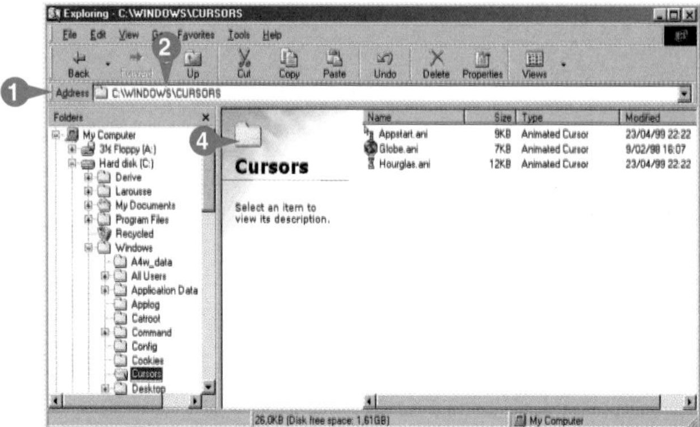

The folder name may be preceded by the drive letter (C:, D:, etc). The root directory is named \ (backslash) and all folder names must be separated by this symbol.

Different ways to view things

View / Folder options / View

Choose View/Folder options, and the Folder options dialogue box will pop up.

If other people use your computer, you can avoid the risk of serious problems by checking the Do not show hidden or system files box. This way, they will stay invisible and the user won't be able to delete them.

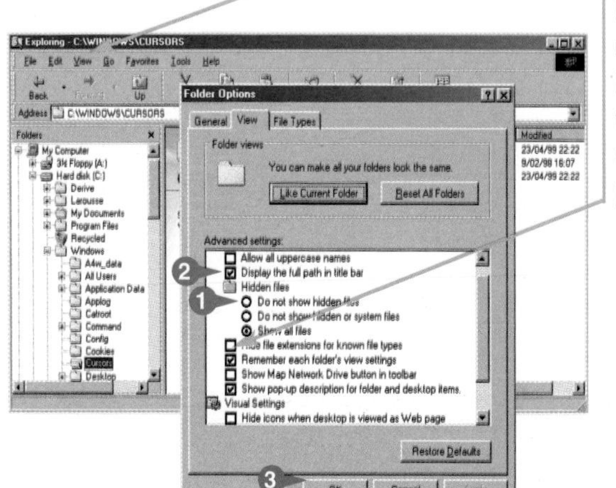

Click not to have file extensions (the three letters which follow the filename and dot) displayed in the right pane.

Checklist

1. Click the *Do not show hidden or system files* button to prevent Explorer displaying hidden and system files. System files are essential to make your computer and programs run properly.
2. To show the path for the selected file or folder, check the *Display the full path in the title bar* box.
3. Click the *OK* or *Apply* buttons to confirm the new settings.

View / Folder options / File types

Every time you install a new application, the new file extensions relating to the kind of files that the program can create are stored in this dialogue box. If Windows 98 cannot find an application that relates to the file type, it offers you a box from which you can choose a program to open it with.

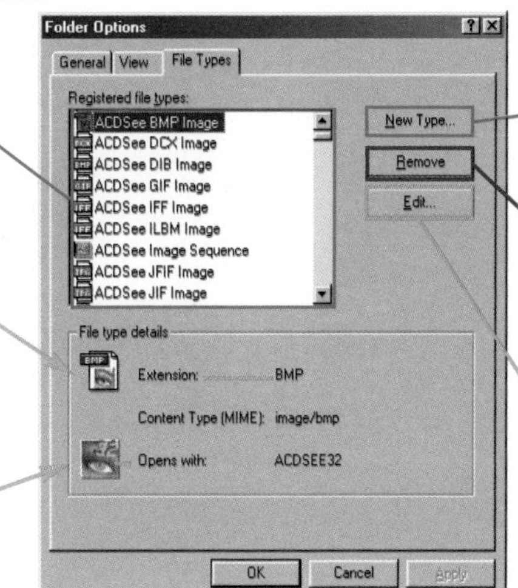

Explorer shows all the file types recorded.

The extensions (3 letters after the filename and dot) of files of the selected type.

The name of the program you can use to open the selected file.

Click to record a new file type.

Click to delete a selected file type.

Click to change the settings associated with the type of file selected.

Connecting up to a network 

Tools / Map Network Drive

Checklist

1. Click the *Map Network Drive* icon.
2. Enter a drive name, or select it from the drop-down box.
3. In the *Path text* box, enter the path to the drive, using the command string: \\name_remote_computer\shared_drive_letter.
4. Click *OK* for Windows 98 to make the connection and display it directly in Explorer.

Explorer shows the remote drive.

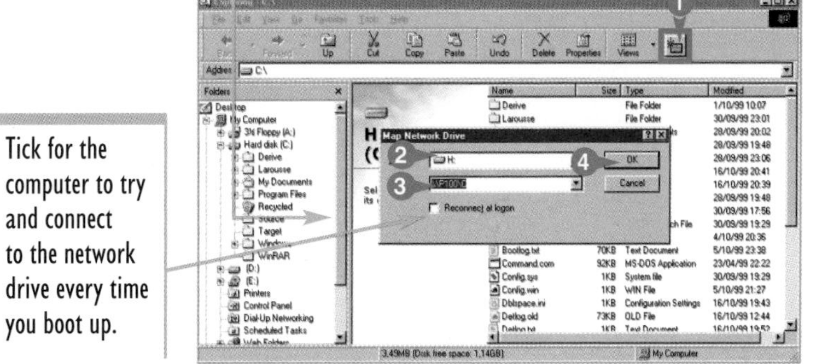

Tick for the computer to try and connect to the network drive every time you boot up.

To show the Map Network Drive icon in the standard toolbar, check the Show Map Network Drive button in the toolbar option in the Folders Options dialogue box (View tab).

To share a drive, the remote computer must have chosen the File and Print Sharing option for Microsoft networks via the Networks icon in the Control Panel.

Checklist

1. Click the toolbar *Disconnect Network Drive* button.
2. Select the network drive to disconnect.
3. Click *OK* to disconnect the network drive.
4. A dialogue box pops up asking you to confirm the disconnection: Click *Yes*.
5. The name assigned to the shared network drive disappears from Explorer.

Disconnection from a network

Tools / Disconnect Network Drive

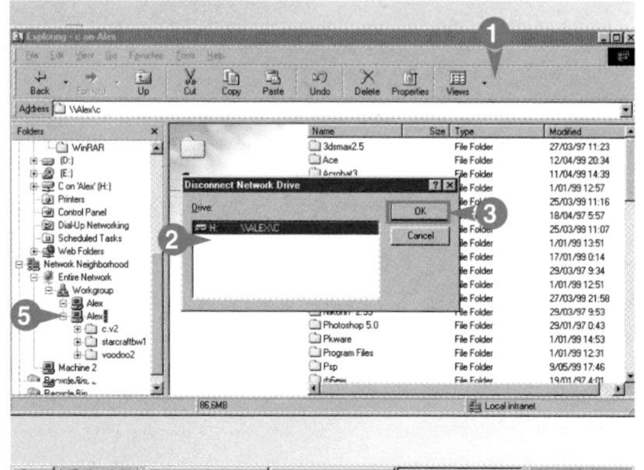

Even if the remote computer which shared the drive is switched off, the drive will still be disconnected and Windows 98 will remove the drive's icon from Explorer.

Rearranging icons

View / Arrange icons

Arrange icons/by Name
sorts files by filename.

Arrange icons/by Type
sorts and arranges files by extension.

Arrange icons/by Size
sorts files by ascending or descending order of size.

Arrange icons/by Date
sorts files by the date when they were created/modified.

Explorer immediately refreshes the display and shows the files sorted according to the command.

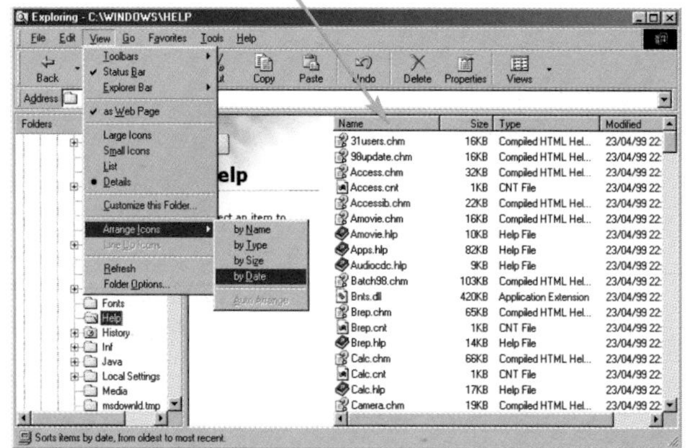

Checklist

The *Arrange Icons* command lets you sort the items viewed in Explorer's right pane. You can sort them by name, date, type or size. You can also sort in ascending or descending order by clicking on the column header in the right pane.

Clicking on the *Name*, *Size*, *Type* or *Modified* headers in the right pane is the same as choosing the corresponding *View/Arrange Icons* commands.

Copying or moving files

Checklist

1. Select the files to be copied by clicking on them. To select files that are next to each other, click on the first one, hold down the *Shift* key and click on the last one. For files that are not next to each other, press the *Ctrl* key and click on each one.

2. To copy the files to another folder, press *Ctrl* and click on the selected files. To move the files to another folder, just click on the selected files.

3. As you move the mouse, Explorer shows a plus sign if you have pressed *Ctrl* to copy.

4. When you release the mouse button, a dialog box pops up to show how the copying is progressing.

2 Click, hold the mouse button down and drag the pointer to the destination folder.

1 Select the files to copy.

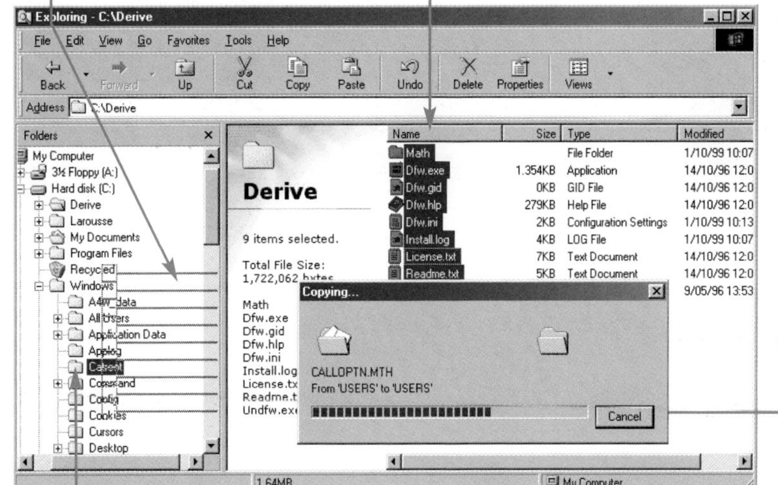

3 Put the mouse pointer on the destination folder so that its name is highlighted.

4 Let go of the button to copy the files.

If you do not press the Ctrl key, Explorer will move the files if you are working with two folders on the same drive. If you are working with two folders on different drives, however, Explorer will just copy them (leaving the files in their original folder).

To cancel the copy, do not release the mouse button but simply press the Esc key. If you have already let go of the button, press Ctrl+Z.

With the context menu displayed:

Choose *Move Here* to move the selected files,

Choose *Copy Here* to copy the files (the originals remain in the source folder).

Choose *Create Shortcut(s) Here* to create shortcuts to the selected files in the destination folder.

Choose *Cancel* to stop copying and return to Explorer.

Right-clicking to copy a file

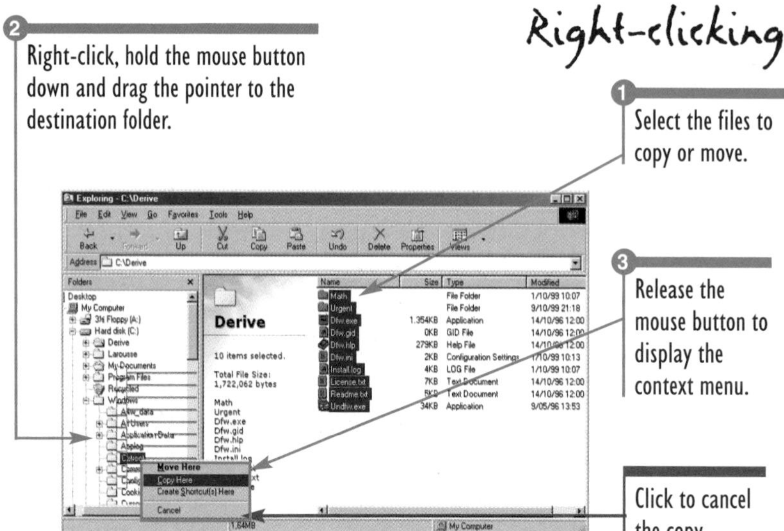

1. Select the files to copy or move.

2. Right-click, hold the mouse button down and drag the pointer to the destination folder.

3. Release the mouse button to display the context menu.

Click to cancel the copy.

You can also cancel the copy by pressing the Esc key. The context menu will vanish and the files will not be copied.

Deleting a file

You can always recover deleted files by looking in the Recycle Bin. But if you press the Shift+Del keys, the files will be purged from your system. They will not go into the Recycle Bin and you will not be able to recover them.

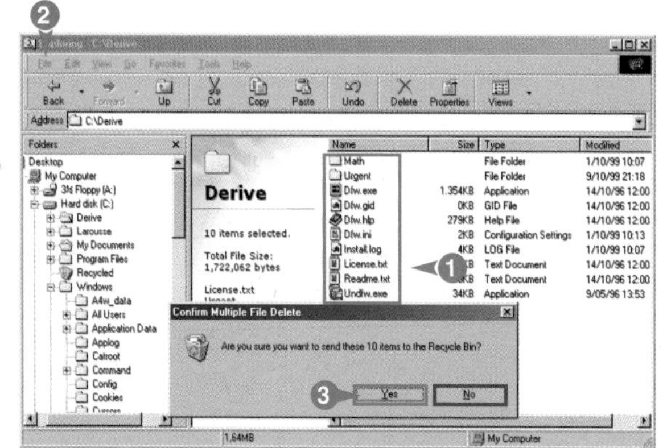

Checklist

1. Select the files to be deleted in the right pane. To delete an entire folder, click on the folder in the left pane.
2. Select the *File/Delete* command or press the *Del* key to bring up a warning box.
3. Windows 98 displays a warning box. Click *Yes* to confirm that you want to delete the files and send them to the *Recycle Bin*.

Renaming a file

If you change your mind about renaming and you click on No in the Rename box, Windows 98 returns to Explorer with the highlight cursor flashing and the name changed. To return to the previous name, simply press Esc.

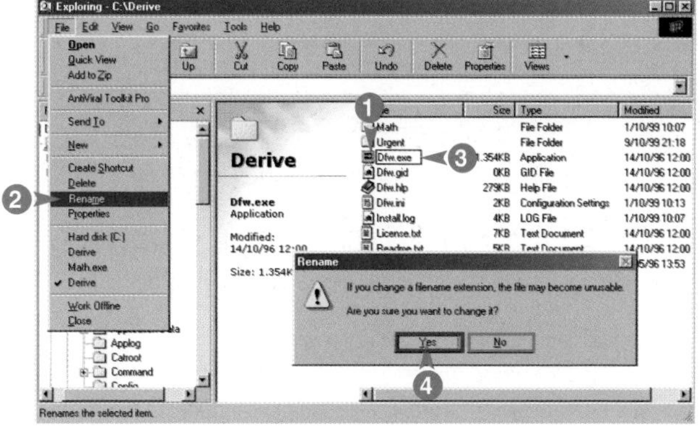

Checklist

1. Click on the name of the file or folder you want to rename.
2. Choose the *File/Rename* command or simply press [F2].
3. Type in a new name and press *Enter* to confirm.
4. If you give a file a different extension, the program it was created with may refuse to open it.

Creating a new folder

Checklist

1. Click on the folder or drive letter in which you want to create a folder.
2. Choose the *File/New/Folder* command to create a new folder named *New Folder*.
3. Explorer highlights the name with the cursor box around it, so you can rename it immediately.
4. Press the *Enter* key or click on a blank area of the window pane to confirm your choice of folder name.

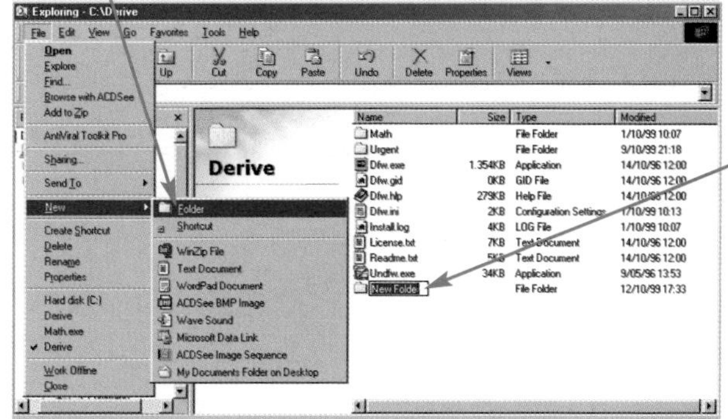

1 Select the location where the new folder is to be created.

2 Choose the File/New/Folder command.

3 Explorer creates the empty folder with the name New Folder.

You create a new file in just the same way. All you do is choose the type of file to be created from the list displayed in the New submenu. The list of file types depends on what programs you have installed on your system.

Most files stored in a folder belong to a parent application, i.e. the program used to create them. When you double-click on a file, Windows 98 launches the parent program, loads the selected file and displays it on screen.

To run a program, look for an associated filename with the extension *.exe*, *.com* or *.bat* and double-click on it.

Launching an application or opening a file

2 Windows 98 automatically opens the file (in this instance with the Wordpad program).

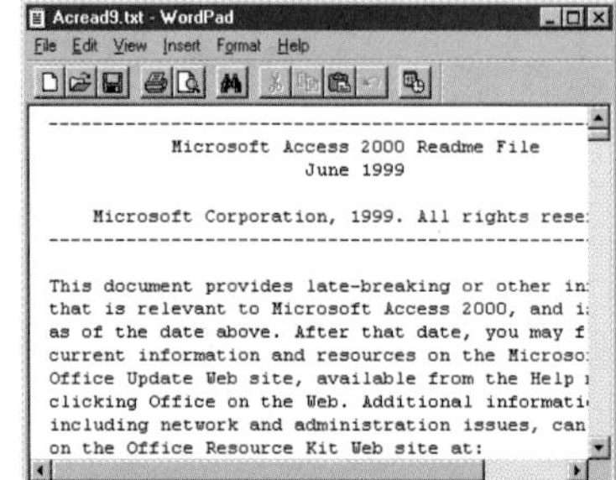

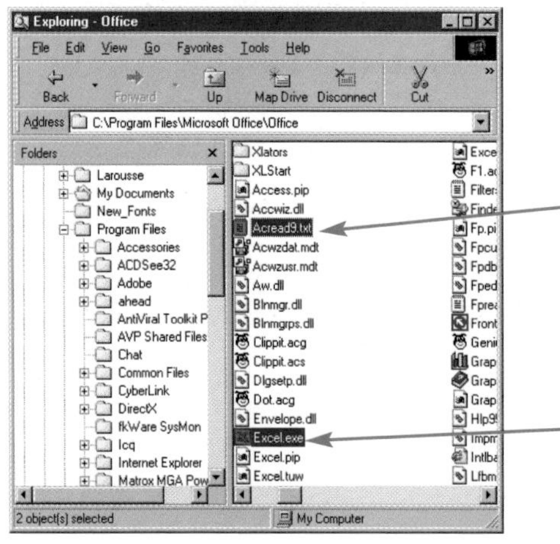

1 Double-click on the chosen file name.

3 Double-click on the chosen program name.

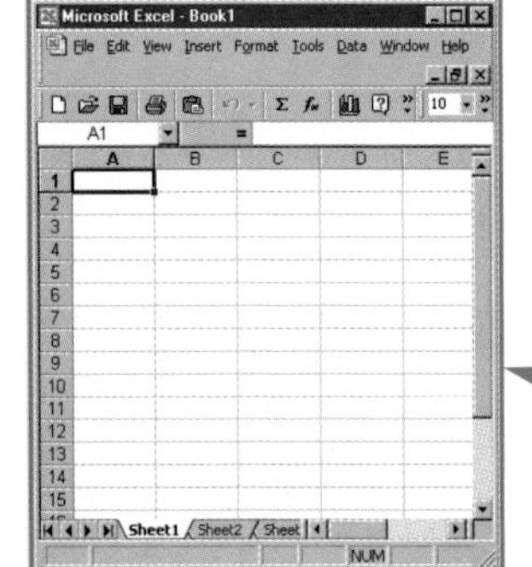

4 Windows 98 runs the associated program.

In either case, you can right-click on the filename and select the Open command to run the associated program or view the file contents. If you select a group of files, Windows 98 will run or open allo the applications associated with all the files in turn.

If no application is associated with the file, Windows 98 displays the Open with dialogue box so you can choose the program with which you wish to view the file's contents.

Chapter 4

Customising Windows 98

Personalising your display

Control Panel / Display

The general appearance of the Windows 98 desktop influences your screen display: too bright or jazzy a background, garish colours for dialogue boxes or window scroll bars can give you sore eyes and shorten your working time. The *Display* icon in *Control Panel* lets you choose the wallpaper Windows 98 uses as the background to your screen. But that's not all. The same dialogue box also lets you choose the screen saver that cuts in when your computer is idle. Broadly speaking, you can set the colours of windows, dialogue boxes and all the objects displayed on your screen. You can change the display settings to specify the resolution of your monitor and how many colours are to be used. Video cards are constantly developing, and the dialogue box gives you a quick way to update the drivers used to improve your display. You can also change the desktop's default icons using the *Effects* tab, or add different Internet channel bars that you subscribe to.

HOW TO

You can bring up Display's Properties dialogue box in three ways:

Choose Start/Settings/Control Panel and then double-click the Display icon.

Double-click on My Computer, Control Panel and Display in turn.

Right-click on a blank area of the desktop; Windows 98 will bring up a context menu in which you can select the Properties command.

TIP

To update the drivers (control programs) for the video cards installed in your computer, use the Settings tab in Display's Properties dialogue box. Click on the Advanced button and Windows 98 will open a new dialogue box in which you are able to change the video adapter drivers.

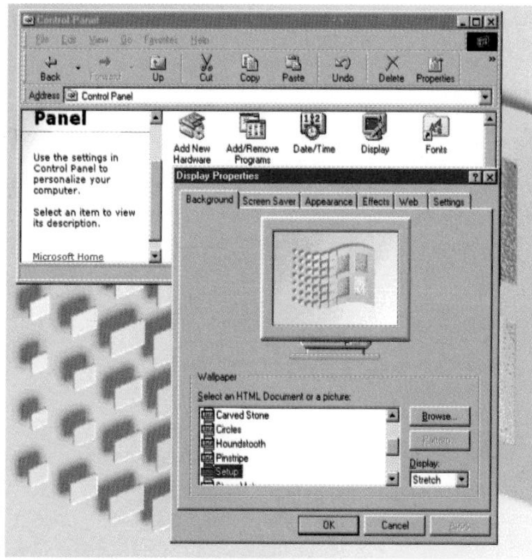

Choosing a background wallpaper

Display Properties
Background | Screen Saver | Appearance | Effects | Web | Settings
Wallpaper
Select an HTML Document or a picture:
Carved Stone
Circles
Houndstooth
Pinstripe
Setup
Browse...
Pattern...
Display:
Stretch
OK | Cancel | Apply

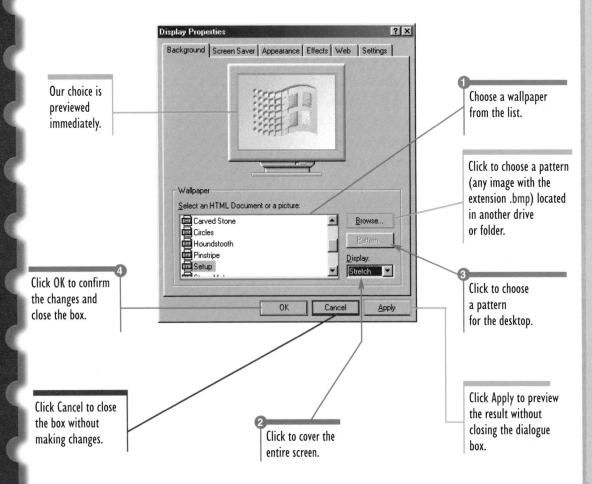

Our choice is previewed immediately.

1 Choose a wallpaper from the list.

Click to choose a pattern (any image with the extension .bmp) located in another drive or folder.

3 Click to choose a pattern for the desktop.

4 Click OK to confirm the changes and close the box.

Click Cancel to close the box without making changes.

2 Click to cover the entire screen.

Click Apply to preview the result without closing the dialogue box.

Checklist

1. Choose a wallpaper to brighten up the desktop.
2. If you want the wallpaper to be full screen, choose the *Stretch* option in the *Display* drop-down list.
3. To choose a pattern as well as wallpaper, click the *Pattern* button.
4. Click the *OK* button.

Hint

If the *Pattern* button is greyed out, choose the *Center* option from the *Display* drop-down list.

Checklist

1. Choose a screen saver from the scroll-down list.
2. Prevent the screen saver being cleared by using a password. Type a password into the dialogue box text box.
3. Set how many minutes with no screen activity there should be before the screen saver starts.
4. Click *OK* to confirm the use of a screen saver.

Choosing a screen saver

Screen Saver tab

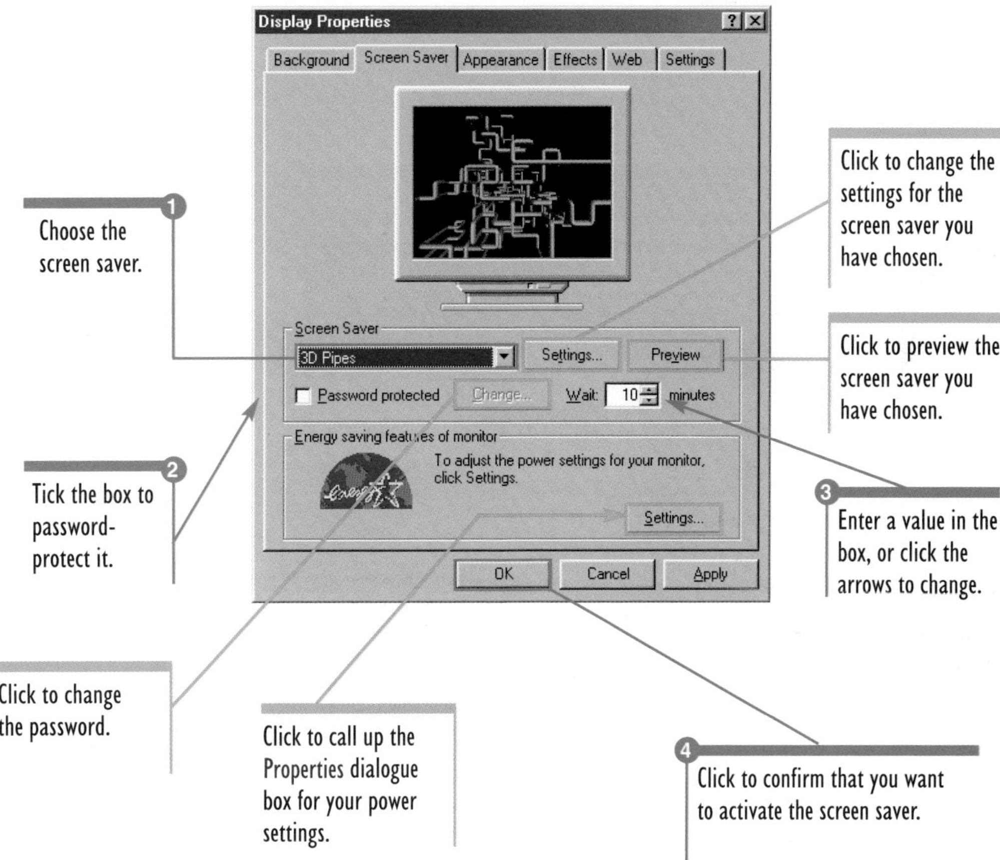

Display Properties
Background
Screen Saver
Appearance
Effects
Web
Settings
Screen Saver
3D Pipes
Settings...
Preview
Password protected
Change...
Wait:
10
minutes
Energy saving features of monitor
To adjust the power settings for your monitor, click Settings.
Settings...
OK
Cancel
Apply
1 Choose the screen saver.
2 Tick the box to password-protect it.
Click to change the password.
Click to call up the Properties dialogue box for your power settings.
Click to change the settings for the screen saver you have chosen.
Click to preview the screen saver you have chosen.
3 Enter a value in the box, or click the arrows to change.
4 Click to confirm that you want to activate the screen saver.

Windows 98 gives you the screen saver for a serious reason. If the same picture is displayed on your monitor for very long periods of time, it may cause damage by burning the image into your screen. The screen saver displays flying objects and other moving patterns at different spots on the screen when your computer is left idle for a specified length of time.

Setting different colours for windows

Appearance tab

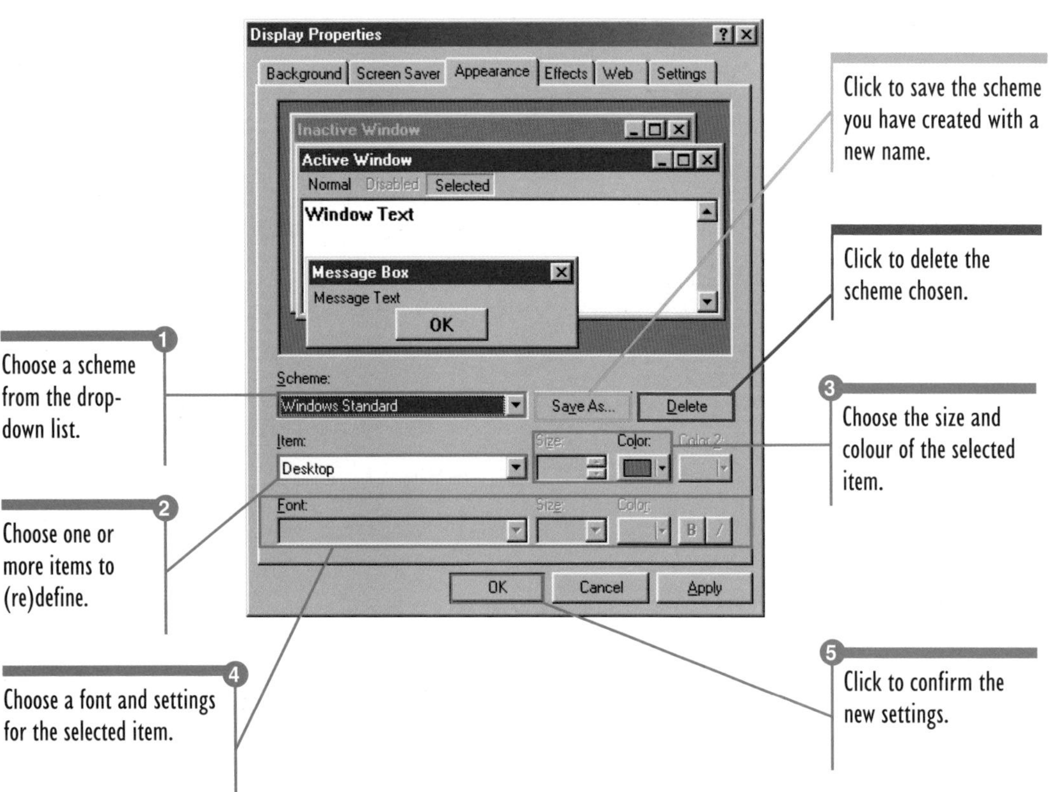

Checklist

1. Choose a scheme you like from the scroll-down menu to save having to define each item separately.
2. To change the appearance of an item, select it from the list.
3. Change the size and colour of the item you have selected.
4. Change the font and attributes of the characters displayed on screen, if you wish.
5. Click *OK* to confirm.

Note

To save having to define each item separately, you can choose one of the schemes supplied with Windows 98. The Windows Standard scheme is the default; it provides restful, simple colours that are easy on the eye.

Changing visual effects

Effects tab

Checklist

1. Click to select the desktop icon to be modified. Slide the bar to see other desktop icons.
2. Click the *Change Icon* button to call up the *Change Icon* dialogue box and choose a new icon. Remember to confirm your choice of new icon by clicking *OK*.
3. To restore the Windows 98 default icons, click on the *Default Icon* button.
4. Click the check boxes to add visual effects.
5. Click the *OK* button to confirm the options chosen.

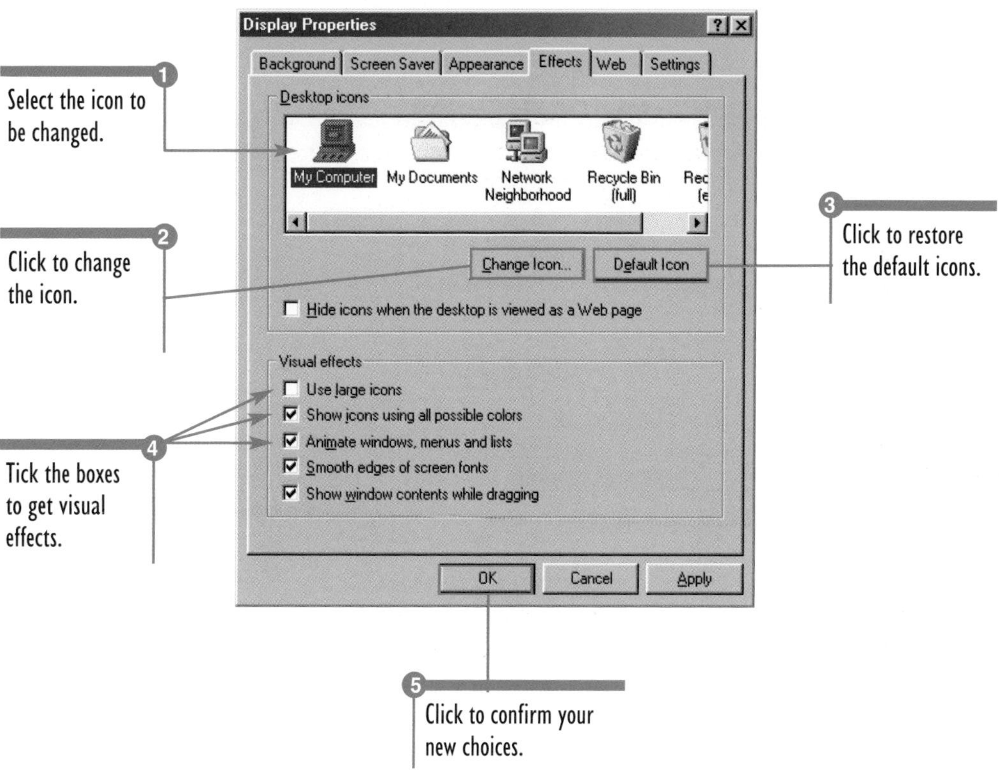

Windows 98 comes with lots of icons. You'll find them in files with the extension .dll in the \Windows\System directory. You can select them in the Change Icons dialogue box by clicking the Browse button.

Setting channels

Web tab

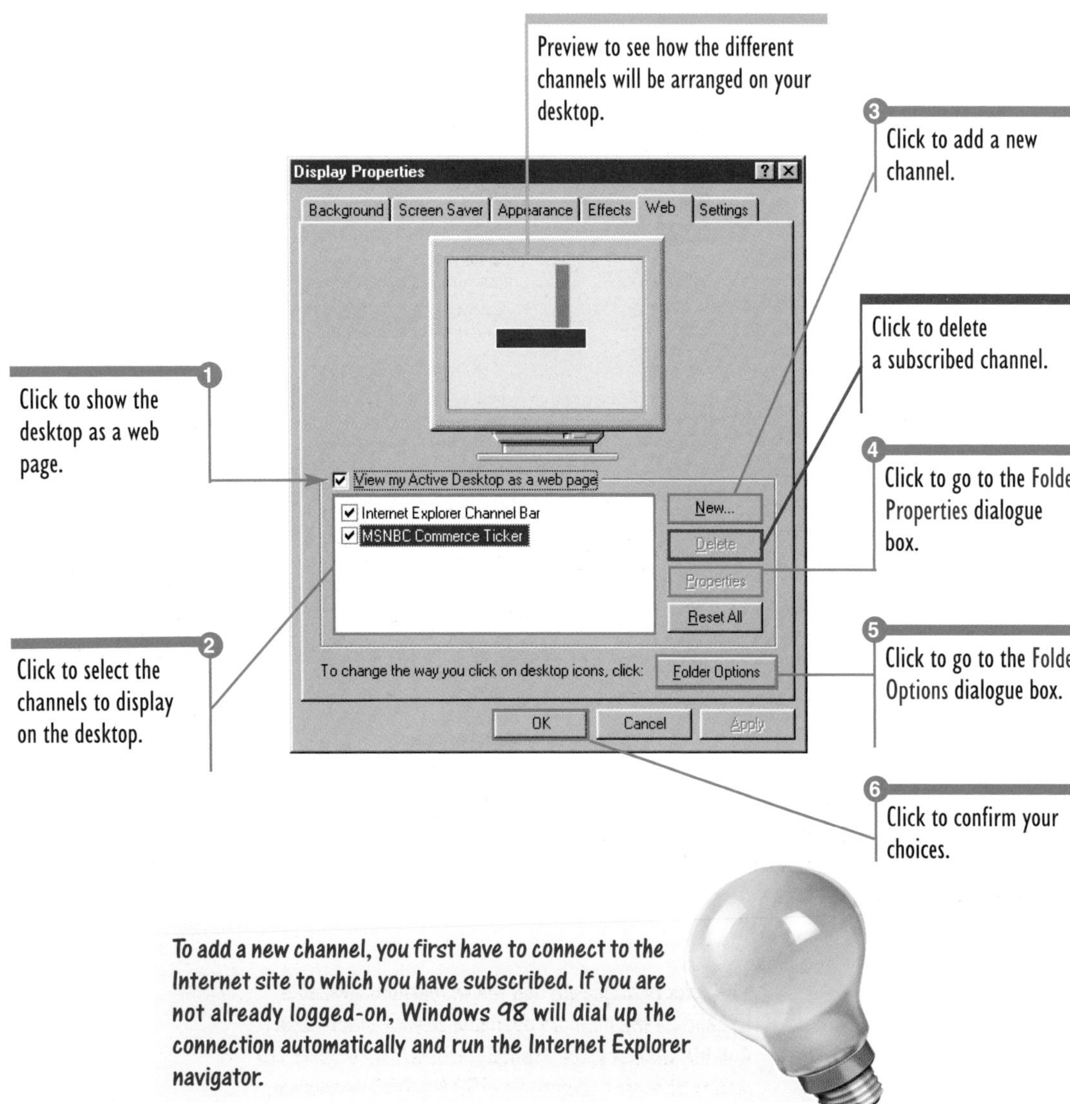
Preview to see how the different channels will be arranged on your desktop.
3 Click to add a new channel.
Click to delete a subscribed channel.
1 Click to show the desktop as a web page.
4 Click to go to the Folder Properties dialogue box.
2 Click to select the channels to display on the desktop.
5 Click to go to the Folder Options dialogue box.
6 Click to confirm your choices.
Display Properties
Background
Screen Saver
Appearance
Effects
Web
Settings
View my Active Desktop as a web page
Internet Explorer Channel Bar
MSNBC Commerce Ticker
New...
Delete
Properties
Reset All
To change the way you click on desktop icons, click:
Folder Options
OK
Cancel
Apply

To add a new channel, you first have to connect to the Internet site to which you have subscribed. If you are not already logged-on, Windows 98 will dial up the connection automatically and run the Internet Explorer navigator.

Ⓐ Tick the *View as a web page* box for Windows 98 to change the desktop screen.

Ⓑ Tick the boxes that represent websites to which you subscribe; Windows will put these on the desktop once you have confirmed.

Ⓒ Manage your subscription channels by clicking on the *New* (to add a newly subscribed channel), *Delete* (to delete a subscribed channel) or *Properties* (to change a subscription) buttons.

Ⓓ Click the *OK* button to confirm your choices.

Checklist

1. Click on the arrow to drop down the list and choose the number of colours.
2. Move the slider to the left for a lower resolution and to the right for a higher one.
3. Click *OK*: Windows 98 will ask you to restart the computer to apply the new resolution settings.

Configuring your display

Settings tab

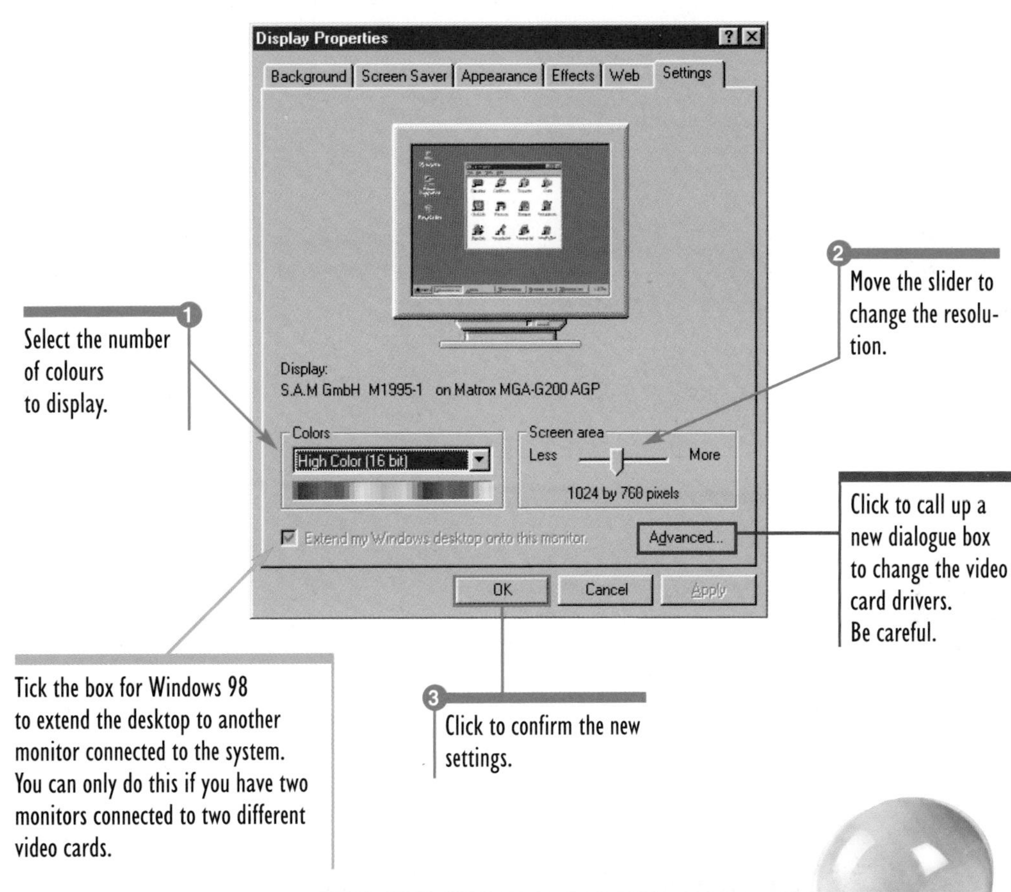

1 Select the number of colours to display.

2 Move the slider to change the resolution.

Click to call up a new dialogue box to change the video card drivers. Be careful.

Tick the box for Windows 98 to extend the desktop to another monitor connected to the system. You can only do this if you have two monitors connected to two different video cards.

3 Click to confirm the new settings.

The colours displayed and the resolutions available depend on the memory available to your video card. A 4 MB memory, for example, will let you display 65 million different colours in a 1024 x 768 resolution.

Flow chart of the Display Properties dialogue box

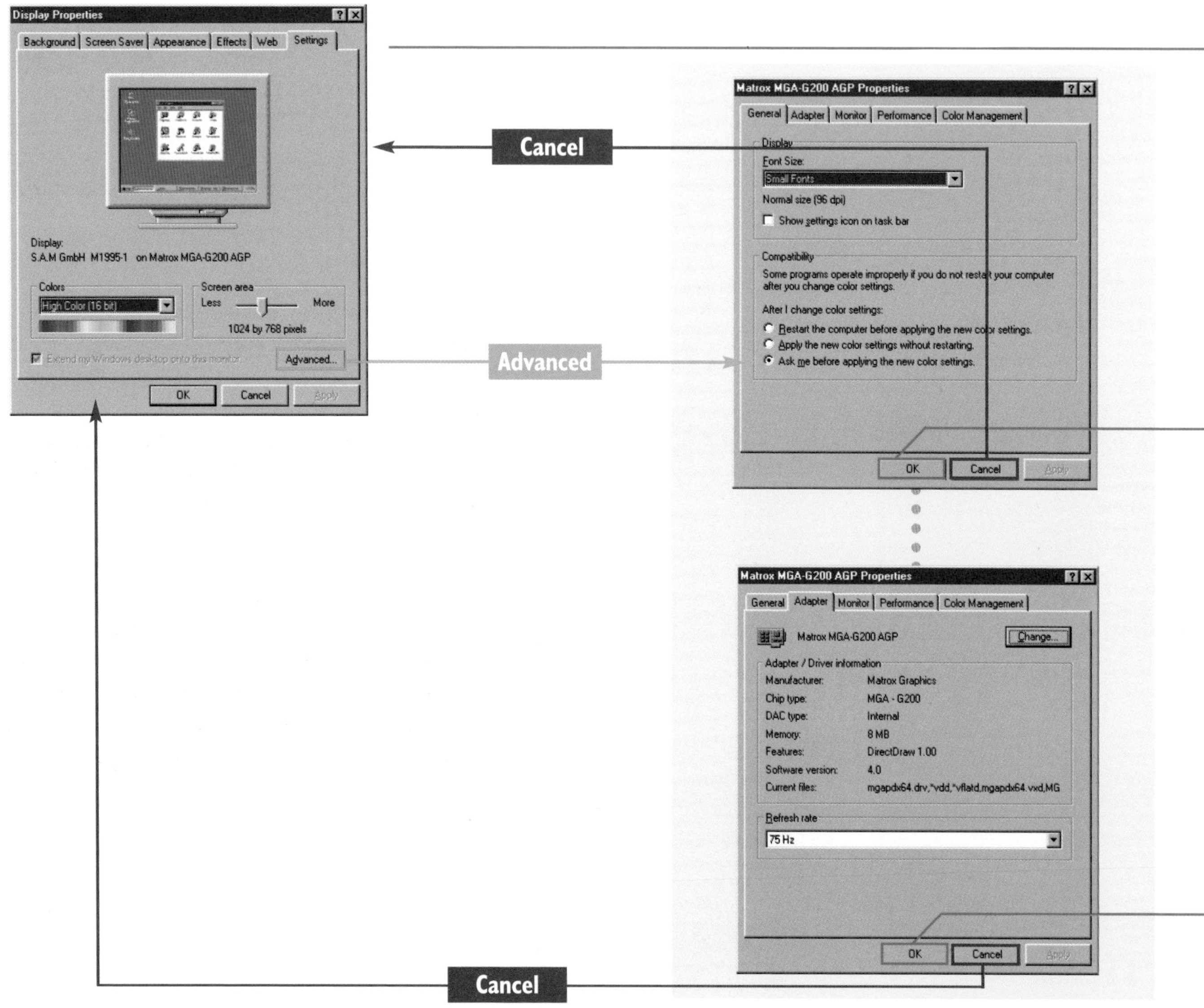

Settings tab — Sets the number of colours and resolution.

General tab — Lets you change the size of screen fonts according to the resolution chosen, and what it should do when colour settings (number of colours and resolution) are changed.

Adapter tab — To change the video card drivers.

In theory

The way your monitor is configured is important to make it easy on the eye. If you have a powerful video card and a large screen (17, 19, 20 or 21 inch) you can choose high resolutions and a huge number of different colours. All these features combine to one end: to stop you getting eye strain.

System and program crashes are frequent occurrences in Windows 98. Very often, they are due to the wrong video card driver being used. If that is the case, you need to get the latest updated driver (either from a supplier or pull it off the Internet). Once you have it, go to the Settings tab, click the *Advanced* button, *Adapter* tab and finally the *Change* button to use the new driver.

Because every video card is different, Windows 98 adapts the *Properties* dialogue box according to the maker. So you may find that the amount of tabs you have and different settings you can choose varies. The page opposite illustrates a system with a *Matrox graphics* MGA-G200 video card installed.

Playing games with a joystick

Control Panel / Game Controllers

All current sound cards have a game port that lets you connect joysticks/gamepads directly to the computer. Once the card is installed, the game port is recognised directly, so all you have to do is plug the joystick in. The *Game Controllers* dialogue box lets you configure your joystick. There are many kinds of joystick, ranging from the basic (a stick and a couple of buttons) to the super-sophisticated (a control surface and more than four buttons). So that Windows 98 can recognise it, you must tell the program what kind of game controller you have connected. Then you need to calibrate it. A 'wizard' (an interactive help utility) will walk you through this. Two dialogue boxes are enough for Windows 98 to centre and fix the controller's handle management. A dialogue box lets you check that everything is working properly by testing the different buttons and the cursor's movement with the rudder.

HOW TO

There are two ways to get to the Game Controllers dialogue box:

Select the Start/Settings/Control Panel command and double-click on the Game Controllers icon.

Double-click in turn on the My Computer, Control Panel and Game Controllers icons.

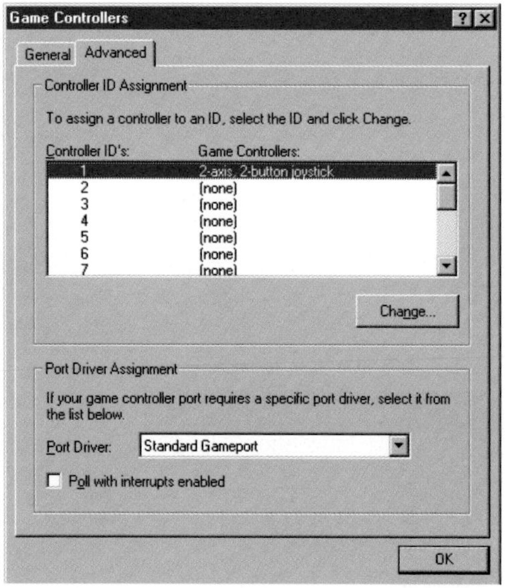

TIP

Your joystick may well work as soon as you plug it in (if the sound card on which the game port is housed is properly configured) but you still need to calibrate it otherwise you may not be able to get the right movements for your favourite simulator.

Calibrating a joystick

Checklist

1. Click in the list of game controllers to select the joystick/gamepad to be configured.
2. Click on the *Add* button to add a new joystick.
3. Click on the *Properties* button to calibrate and test the joystick.
4. Click on the *OK* button to confirm the changes.

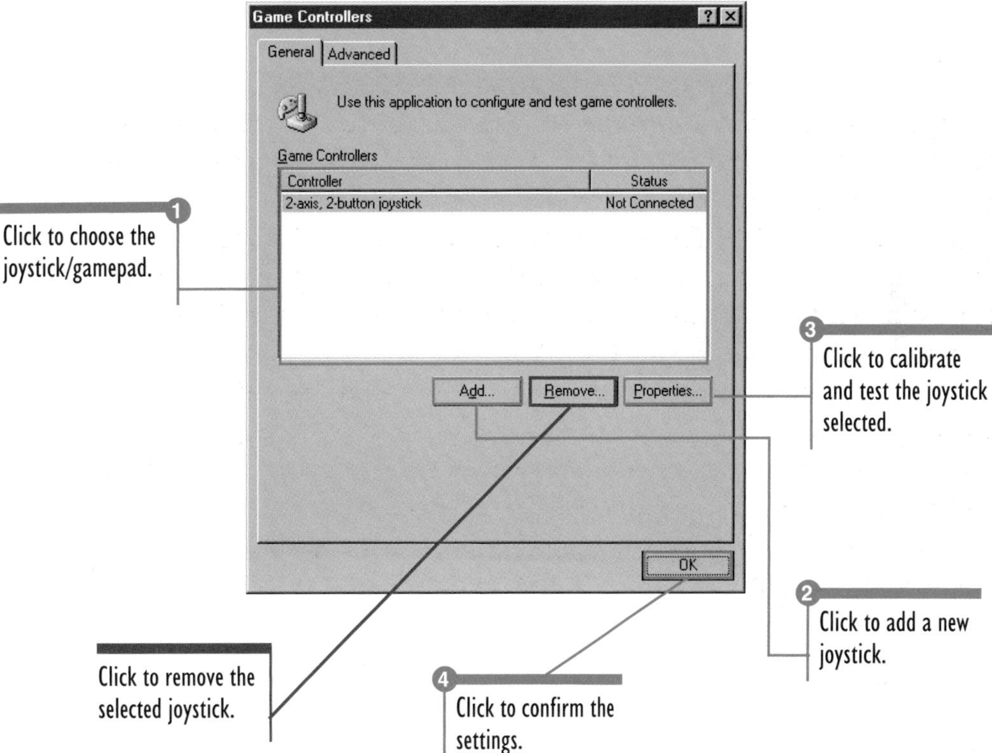

1 Click to choose the joystick/gamepad.

2 Click to add a new joystick.

3 Click to calibrate and test the joystick selected.

4 Click to confirm the settings.

Click to remove the selected joystick.

If you have several joysticks, you should save the configurations so that next time you only need to select from the Controllers list the joystick you wish to use.

Joystick settings

Advanced tab

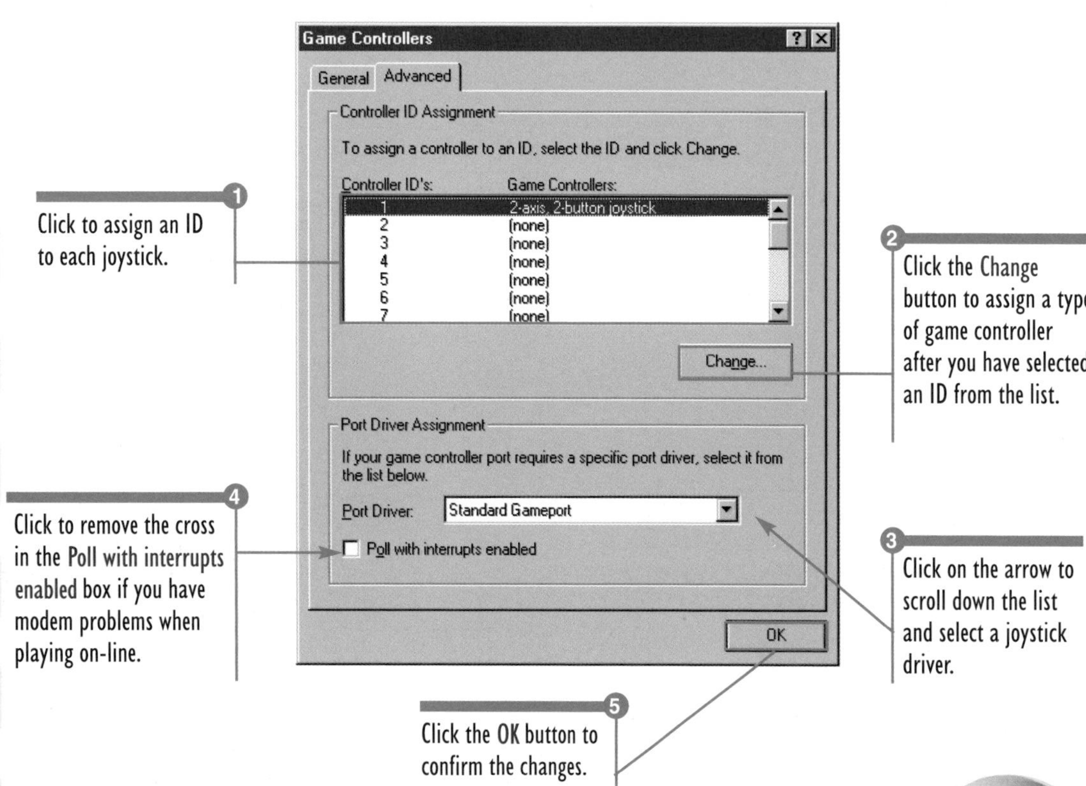

You may not be able to play some MS-DOS games with more modern game controllers. This is because the controllers use special drivers recognised only under Windows 98, which will not work under MS-DOS.

Checklist

1. Click to assign an ID to each game controller.
2. Click on the *Change* button to assign a type of game controller after you have selected an ID from the list.
3. Click on the arrow to scroll down the list and select a game controller driver.
4. Click to remove the cross in the *Poll with interrupts enabled* box if you have modem problems when playing on-line.
5. Click the *OK* button to confirm the changes.

Flow chart of how to calibrate a joystick

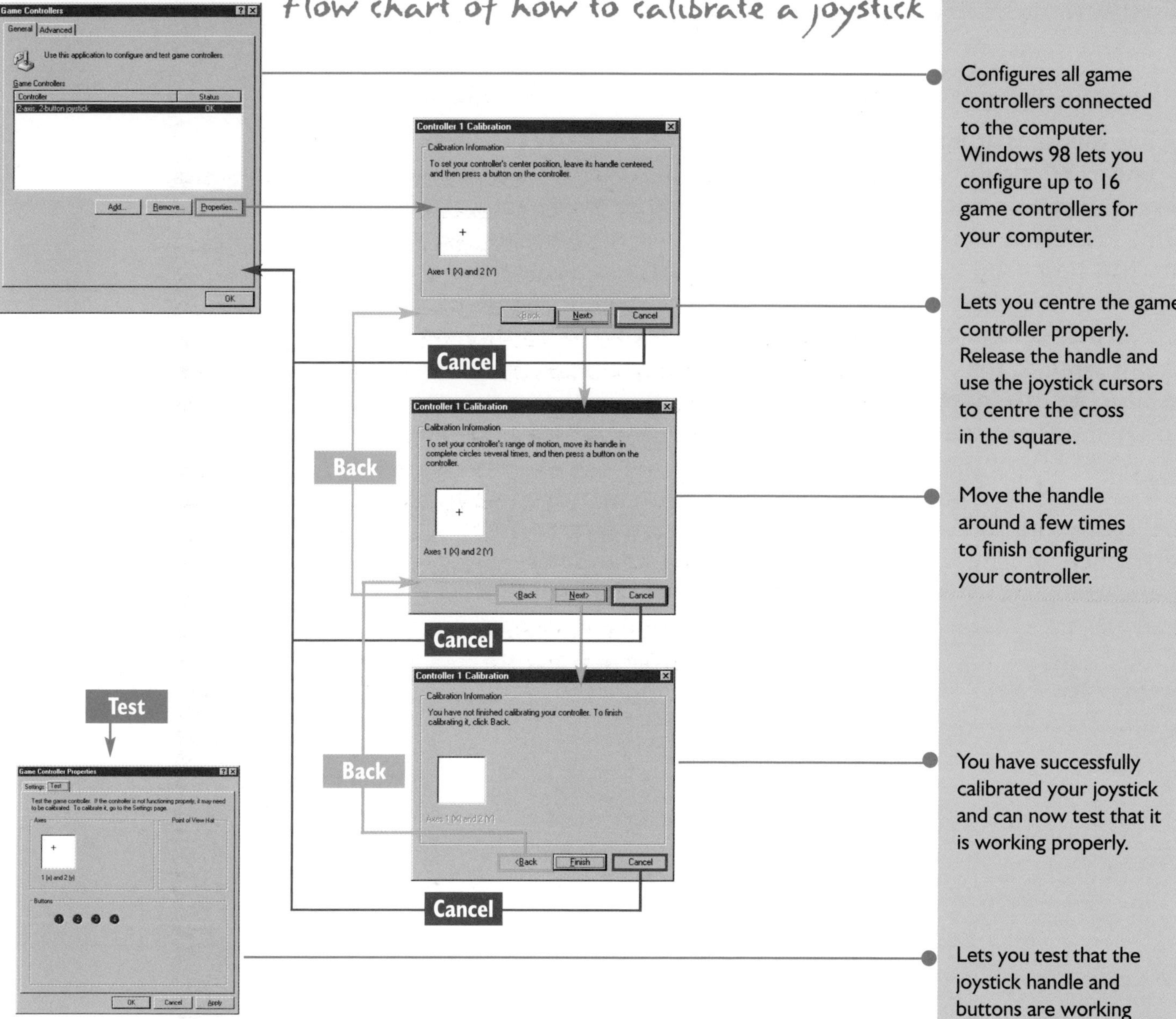

Configures all game controllers connected to the computer. Windows 98 lets you configure up to 16 game controllers for your computer.

Lets you centre the game controller properly. Release the handle and use the joystick cursors to centre the cross in the square.

Move the handle around a few times to finish configuring your controller.

You have successfully calibrated your joystick and can now test that it is working properly.

Lets you test that the joystick handle and buttons are working properly.

Good mouse control

Control Panel / Mouse

Your mouse is at least as important an input device as the keyboard under Windows 98. You simply cannot use the operating system properly if you do not have a mouse connected to your computer. The *Mouse Properties* dialogue box lets you adjust it to work the way that suits you best. You normally use the left button to select and move items, and the right one to call up context menus and for special movements. Left-handed users will almost certainly want to swap the buttons around. You can do that easily from the *Buttons* tab, where you can also set the speed of the double-click that you use for certain operations. There is a special test area to check your settings without closing the box. Windows 98 changes the pointer's appearance as you move the mouse. The default is a white arrow when you click on an item, and an I-beam when entering text. You can change the appearance of any of these pointers using the different schemes supplied with Windows 98, or any other file with the extension *.cur* or *.ani* (for animated cursor). The dialogue box also lets you set the cursor speed and also gives you the option of leaving a trail behind it as it moves on-screen (very useful for the LCD screens on laptops).

HOW TO

There are two ways to get to the Mouse Properties dialogue box:

Select the Start/Settings/Control Panel command and double-click on the Mouse icon.

Double-click in turn on the My Computer, Control Panel and Mouse icons.

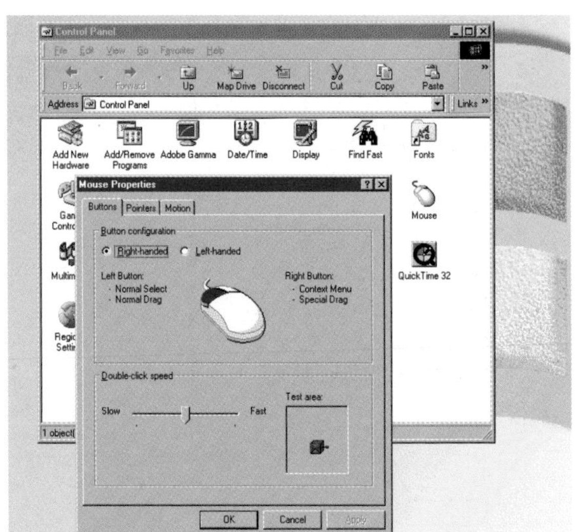

Configuring your mouse

Checklist

1. Choose a left-handed setting (*Left-handed* box) if you want to use the right button for normal selection and moving around.
2. Click the slider and drag it to the right to increase double-click speed or left to slow it down.
3. Double-click on the *Test* box. If the Jack-in-the-box pops out or hides, Windows 98 recognises the mouse double-click.
4. Click *OK* for Windows 98 to store the options chosen.

••••• ***Hint*** •••••

If you clicked on the *Left-handed* option to swap the mouse buttons around, do not run MS-DOS programs in full-screen mode: the mouse will not work. Instead, run them in a window to keep your left-handed user setting.

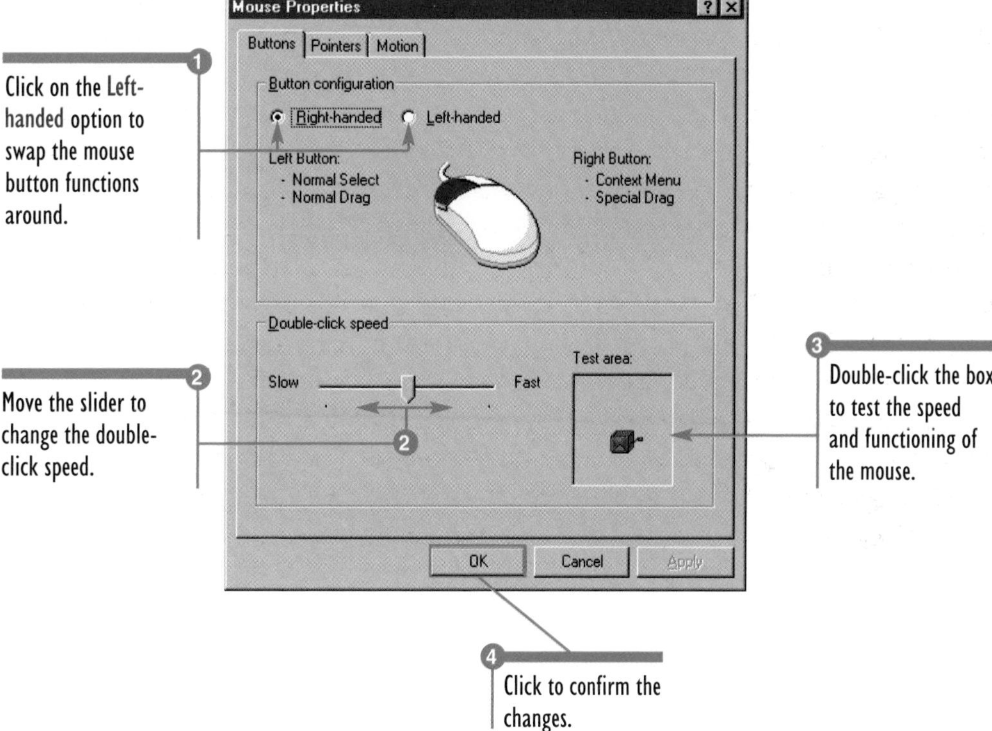

1 Click on the Left-handed option to swap the mouse button functions around.

2 Move the slider to change the double-click speed.

3 Double-click the box to test the speed and functioning of the mouse.

4 Click to confirm the changes.

Changing the pointer

Pointers tab

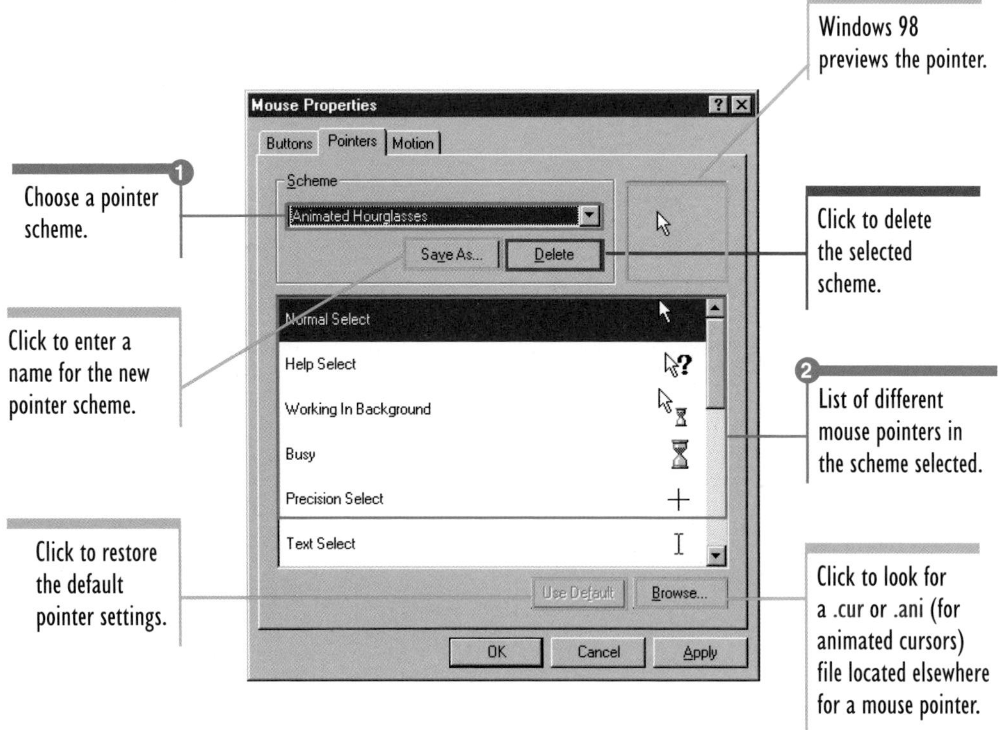

1
Choose a pointer scheme.
Click to enter a name for the new pointer scheme.
Click to restore the default pointer settings.
Windows 98 previews the pointer.
Click to delete the selected scheme.
2
List of different mouse pointers in the scheme selected.
Click to look for a .cur or .ani (for animated cursors) file located elsewhere for a mouse pointer.
Mouse Properties
Buttons
Pointers
Motion
Scheme
Animated Hourglasses
Save As...
Delete
Normal Select
Help Select
Working In Background
Busy
Precision Select
Text Select
Use Default
Browse...
OK
Cancel
Apply

A Select a pointer scheme for Windows 98 to assign the different shapes to the mouse actions.

B Select an action in the list and assign a *.cur* or *.ani* (for animated cursors) file to it by clicking on the *Browse* button.

C If the pointer is animated, you can view how it will work in the *Preview* window.

D Click *OK* to confirm the changes and close the box.

You can choose a different pointer from the Windows 98 default ones through the Browse dialogue box, which calls up a list of files available in the \Windows\Cursors folder. To add new pointers, choose the Add/Remove Programs icon in Control Panel, click on the Windows Setup tab, and then in turn on Accessories, Details and Mouse Pointers in the Components list.

Motions tab

Making your mouse leave a trail is really useful for tracking the pointer's location on LCD screens.

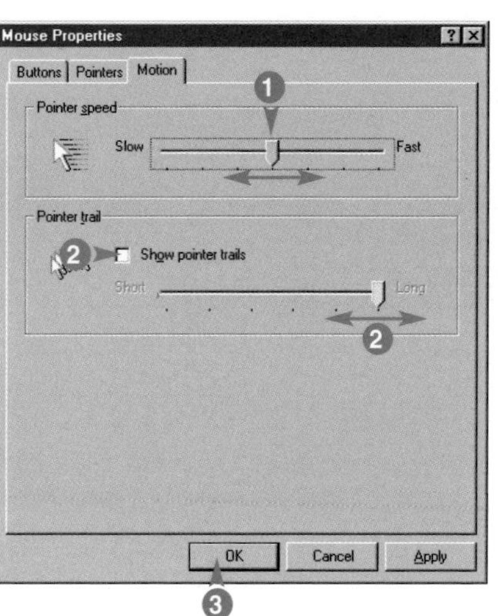

Checklist

1. Move the slider to the left to reduce the pointer speed and right to increase it. The faster the pointer speed, the less you have to move the mouse around on the mouse mat.
2. Activate the mouse pointer trail (tick the *Cursor Trails Enabled* box) and adjust the length by moving the slider.
3. Click *OK* to confirm the options.

Flow chart of the Mouse Properties dialogue box

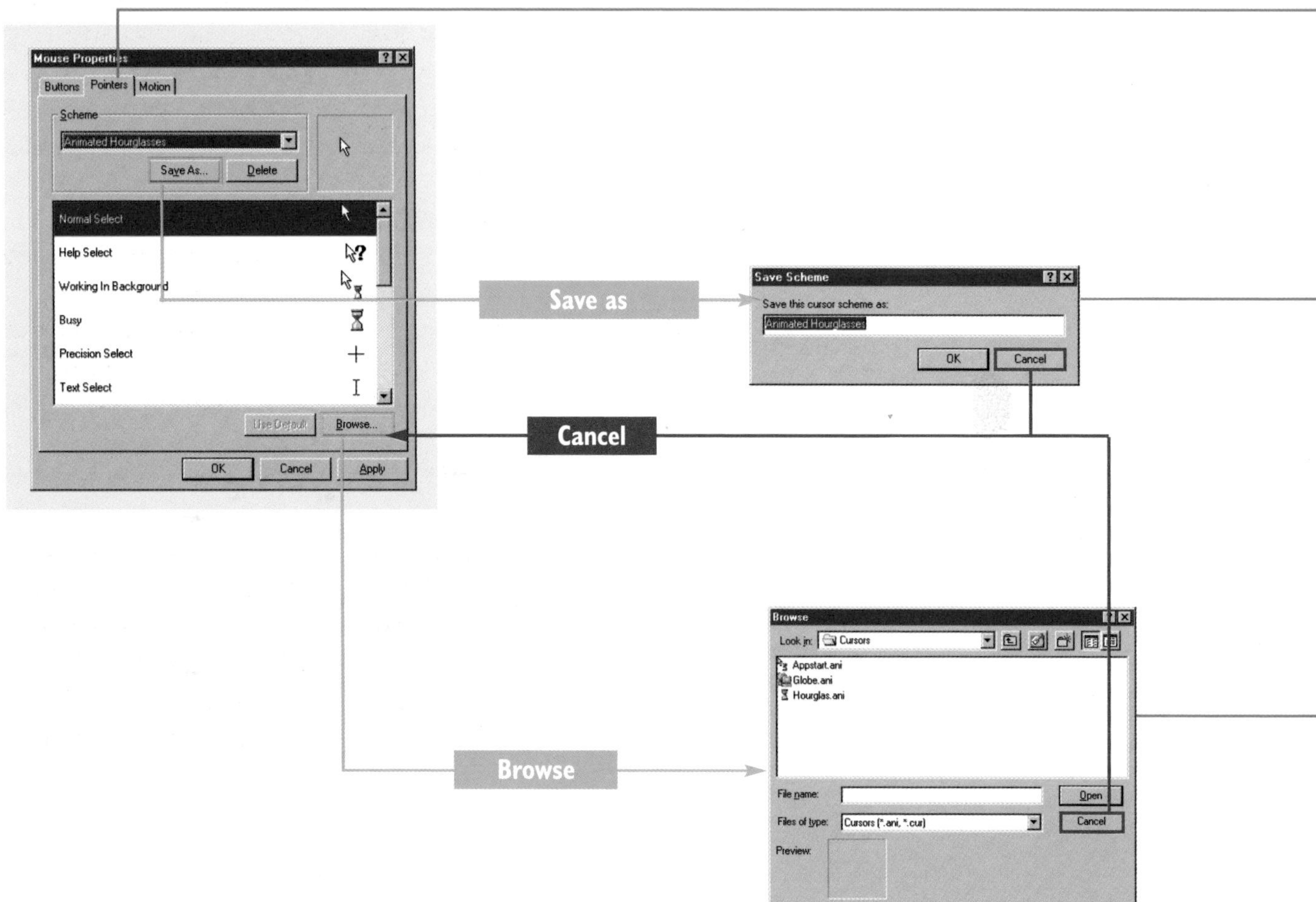

Pointers tab — To choose different pointers for the different mouse actions.

Save a scheme — To save a new mouse pointer scheme.

Browse — Shows the different mouse pointers available; these are files with the extension *.cur* or *.ani* (for animated cursors).

In theory...

To use a mouse under MS-DOS, you had to install a Mouse file and use a special command string. Windows 98 detects your mouse automatically, so that you no longer have to worry about installing anything in a boot file.

If you change your mouse, Windows 98 will automatically recognise that a new device has been added and install the necessary drivers. If you connect a special mouse, the operating system will ask you to insert the disk with the drivers on it into the floppy drive.

Because the operating system uses a graphical interface, you can have different pointers for different tasks. You can also have animated pointers, such as the now-famous hourglass which tells you the system is busy doing something.

Windows 98 – full access

Control Panel / Accessibility Options

Windows 98 offers a range of options to make the keyboard, sounds, display and mouse settings easier for people with physical, sight or hearing impairments. One simple but crucial change for users who have difficulties holding down two keys at once is to make the *Alt*, *Ctrl* and *Shift* keys stay pressed. nThat makes the *Alt+Ctrl+F1* combination easy to perform by pressing the *Alt*, *Ctrl* and *F1* keys in turn. The accessibility tools can help the hard of hearing with the sound warnings that more and more programs are using. The *Accessibility Properties* dialogue box has an option telling Windows 98 to display a message on screen whenever a sound effect comes through the computer speakers. People who experience problems using the mouse can simply replace it with the keyboard arrow keys. All the pointer speed control options are also available through this box. Finally, Windows 98 also allows an auxiliary input device to be connected to the computer's serial port for users who cannot use either the keyboard or the mouse. Windows 98 also provides advanced accessibility options, which include magnifying the area of the screen where the mouse pointer is located. You install these options through the *Add/Remove Programs* icon (*Windows Setup* tab) in *Control Panel*.

HOW TO

There are two ways to get to the Accessibility Options dialogue box:

Select the Start/Settings/Control Panel command and double-click on the Accessibility Options icon.

Double-click in turn on the My Computer, Control Panel and then on the Accessibility Options icon.

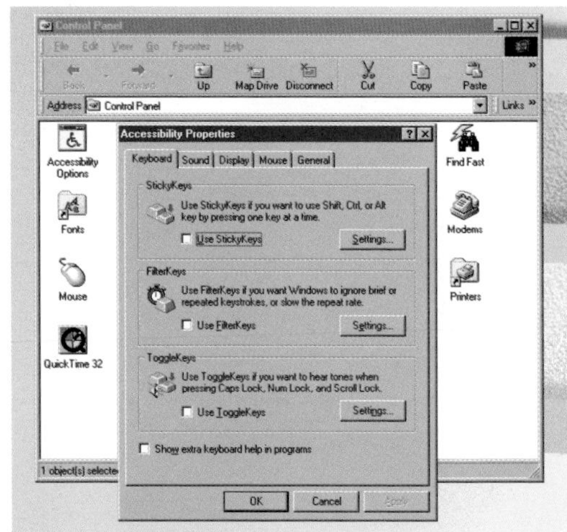

TIP

If the Accessibility Options icon is not already installed in Control Panel, double-click on the Add/Remove Programs icon. Click on the Windows Setup tab and check the Accessibility Options box in the Components list. Click the OK button to confirm.

Keyboard accessibility

Ⓐ Tick the *StickyKeys*, *FilterKeys* or *ToggleKeys* boxes to activate the option you want.

Ⓑ Click on one of the *Settings* buttons to set extra features for any of the three options.

Ⓒ Confirm your settings by clicking the *OK* button.

❶ Click on the box to keep the Ctrl, Alt and Shift keys held down until pressed again.

❷ Tick for Windows 98 to ignore accidental or repeated keystrokes.

❸ Tick this box for Windows 98 to emit a high- or low-pitched sound when the Caps Lock, Num Lock or Scroll Lock keys are pressed or released.

Accessibility Properties

Keyboard | Sound | Display | Mouse | General

StickyKeys

Use StickyKeys if you want to use Shift, Ctrl, or Alt key by pressing one key at a time.

Use StickyKeys — Settings...

FilterKeys

Use FilterKeys if you want Windows to ignore brief or repeated keystrokes, or slow the repeat rate.

Use FilterKeys — Settings...

ToggleKeys

Use ToggleKeys if you want to hear tones when pressing Caps Lock, Num Lock, and Scroll Lock.

Use ToggleKeys — Settings...

Show extra keyboard help in programs

OK | Cancel | Apply

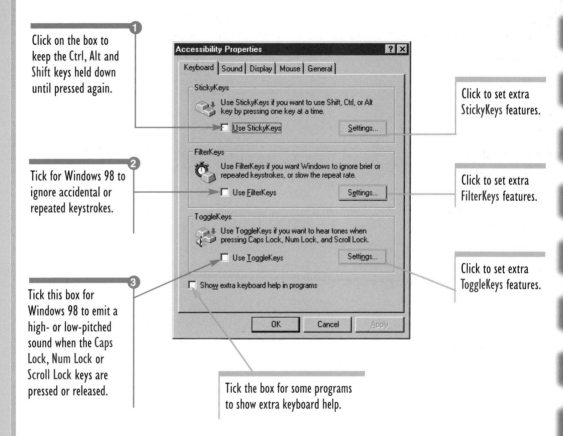

Click to set extra StickyKeys features.

Click to set extra FilterKeys features.

Click to set extra ToggleKeys features.

Tick the box for some programs to show extra keyboard help.

Checklist

1. Tick the box for Windows 98 to make part of the screen flash when a sound cue is given.
2. Click the *Settings* button to specify which part of the screen should flash when a sound cue is given.
3. Tick the box for Windows 98 to display a visual message on screen when a sound cue is given.
4. Click *OK* to confirm the visual cue options.

Sound tab

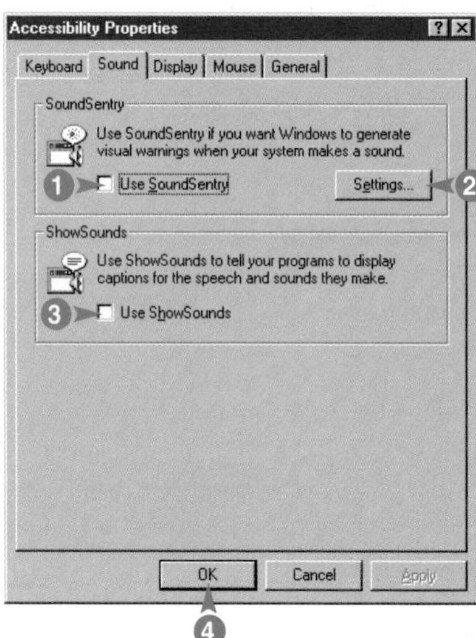

Display tab

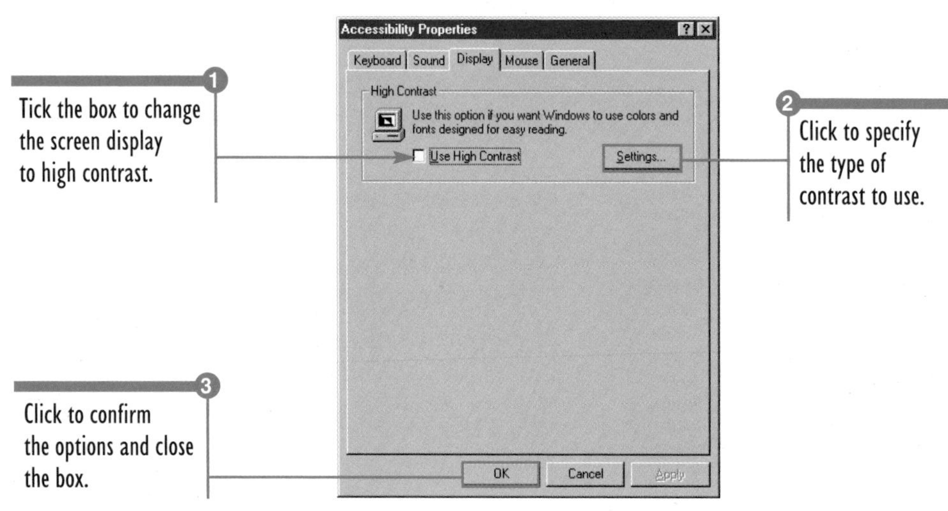

1. Tick the box to change the screen display to high contrast.
2. Click to specify the type of contrast to use.
3. Click to confirm the options and close the box.

Using a high contrast makes the screen easier to read for users who have problems with the Windows 98 standard display. Click the *Use High Contrast* box to change the display settings and the *Settings* button to select the type of high contrast to use.

Mouse tab

Using MouseKeys does not mean you can do without a mouse in Windows 98. The operating system will simply refuse to load if it fails to detect a mouse connected to the computer.

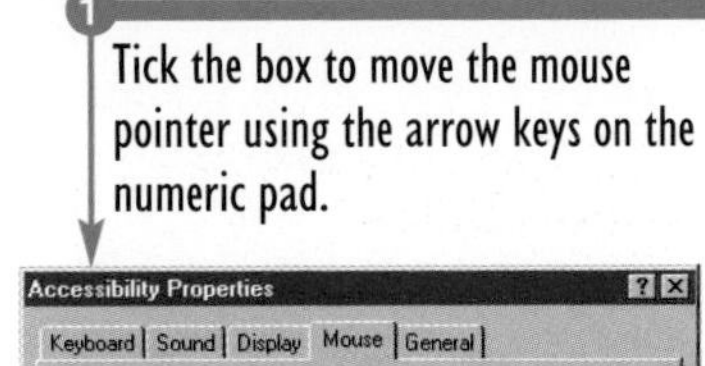

1 Tick the box to move the mouse pointer using the arrow keys on the numeric pad.

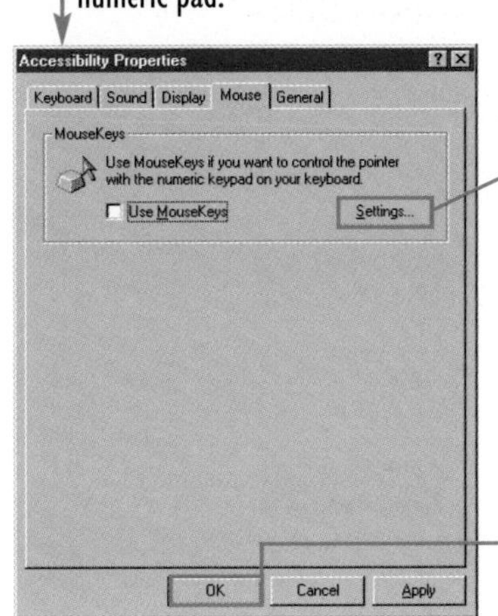

2 Click to set extra features for the arrow keys to move the pointer (pointer speed, showing MouseKey status on screen, etc.).

3 Click to confirm the options and close the box.

Note

To use the keyboard arrow keys to control the pointer, tick the *Use MouseKeys* box. Then click the *Settings* button to set the pointer speed and other *MouseKey* options. Finish by clicking the *OK* button.

General tab

If more than one person is using the same computer, you can have the special accessibility options turned off after a set time. To do that, tick the *Turn off accessibility features after idle for* box and enter a time in the text box. Because the accessibility options can be turned on by a keyboard shortcut, tick the *Give warning message...* or *Make a sound...* boxes so as not to turn them on accidentally. Remember to confirm your options by clicking the *Apply* or *OK* buttons.

Tick the box for Windows 98 to display a text message whenever an accessibility option shortcut key is pressed.

Tick the box to turn off the accessibility options after the time set in the text box.

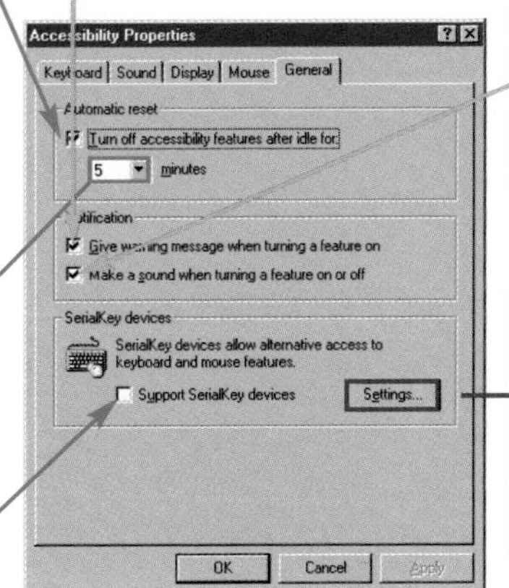

Tick the box for Windows 98 to give an audible signal whenever an accessibility option shortcut key is pressed.

Enter a time after which the accessibility options will be turned off.

Tick the box to use an input device other than the keyboard or mouse.

Click to set the serial port to which the auxiliary input device is connected.

If the Turn off accessibility features after idle for box is ticked, Windows 98 turns off all the accessibility options chosen after the time set, apart from the auxiliary input device. For that, simply click the box to clear the tickmark.

Flow chart of the Accessibility Properties dialogue box (keyboard tab)

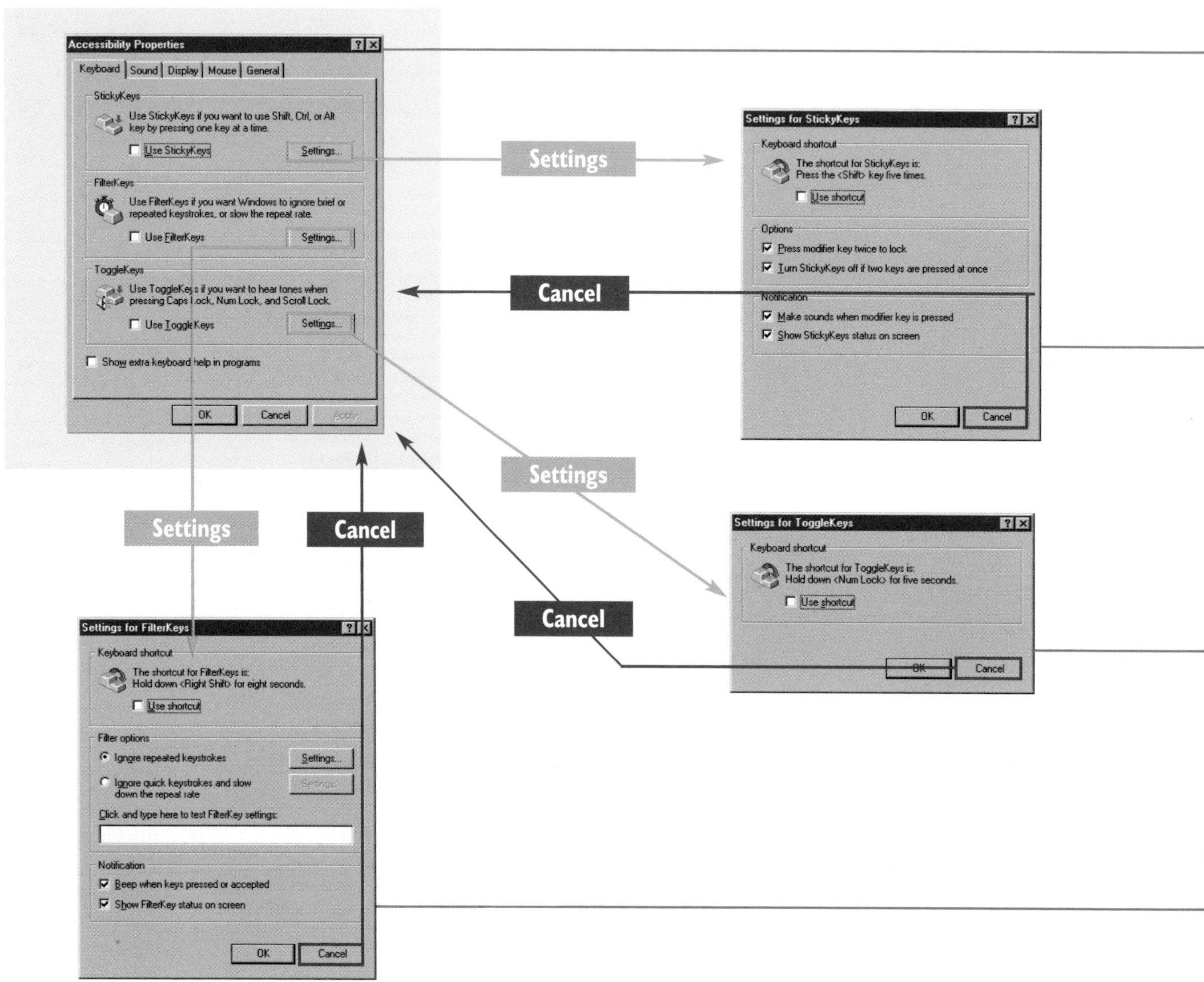

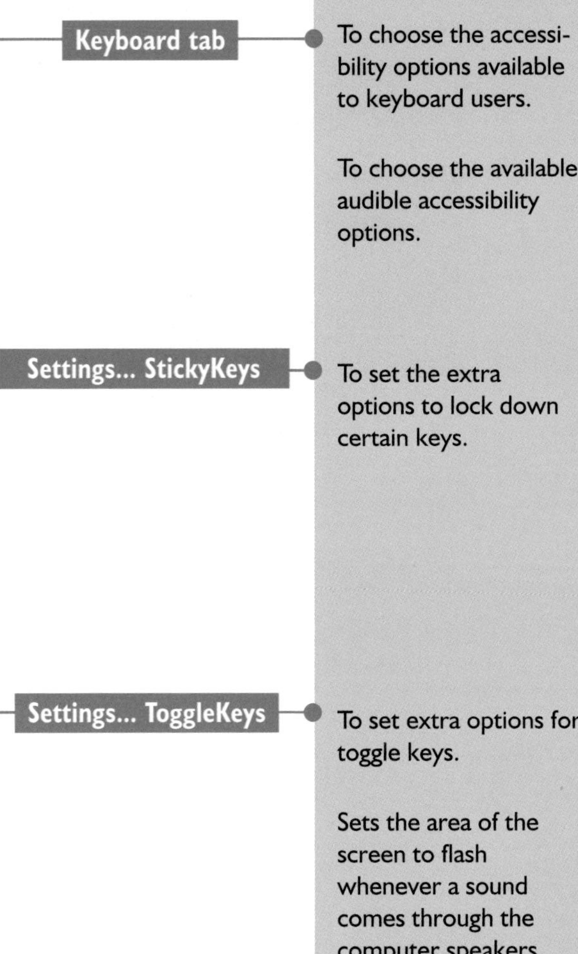

To choose the accessibility options available to keyboard users.

To choose the available audible accessibility options.

To set the extra options to lock down certain keys.

To set extra options for toggle keys.

Sets the area of the screen to flash whenever a sound comes through the computer speakers.

Sets extra options for bounce keys.

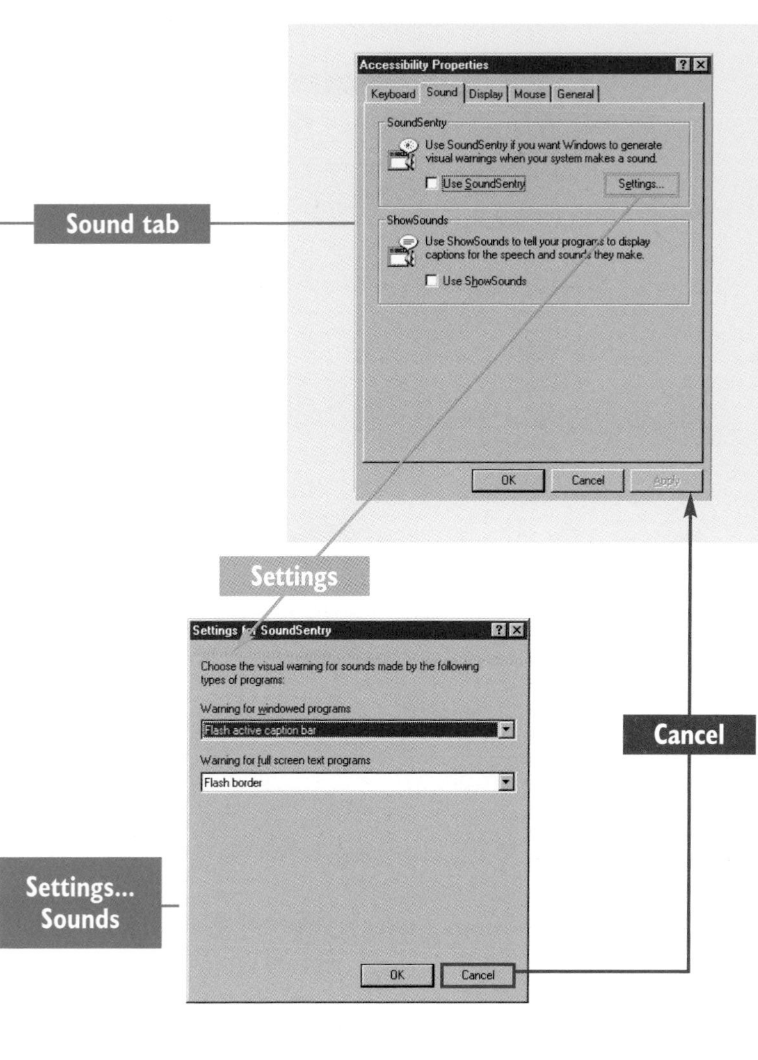

Flow chart of the Accessibility Properties dialogue box (other tabs)

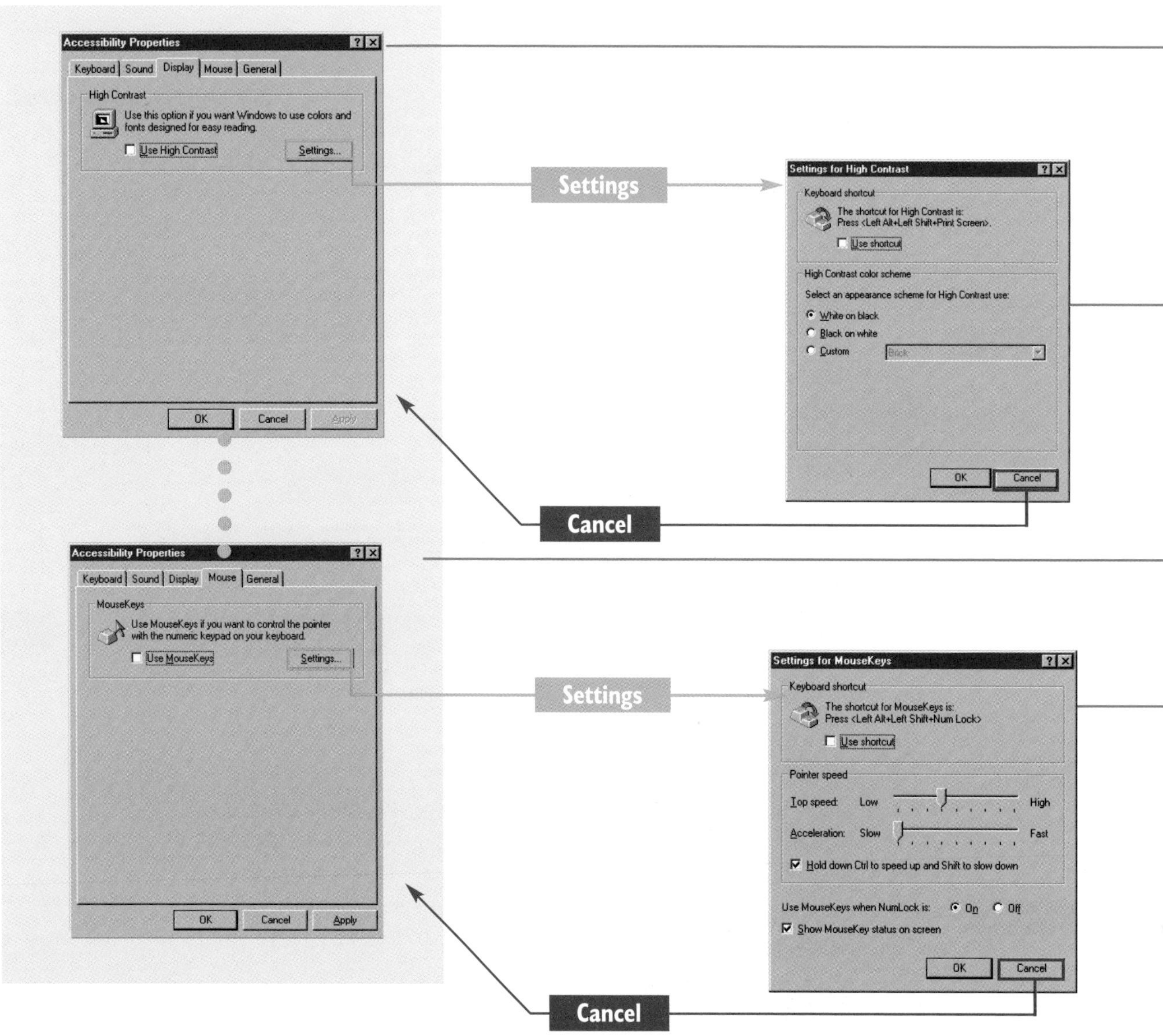

Display tab

To choose the accessibility options for display.

General tab

To turn off the accessibility options or warn the user that they are on.

High Contrast Settings

Sets the keyboard shortcut to turn on high contrast, and the type of high contrast to use.

Mouse tab

To choose the accessibility options available for the mouse.

MouseKeys Settings

To specify the pointer speed and other features when using the keyboard arrow keys to move the pointer.

To specify the serial port and baud rate for an auxiliary input device.

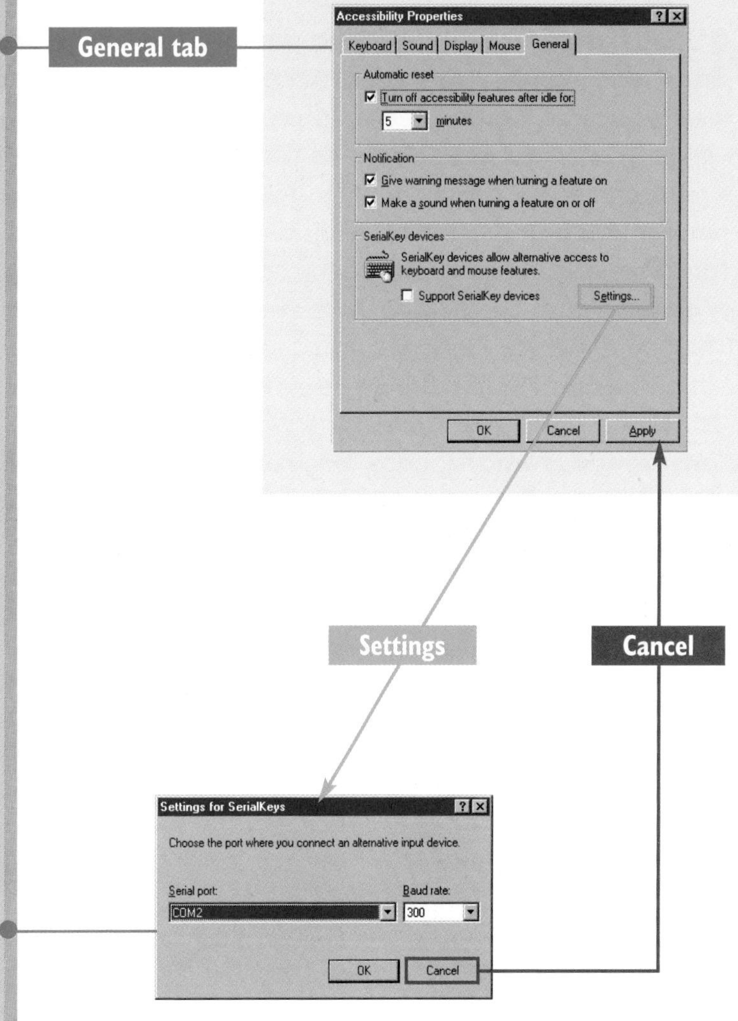

E-mailing with MS Exchange

Control Panel / Mail

MS Exchange is a multiservice e-mail program which you can use to send faxes, messages over local networks, or e-mail on networks such as CompuServe, Microsoft Network or the Internet. It also gives you an address book. To use all these features properly, you must configure the program first. You start by adding services to MS Exchange; you'll find a list of available services by clicking on the *Add* button. This requires you to specify the different settings for each service: if you want to include Internet e-mailing, you must give the address, mail server, account number and password for the mailbox. The information MS Exchange requires varies with the service being added. Once you have done all this, you can use the dialogue box buttons to add, remove, copy or change a service. MS Exchange also lets you define different profiles for multiple users all using different services. The *Exchange* box also lets you specify the properties for sending and receiving e-mail (*Delivery* tab) and options relating to the address book.

HOW TO

There are two ways to get to the MS Exchange Settings Properties dialogue box:

Select the Start/Settings/Control Panel command and double-click on the Mail icon.

Double-click in turn on the My Computer, Control Panel and Mail icons.

TIP

Before trying to send a fax from your computer, check that the fax service is installed in MS Exchange. If it is not, you won't be able to do this. Use the MS Exchange Settings Properties dialogue box and the Add button to add it to, and configure it, in MS-Exchange.

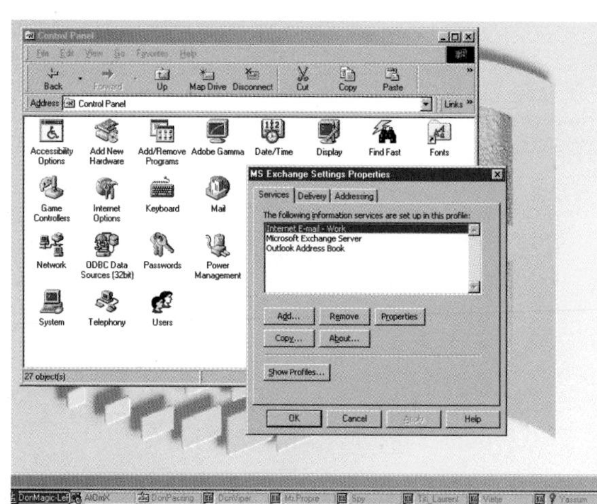

Choosing services

Ⓐ Start by clicking on *Add* to view a list of services and choose one.

Ⓑ Use the *Remove* button to delete a service from the program or the *Properties* button to change its settings.

Ⓒ To create a new user profile, click the *Show Profiles* button.

Ⓓ Confirm by clicking *OK*.

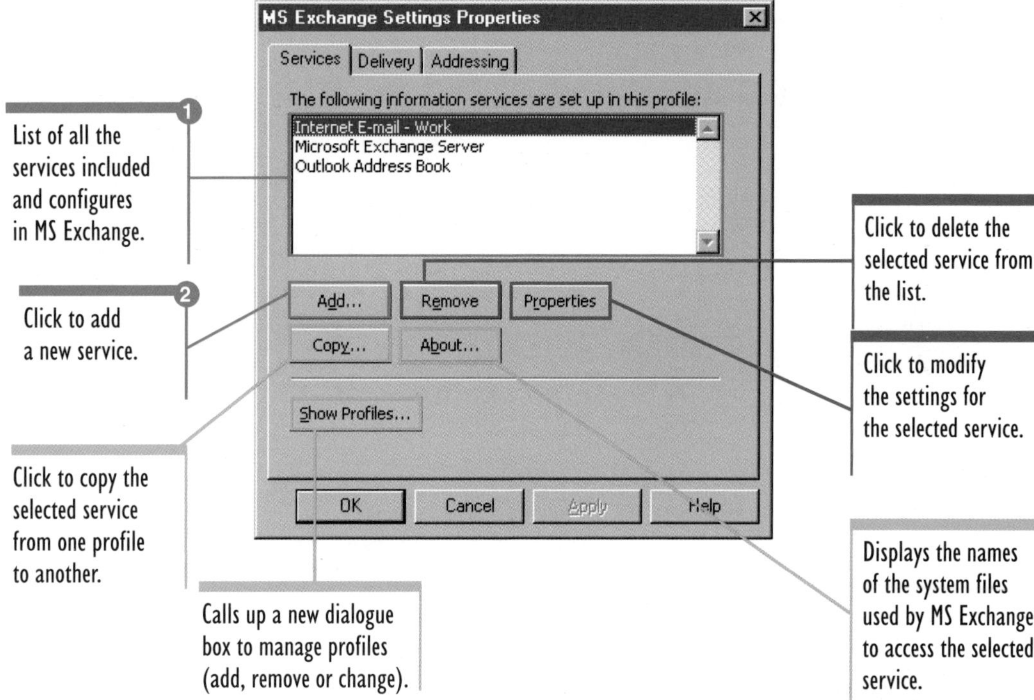

1 List of all the services included and configures in MS Exchange.

2 Click to add a new service.

Click to copy the selected service from one profile to another.

Calls up a new dialogue box to manage profiles (add, remove or change).

Click to delete the selected service from the list.

Click to modify the settings for the selected service.

Displays the names of the system files used by MS Exchange to access the selected service.

Some services are separate from Windows 98 and not automatically installed with the operating system. To use one of these services, click on the Add button, then on Have Disk in the Add Service to Profile dialogue box and insert the disk with the service on into the drive. It will then show up in the list of available services and you can include it in a user profile.

Continued (Delivery and Addressing tabs) on page 118

Flow chart of MS Exchange Settings Properties (Services tab)

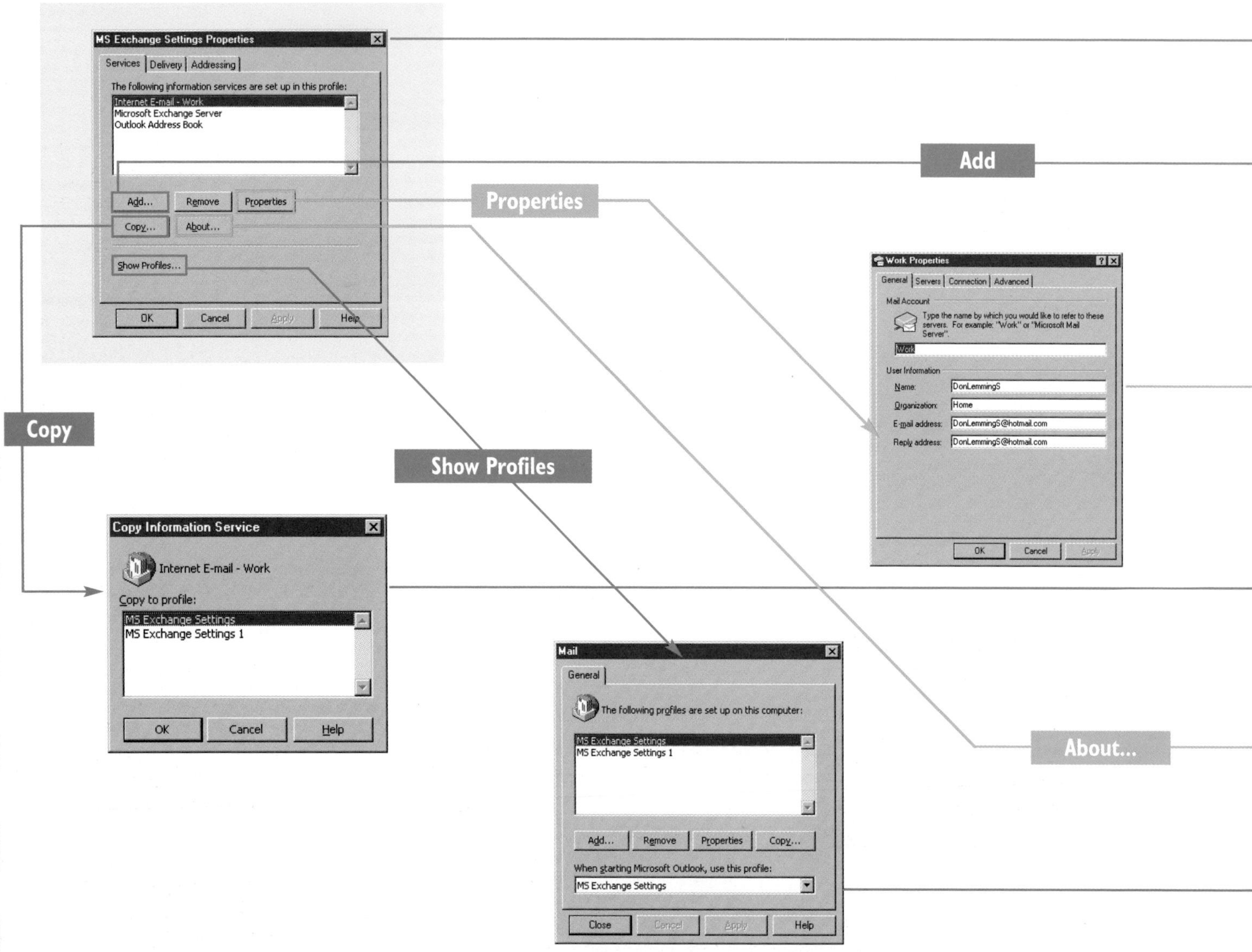

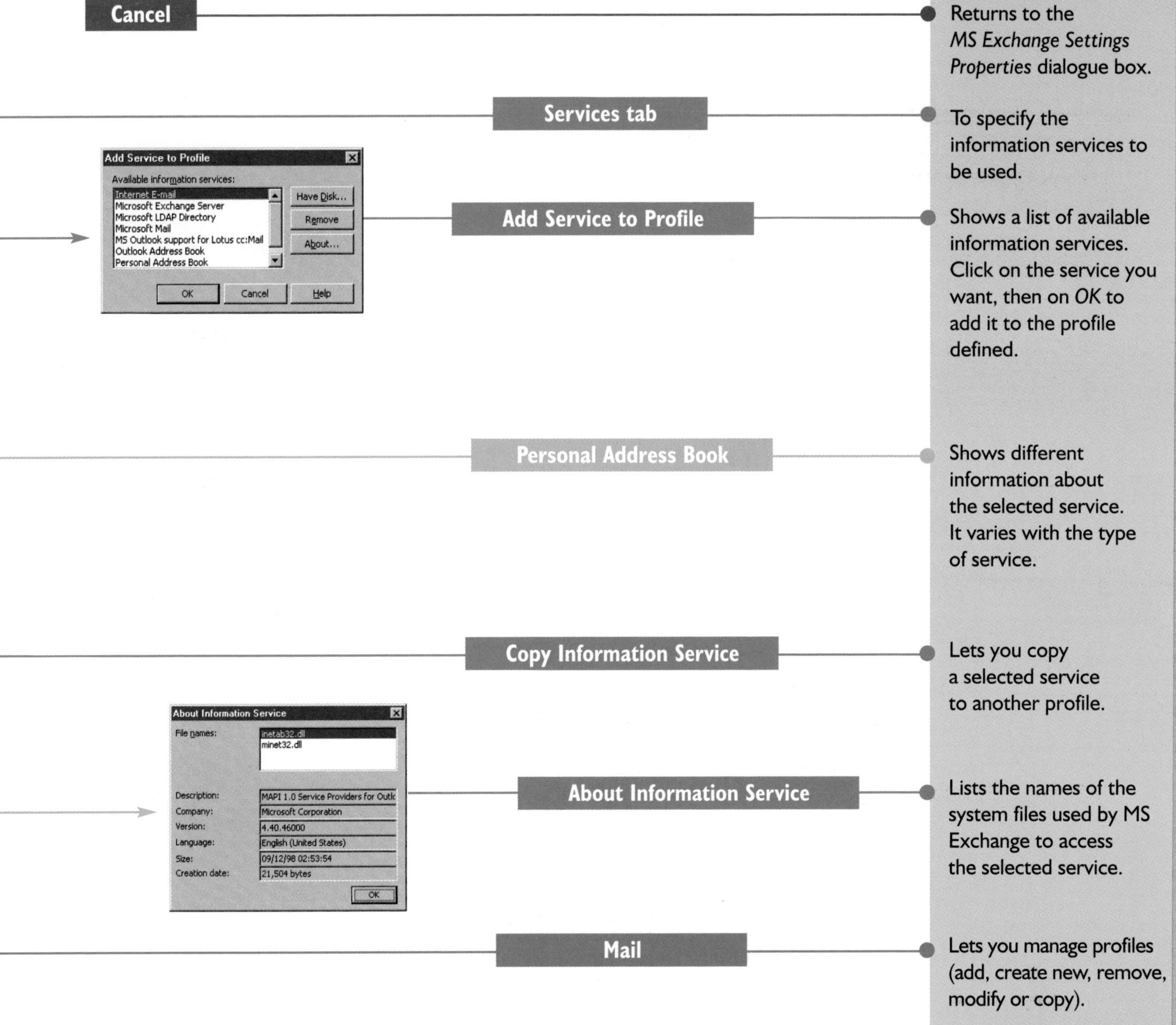

Cancel

Returns to the *MS Exchange Settings Properties* dialogue box.

Services tab

To specify the information services to be used.

Add Service to Profile

Shows a list of available information services. Click on the service you want, then on *OK* to add it to the profile defined.

Personal Address Book

Shows different information about the selected service. It varies with the type of service.

Copy Information Service

Lets you copy a selected service to another profile.

About Information Service

Lists the names of the system files used by MS Exchange to access the selected service.

Mail

Lets you manage profiles (add, create new, remove, modify or copy).

Flow chart of MS Exchange Settings Properties (addressing tab)

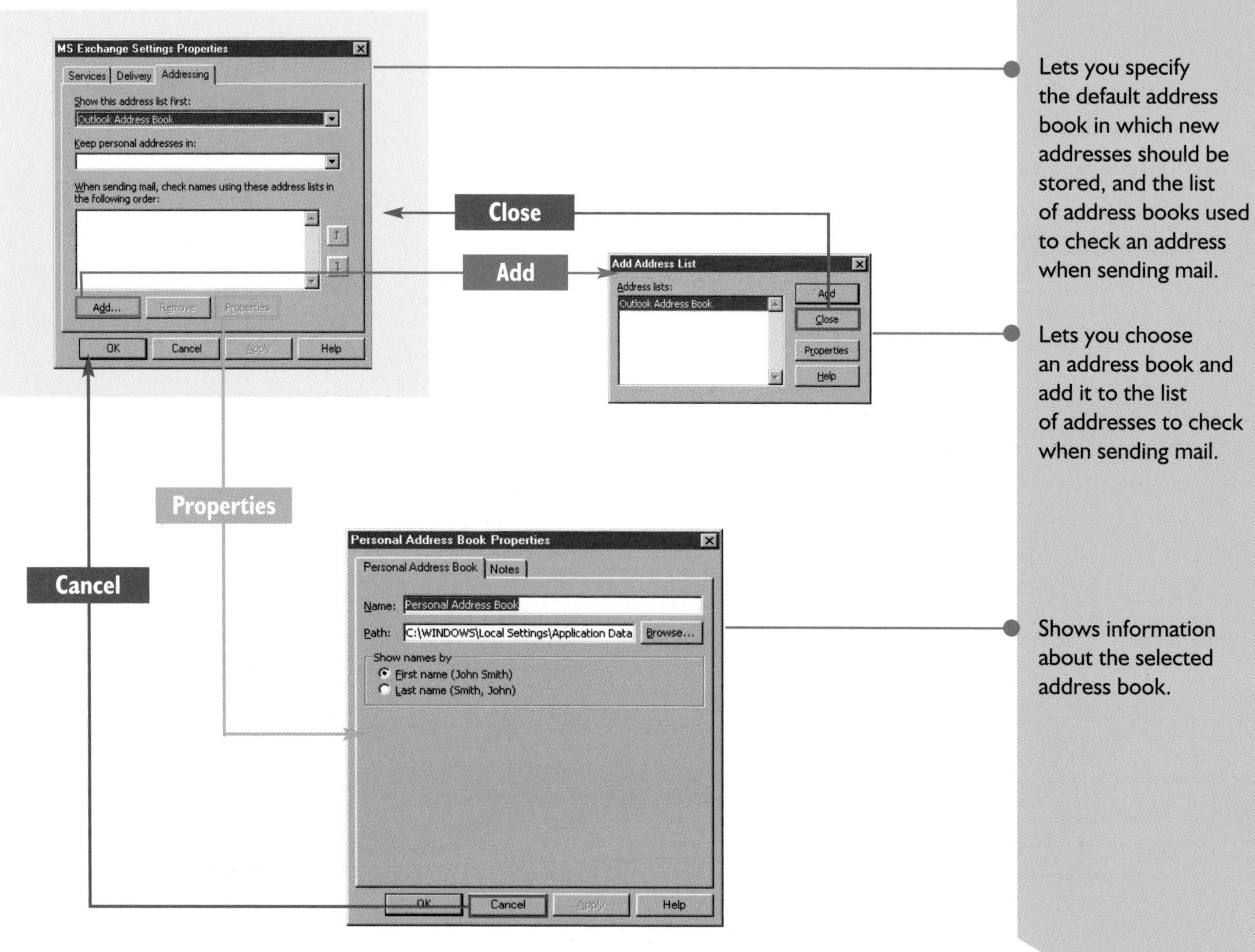

Lets you specify the default address book in which new addresses should be stored, and the list of address books used to check an address when sending mail.

Lets you choose an address book and add it to the list of addresses to check when sending mail.

Shows information about the selected address book.

In theory...

MS Exchange is a MAPI (Mail Application Programming Interface) mailing program, which lets you work with service providers who use the same system. MAPI has a range of features which MS Exchange uses to handle messages sent to or received from on-line services such as the Internet, CompuServe or MSN, and to manage all the addresses involved. The value of this type of interface is that service providers only have to supply a MAPI-type application for MS Exchange to be able to handle the e-mail sent using it.

The MAPI interface allows MS Exchange to handle:

Personal address books, in which you can store the contact details and e-mail addresses of your correspondents.

Personal Folders, containing all the mail, messages and faxes sent and received.

Faxes, letting you send and receive faxes.

E-mail, to manage messages transmitted over a network.

Internet Mail, to send and receive messages from other on-line service subscribers.

CompuServe Mail, to send and receive messages from other on-line service subscribers.

MSN Mail, to send and receive messages from other on-line service subscribers.

Microsoft Mail Exchange between computers connected to a service using the Microsoft Exchange Server.

Checklist

1. Start by telling MS Exchange where to store your mail.
2. Give an order of preference for the services used to send mail. Put the service you want MS Exchange to use to send mail in preference to any other at the top.
3. Click *OK* to confirm the settings and close the box.

Delivery tab

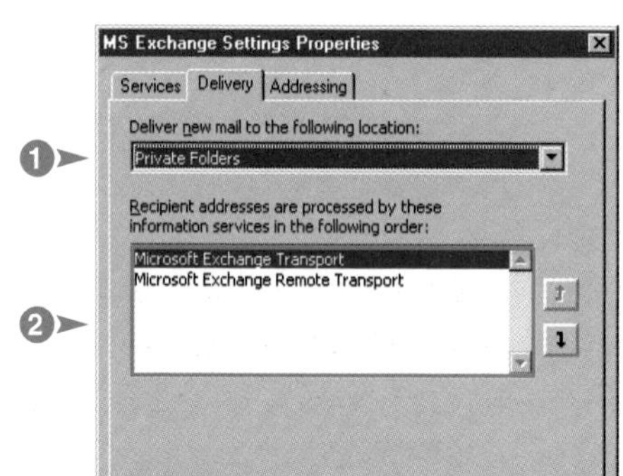

The order of preference is only relevant if you have more than one service handling the same e-mail addresses.

Addressing tab

It's well worth grouping all the information about your contacts together in a single address book.

Unfortunately, Windows 98 offers several, and the temptation is to use more than one...

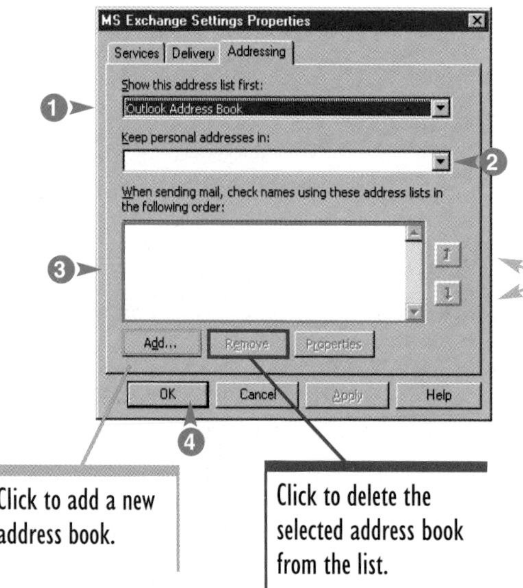

Click to add a new address book.

Click to delete the selected address book from the list.

Click to change the order of preference for checking addresses by moving the selected address book up or down the list.

Checklist

1. First select your default address book (the one that will pop up when you click an *Address Book* icon).
2. Then choose the name of the default address book to use when adding new contact names.
3. List the different address books used to check addresses when sending messages by order of preference. Use the *Add* and *Remove* buttons, and the up-down arrows at the side of the list.
4. Click *OK* to confirm.

Installing new fonts

Control Panel / Fonts

Windows 98 stores all fonts together in a separate folder called *\Windows\Fonts* with a shortcut via the *Control Panel*. The most commonly-used ones are TrueType fonts identified by their *.ttf* extension. You can perform all font management operations through the *Fonts* window. You can easily add new fonts to your system with the *File/Install New Font* command. Once installed, the new font will be immediately available to all your applications. There is another way: simply copy the font file directly into the *\Windows\Fonts* folder. Double-clicking on a *.ttf* file calls up a special window showing the name and properties of that font. Windows 98 also displays samples of text showing the appearance of the font in sizes from 12 to 72 points. To remove a font, just delete the relevant file from the *Fonts* folder.

HOW TO

There are two ways to get to the Fonts folder:

Select the Start/Settings/Control Panel command and double-click on the Fonts icon.

Double-click in turn on the My Computer, Control Panel and Fonts icons.

TIP

Installing dozens of different fonts just clutters up your system. Really, the maximum number of fonts you want on any page is three. Too many different fonts makes the text painful to read, and too many fonts installed will slow down your computer.

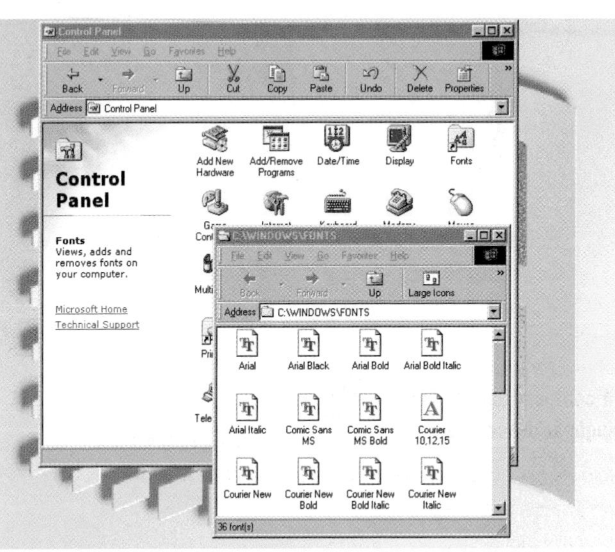

Viewing fonts

All the fonts are in the Fonts folder.

Clicking on the list shows you that Fonts is a subfolder of the Windows folder, where the operating system files are stored.

Each filename stands for a font.

Windows 98 shows the number of fonts on your computer.

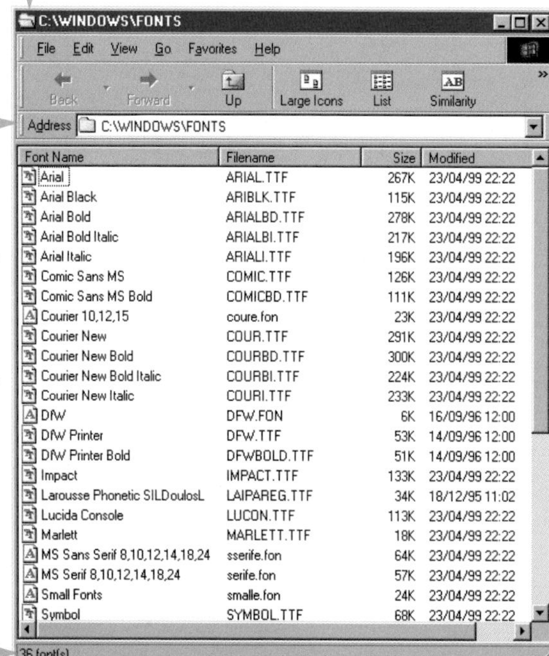

Note

All the fonts on your computer are stored in the *Fonts* folder. To add a new font, open the folder and use the font management commands (from the *File* menu).

Hint

Windows 98's default is to show all the files that stand for fonts in the *Fonts* window. To view only the basic font, but not its bold and italic variations, select the command *View/Hide Variations*.

Checklist

1. First, tell Windows where the new font files are located (drive + folders). In the sample screen, the fonts are in the *New fonts* folder on a zip disk in the E: drive.
2. Windows 98 shows the names and types of fonts found in the *List of fonts* box. Select the font to add; press and hold down the *Ctrl* key if you want to add more than one.
3. Click on the *Select All* button for Windows 98 to select all the fonts in the list.
4. By default, Windows 98 will always put new fonts in the *Fonts* folder; make sure it does so by seeing that the *Copy fonts to Fonts folder* box stays ticked.
5. Click *OK* to start the installation procedure.

Adding a new font

File / Install New Font

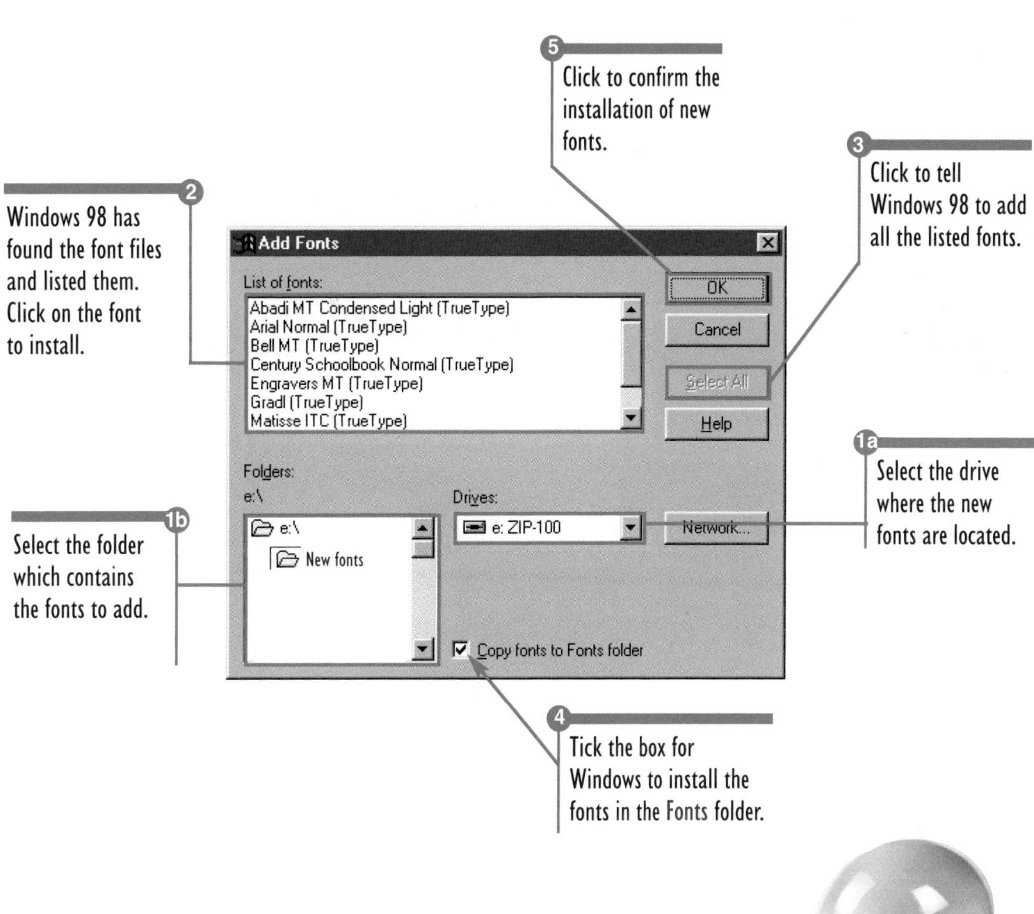

5 Click to confirm the installation of new fonts.
3 Click to tell Windows 98 to add all the listed fonts.
2 Windows 98 has found the font files and listed them. Click on the font to install.
Add Fonts
List of fonts:
Abadi MT Condensed Light (TrueType)
Arial Normal (TrueType)
Bell MT (TrueType)
Century Schoolbook Normal (TrueType)
Engravers MT (TrueType)
Gradl (TrueType)
Matisse ITC (TrueType)
OK
Cancel
Select All
Help
Folders:
e:\
e:\
New fonts
Drives:
e: ZIP-100
Network...
Copy fonts to Fonts folder
1a Select the drive where the new fonts are located.
1b Select the folder which contains the fonts to add.
4 Tick the box for Windows to install the fonts in the Fonts folder.

You can bypass the Add Fonts dialogue box by simply copying .ttf files into the Fonts folder.

To remove a font, click on its name and run the File/Delete command.

Note

To see what an installed font looks like, double-click on its name or run the *File/Open* command. Windows 98 will show a sample of text in different sizes of the selected font. Click on the *Print* button to print it out.

Viewing a font's appearance

File / Open

Click to close the window.

Click to print the sample and see what the font looks like on paper.

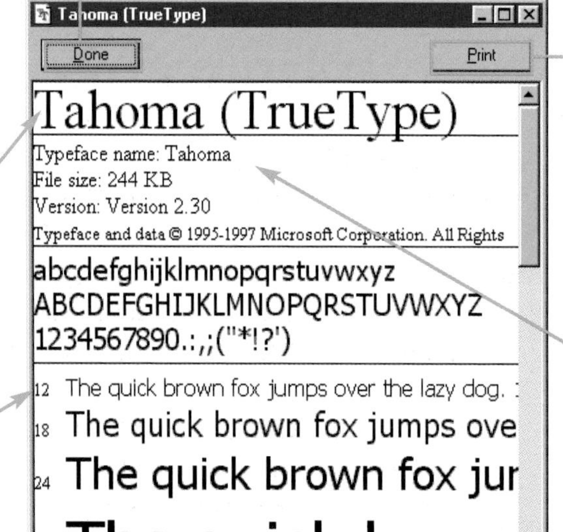

Windows 98 shows the font name and type (TrueType).

Windows 98 shows other information about the font.

A few lines of text to illustrate the font in different sizes.

Painless printing

Control Panel / Printers

Along with the screen, the printer is the most used output device. That's why Windows 98 has tried to make it as easy as possible to use. Installing a printer is made much easier by a wizard, which guides you through the settings you need to define in a series of dialogue boxes. Once installed, the printer is available to all applications running under Windows 98. You can have several printers installed, which Windows 98 stores in a folder called *Printers*. You define your printer settings in a single dialogue box entitled (printer name) *Properties* (eg *HP LaserJet Properties*). In it, you can set the drivers needed to make the printer work properly, the resolution, paper size and orientation, number of copies to print and much more besides. The printer manager gives extra help with information on jobs being printed. If you are printing several documents, the manager lists them in order of printing, and shows how the current print job is progressing. You can pause, resume or cancel printing of the current document at any time. You call up the printer manager box by double-clicking on the printer icon in the *Printers* folder.

HOW TO

There are two ways to get to the Printers folder:

Select the Start/Settings/Printers command.

Double-click in turn on the My Computer Control Panel and Printers icons.

TIP

Even if you don't have a printer connected to the computer, you can still install a notional printer. Run the Add Printer Wizard and select Generic from the Manufacturers list. In the dialogue box, click on FILE: and continue until Windows 98 asks you to insert the installation CD-Rom. Everything you print will be put in a text file on your computer's hard disk.

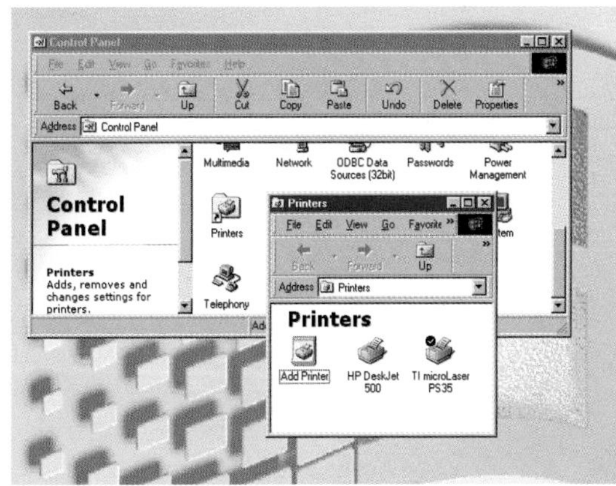

The Printers folder

Windows 98 shows that a Hewlett-Packard printer is installed.

Windows 98 shows the folder name: Printers.

1 Double-click on this icon to add a new printer.

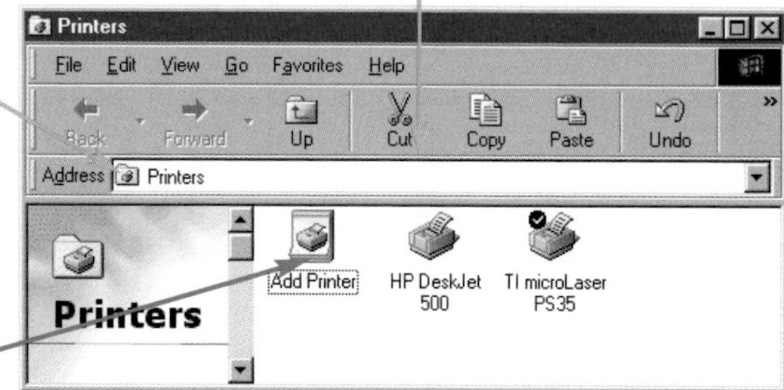

2 The printer manager commands.

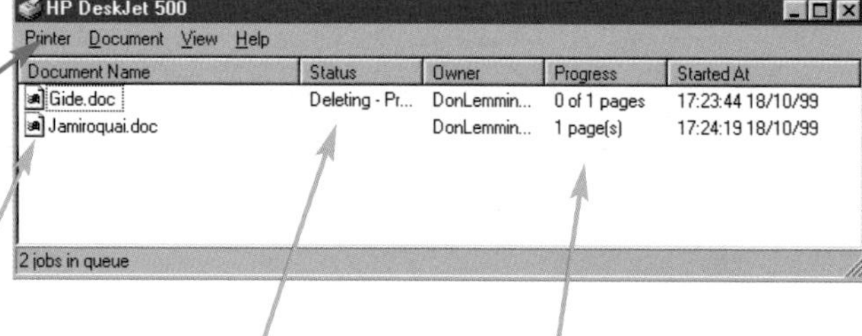

Documents queued for printing.

The status of documents in the print queue.

The manager shows how the print job is progressing and how many pages are still to print.

When a document is being printed, Windows 98 puts a printer icon on the far right of the taskbar. Double-clicking on it calls up the printer manager immediately.

- A Use the *Add Printer* icon to add a new printer.
- B Double-click on the printer's icon to display its manager and view print jobs in progress.
- C The *Printer* menu gives you the commands to pause, clear and resume a print job.
- D The manager is a good way to keep an eye on progress with a print job, and any problems.
- E Click the close button (X) or select the *Printer/Close* command to hide the print manager.

Printer properties

<*printer name*> Properties command

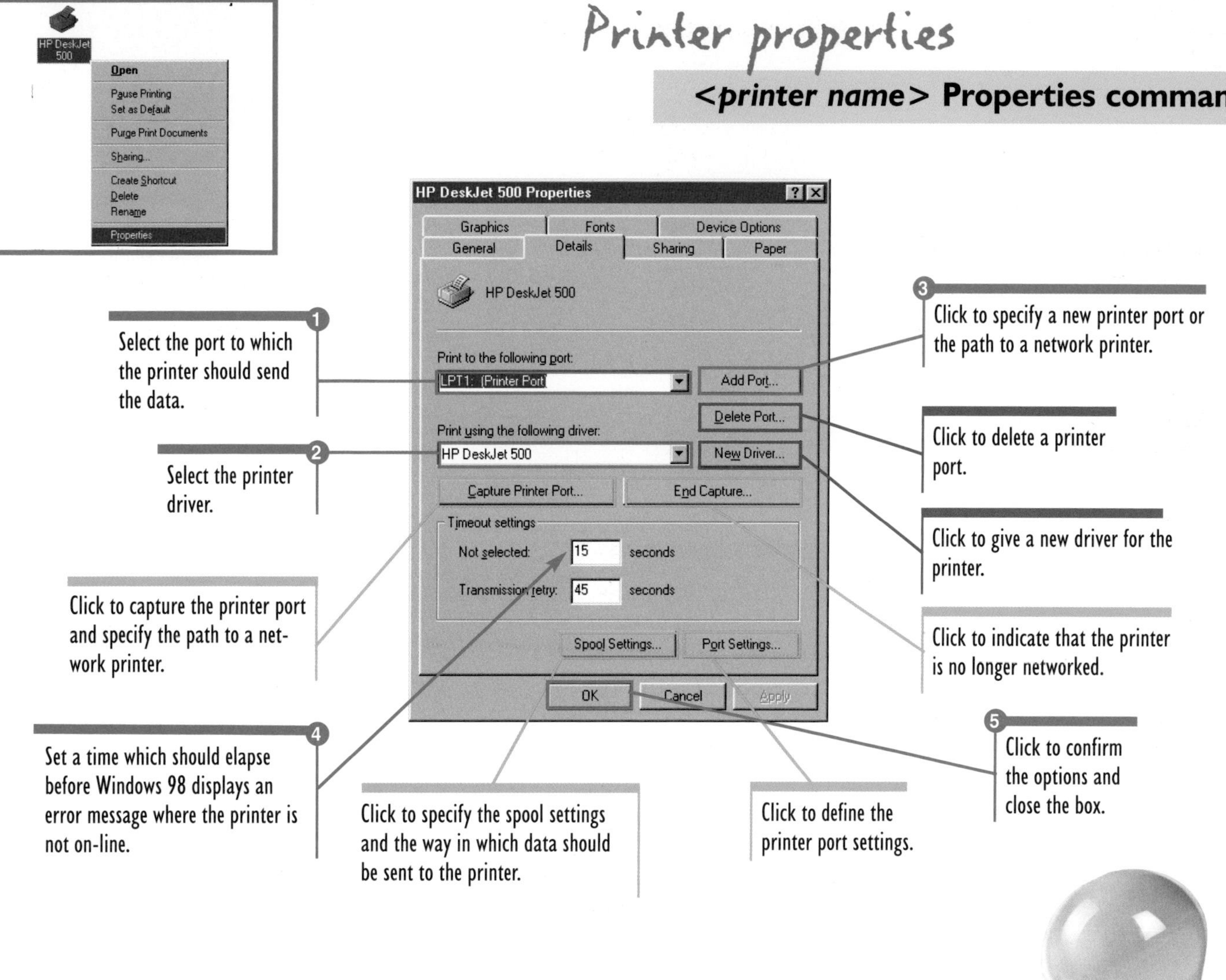

1 Select the port to which the printer should send the data.

2 Select the printer driver.

Click to capture the printer port and specify the path to a network printer.

4 Set a time which should elapse before Windows 98 displays an error message where the printer is not on-line.

Click to specify the spool settings and the way in which data should be sent to the printer.

3 Click to specify a new printer port or the path to a network printer.

Click to delete a printer port.

Click to give a new driver for the printer.

Click to indicate that the printer is no longer networked.

5 Click to confirm the options and close the box.

Click to define the printer port settings.

The spool is an area of the hard disk where Windows 98 temporarily stores the information to be printed. You can speed up printing by asking Windows 98 not to use the spool but print directly to the printer. To do that, click the Spool Settings button, then click on the Print directly to the printer option. Note that this option is not available if the printer is shared in a network.

Checklist

1. Click and select the printer resolution: 300, 600 or 1200 dpi are the most common.
2. Click a button to select the type of printing for images.
3. Move the slider to change print intensity (default is 100).
4. Click to restore the default settings.

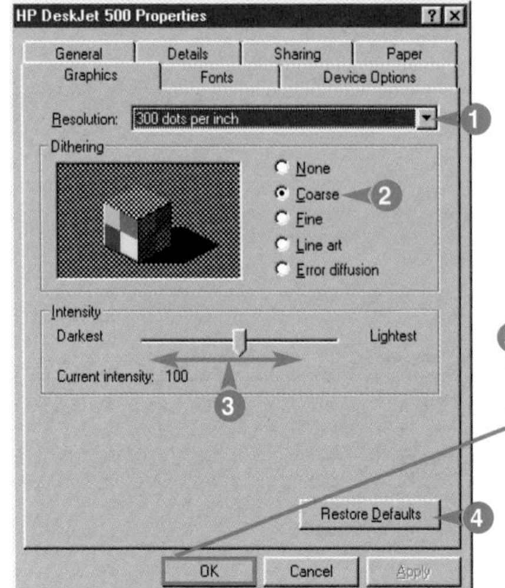

5. Click to confirm the options and close the box.

Graphics tab

If your printer does not have enough memory to print a greyscale image, click on the **None** option of **Dithering** (a graphic technique that is used to create additional colours from the existing palette).

Fonts tab

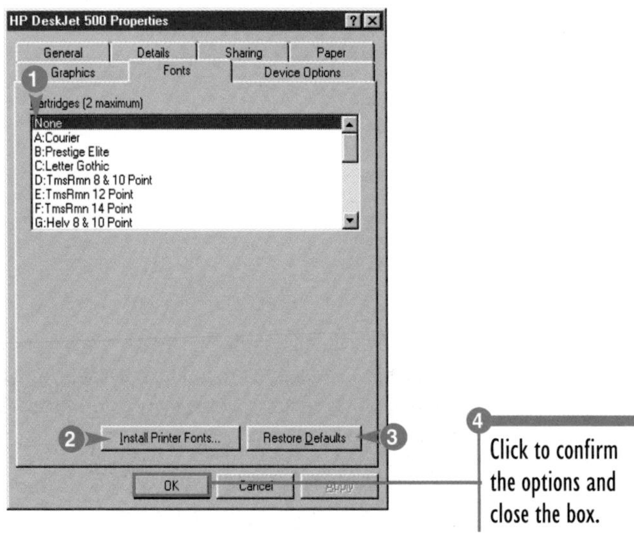

4. Click to confirm the options and close the box.

Checklist

1. Click on the font cartridges your printer uses.
2. Click to install new fonts or cartridges.
3. Click to restore the printer's default settings.

Checklist

1. Choose your printer's memory size.
2. Move the slider to tell Windows how to manage your printer's memory.
3. Click to restore the default settings.

Device Options tab

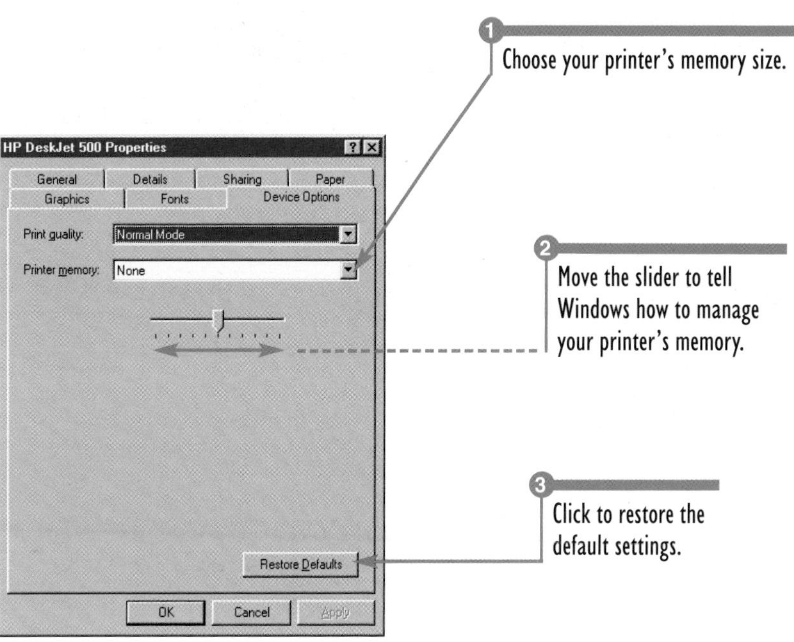

If you choose conservative printer-memory tracking, the printer manager will cautiously avoid printing complicated images so as not to exceed the printer's available memory. Choosing aggressive will make it try and print complicated images at the risk of exceeding available memory.

Paper tab

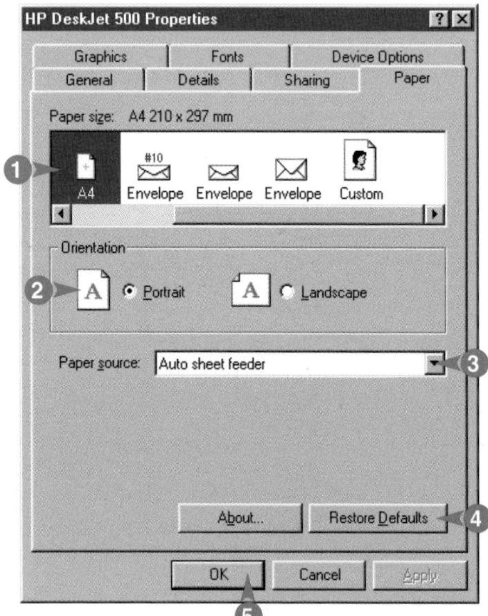

If you choose the **Envelope** option under **Paper size**, you will also have to change the feed setting to **Manual feed envelopes** in the **Paper source** box.

Checklist

1. Choose the type of paper for the printer to use.
2. Choose the paper orientation.
3. Choose the paper source.
4. Click to restore the default settings.
5. Click OK to confirm your choices.

Note

Some printers display more options, such as :

The number of copies to be printed.

An option to specify the printable areas (some printers cannot print right to the edges of the paper).

General tab

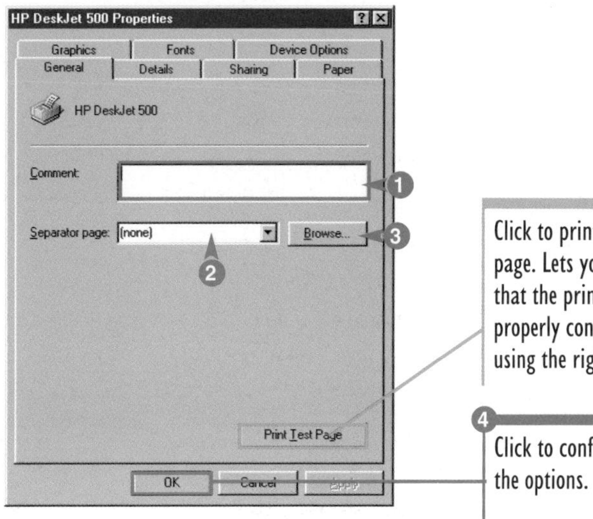

Click to print a test page. Lets you check that the printer is properly connected and using the right driver.

4 Click to confirm the options.

Checklist

1. Insert a comment identifying the printer; all network users of the printer will see the comment.
2. Select a separator page; this is useful if you are printing multiple documents, or the printer is used by several people.
3. Click to choose a separator page (any metafile with the extension *.wmf*).

Sharing tab

Checklist

1. Click on the button to stop other network users using the printer.
2. Click on the button to allow other network users to use the printer.
3. Give the printer name.
4. Enter a comment, which all network users will be able to see.
5. Enter a password, which all other network users must give in order to print to the printer.

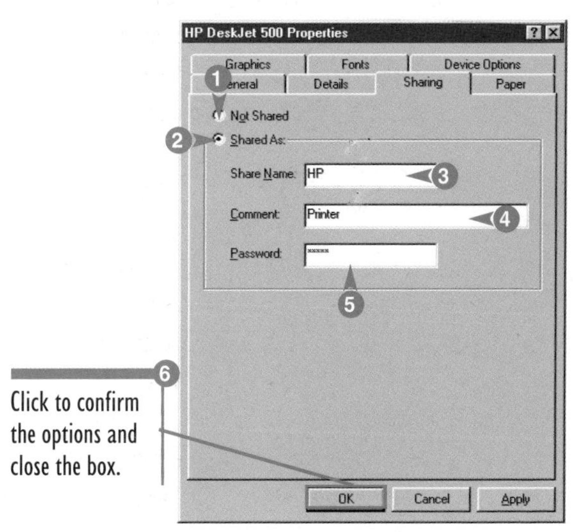

6 Click to confirm the options and close the box.

In a network, all users who want to print to a printer must enter a path. If computer_name is the name of the computer to which the shared printer is connected, the command string for the path will be:

\\computer_name\printer_name .

Flow chart of how to add a printer

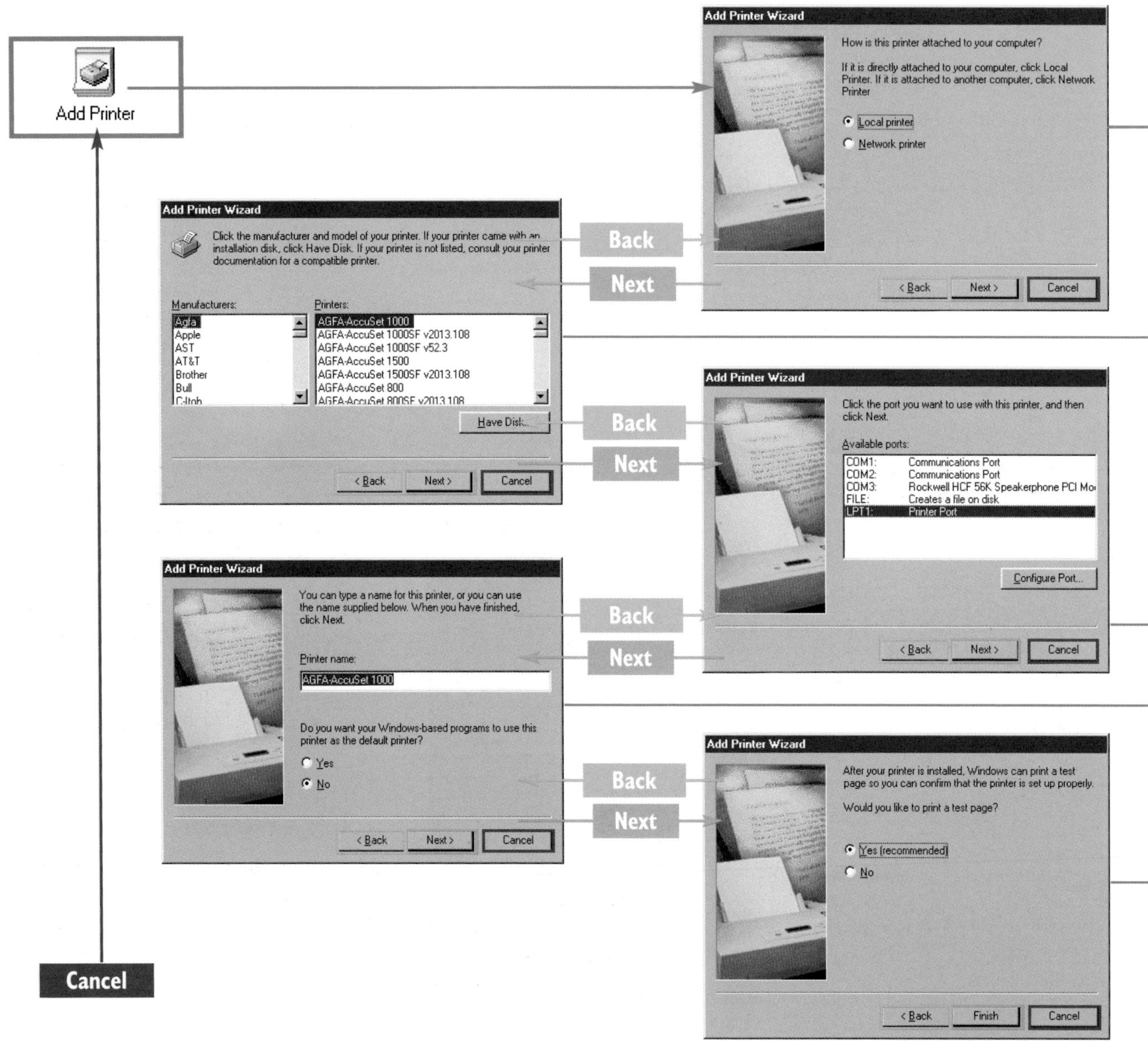

Specify whether the printer is to be shared in a network or used by only one user. If it is to be used in a network, you must set a path for it in the form \\<*computer_name*>\ <*printer_name*>, where <*computer_name*> is the name of the computer to which the printer is physically connected. You can easily get to the computer and printer's name using the *Browse* button.

Specify the manufacturer and model of printer. For a very recent model, you should use the diskette supplied by the manufacturer. Insert it in the drive and click on the *Have Disk* button. Windows 98 will display the printer name. Simply click on it to move to the next stage.

Specify which port the printer is connected to. You will not get this box if it is a network printer.

Enter the printer name and whether Windows 98 should use it as the default for all programs.

Test whether the printer is properly connected and using the right driver. If the test page does not print, it is not connected properly.

There are many ways to print a document

1: Directly from within the program with the *File/Print* command. This is the easiest way.

2: From the *Print* command in the document's context menu. Here, Windows 98 will open the document's parent application, start the print process and close the application once the print job is completed.

3: By dragging and dropping the document icon onto a printer icon. Click on the icon which stands for the document and hold the mouse button down. Move the mouse so that the document icon is placed on top of the printer icon. It should be highlighted. Let go of the mouse button for Windows 98 to open the document's parent application and start the print process. You'll get the same result by dropping the icon into the printer manager.

4: By using the *Send To* command in the document's context menu. But to send the document to the printer, you first have to include the printer in the list of recipients. To do that, simply use Explorer to put a shortcut to the printer in the *\Windows\Send To* folder. You'll then see that the *Send To* subcommand will contain the defined printer, so all you need do is select it to start printing.

5: From the *Print* command in the folder's *File* menu. Simply open the folder in which the document to print is located. Click on its icon and choose the *File/Print* command. Windows 98 will open the document's parent application, print it, then close both the document and the parent application.

Adding and Removing programs

Control Panel / Add / Remove Programs

Although the procedure for installing a new program is now fairly easy, Windows 98 can even do that for you. The *Install/Uninstall* tab in the *Add/Remove Programs Properties* box will search either the floppy disk drive or CD-Rom for an installation file. Just click on the *Finish* button to start installing the program. You can also uninstall a program already on your hard disk quickly and cleanly from the same tab. Obviously, you can only use this feature if the program is recognised by Windows 98. The operating system comes supplied with a set of components, including various utilities and other programs. They are all on the Windows 98 CD-Rom, but not all of them are copied to your disk when you install it. To add (or remove) any, click the *Windows Setup* tab, then click the box for the program you want to be installed on your hard disk. One important thing: when you start up your system for the very first time, make sure to create a startup disk (from the *Startup Disk* tab). It might be a lifesaver one day when your system starts playing up!

HOW TO

There are two ways to get to the Add/Remove Programs Properties dialogue box:

Select the Start/Settings/Control Panel command, then double-click on the Add/Remove Programs icon.

Double-click in turn on the My Computer, Control Panel and finally the Add/Remove Programs icons.

NOTE

All programs nowadays come with a special self-installing feature. Once you have loaded the CD-Rom with the program on it, it will start to run automatically and the first installation dialogue box will pop up on the screen.

Installing and removing software

A To auto-run a new program's installation procedure, Windows 98 first looks for a *Setup.exe* or *Install.exe* file on a floppy disk in drive A:. If there is no disk present, it checks the CD-Rom drive for the same thing. If it finds either of the files, the program installation procedure can start.

B To remove a program or add new components of one already installed, simply select it from the list and click on the *Add/Remove* button.

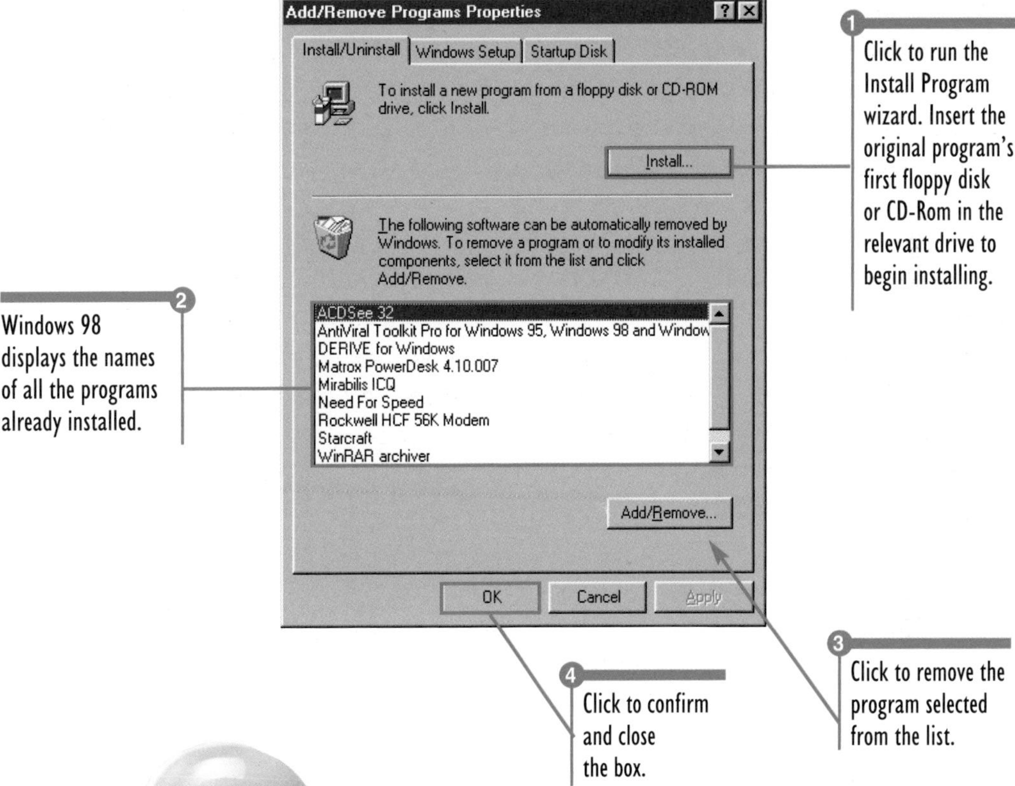

1 Click to run the Install Program wizard. Insert the original program's first floppy disk or CD-Rom in the relevant drive to begin installing.

2 Windows 98 displays the names of all the programs already installed.

3 Click to remove the program selected from the list.

4 Click to confirm and close the box.

Never remove a program just by going into its installation folder and deleting all the files. Always use the procedure described here, because all programs store some files in the Windows directory which you won't be able to find and delete afterwards.

Windows Setup tab

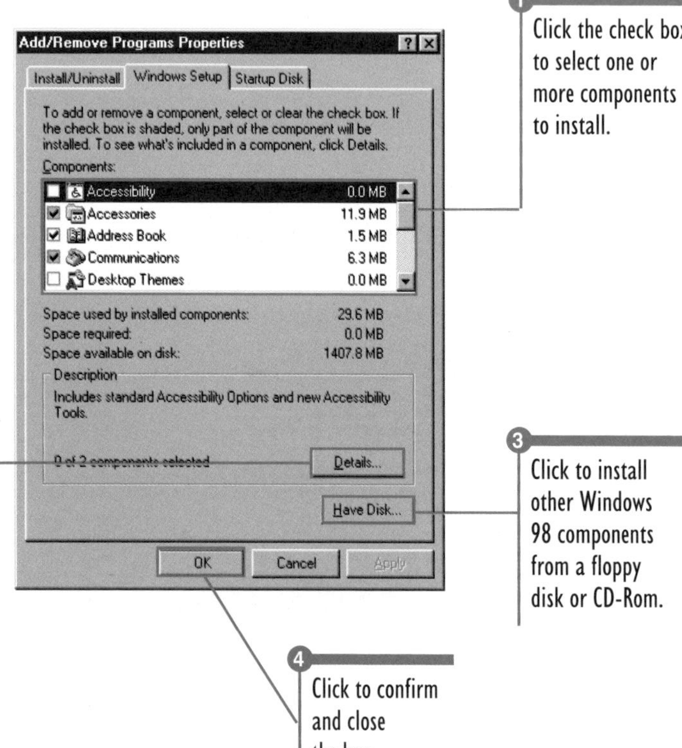

1 Click the check box to select one or more components to install.

2 Click for a list of utilities and select them by clicking on the check boxes.

3 Click to install other Windows 98 components from a floppy disk or CD-Rom.

4 Click to confirm and close the box.

Note

By default, Windows 98 does not install all its components and utilities when you first load it.

To see which ones have not been installed, view the list of components; a greyed-out check box means its associated programs have not been installed. To install them, click the *Details* button and then tick the relevant boxes.

Click *OK* to confirm. Windows 98 will ask you to insert the original CD-Rom and install the new components.

You can use the same procedure to remove parts of Windows 98 from the hard disk. Simply click the box of the component concerned to remove the tick. Click the OK button to confirm and Windows 98 will remove all the programs concerned from the hard disk.

Checklist

Just click the *Create Disk* button to start the disk creation procedure. After a few seconds, Windows 98 will show a message asking you to insert a blank disk in drive A:. Do that and leave it to carry on. After a few minutes, you will have a startup disk to rescue you in case of a system failure!

Startup Disk tab

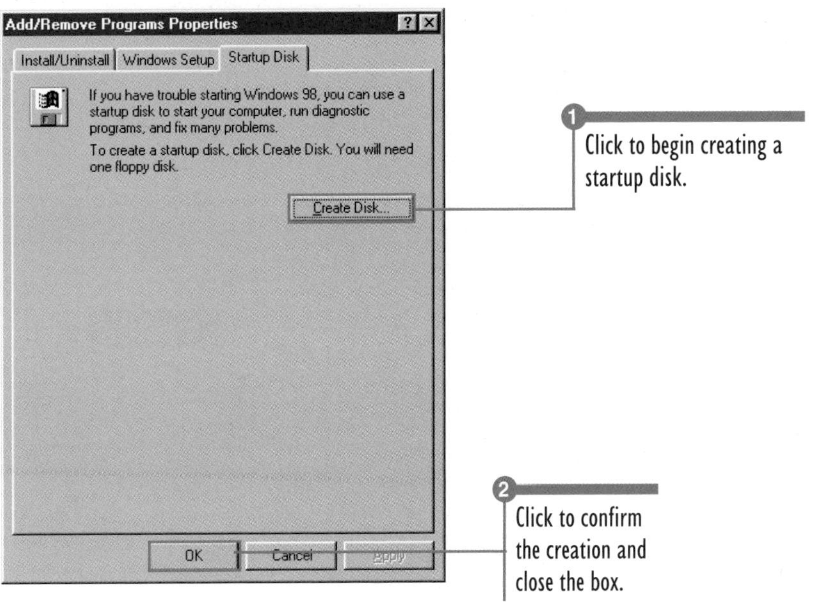

If your computer refuses to boot up due to a disk error or corrupted boot files, use your startup disk. Insert it in the floppy drive and turn your computer on. After a few minutes (it takes a little longer, because the floppy drive is slower than your hard disk), Windows 98 will start up via the disk and display the A: prompt.

Flow chart for adding a program

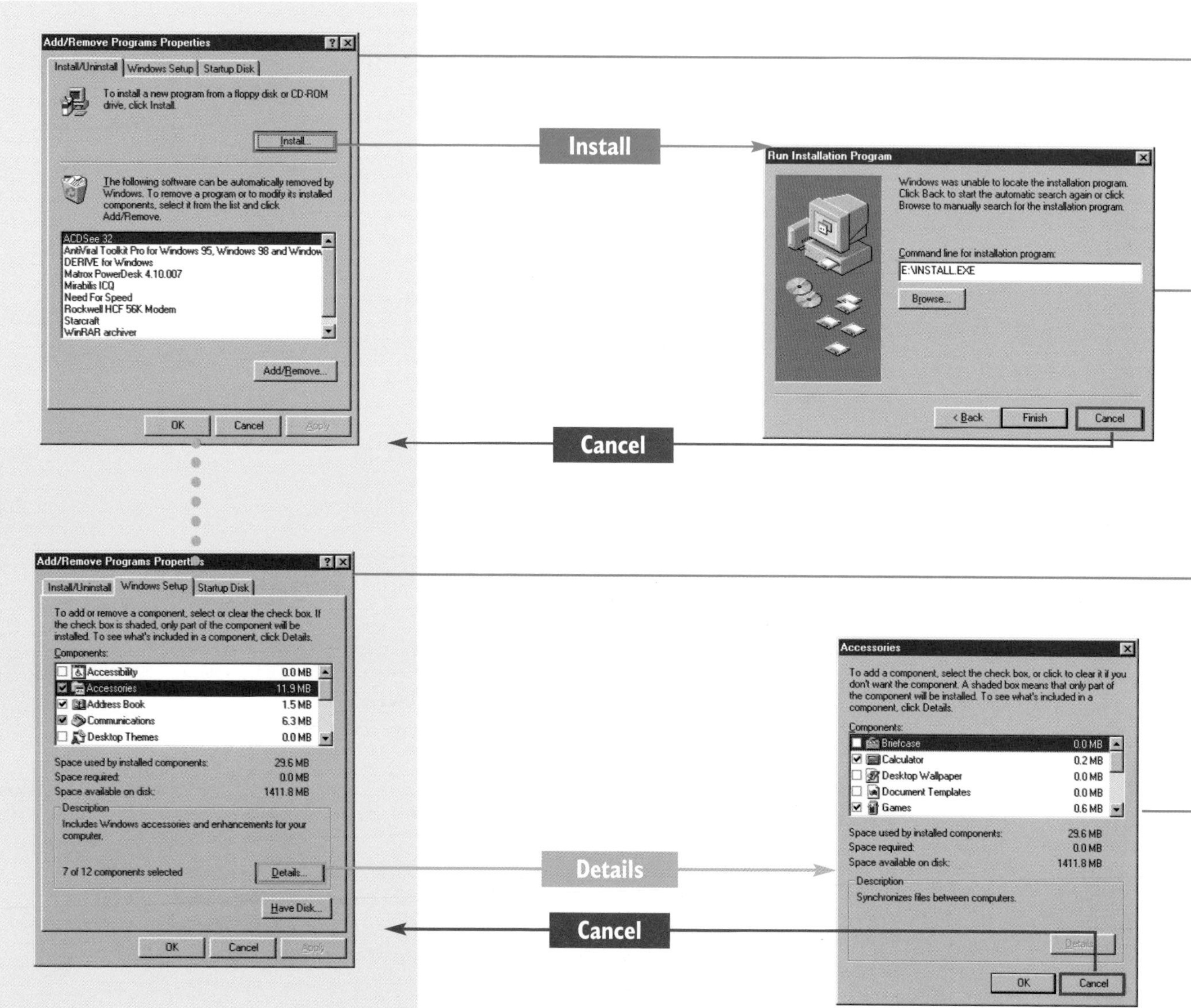

Lists the installed programs so that you can select the one you want removed from your hard disk.

Windows 98 displays the program's executable installation file. Click on the *Finish* button to start the installation program.

Lists the Windows 98 components installed on your computer. To add components, click the check boxes and *OK* to confirm.

Shows the utilities contained in the *Accessories* component, so that you can select them individually. Each component has one or more utilities that can be installed or uninstalled.

Adding new hardware

Control Panel / Add New Hardware

The **Add New Hardware Wizard is an invaluable help when you want to add a new modem, video adapter or other hardware. Once you have physically put the hardware into place on your computer, you will still have to configure it. This is when you give Windows 98 all the information it needs to make the new equipment work. In stage one, you do nothing: Windows 98 will automatically try and detect the device if it is Plug and Play. If it does detect it the problem is solved. Windows 98 will copy the drivers onto your computer's hard disk, and all you need do then is restart the computer for the equipment to work properly. If it isn't detected, you move to stage two: selecting the type of hardware (sound card, network card, video card, modem, etc.). Then you have to select the manufacturer and model so that Windows 98 can install the right drivers for it. Restart the computer, and you can start using the equipment. In an intermediate dialogue box, the operating system shows the resources assigned to the new device (needed for it to work properly); in some cases there may be a conflict with another device. If so, Windows 98 will help you resolve it by calling up the *System Properties* dialogue box (covered in the Managing your system section hereafter).**

TIP

Always start by asking Windows 98 to detect your new device — it's much easier. If it can't, you'll have to install it by hand, telling Windows the type, manufacturer and model of the new equipment.

HOW TO

There are two ways to get to the Add New Hardware Wizard dialogue box:

Select the Start/Settings/Control Panel command, then double-click on the Add New Hardware icon.

Double-click in turn on the My Computer, Control Panel and Add New Hardware icons.

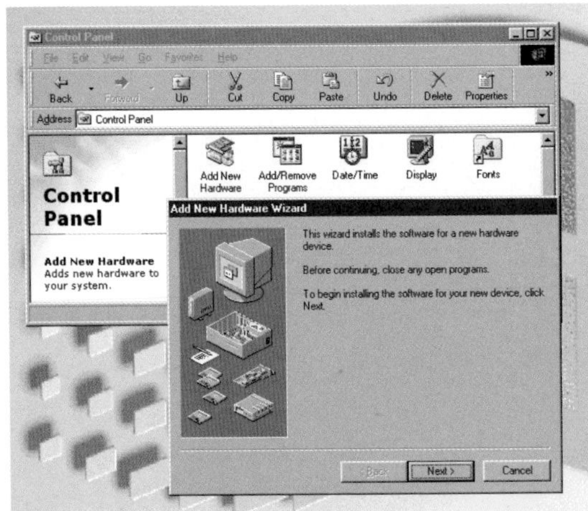

Adding new hardware

Checklist

1. Choose the *Yes (Recommended)* option to start automatic detection. After a few minutes (up to ten on slower machines), Windows 98 will display a list of all the new devices it has detected.
2. Click the *No* option if you are installing a recent device and have a disk supplied by the manufacturer with the driver files on it.
3. In either case, click *Next>* to continue.

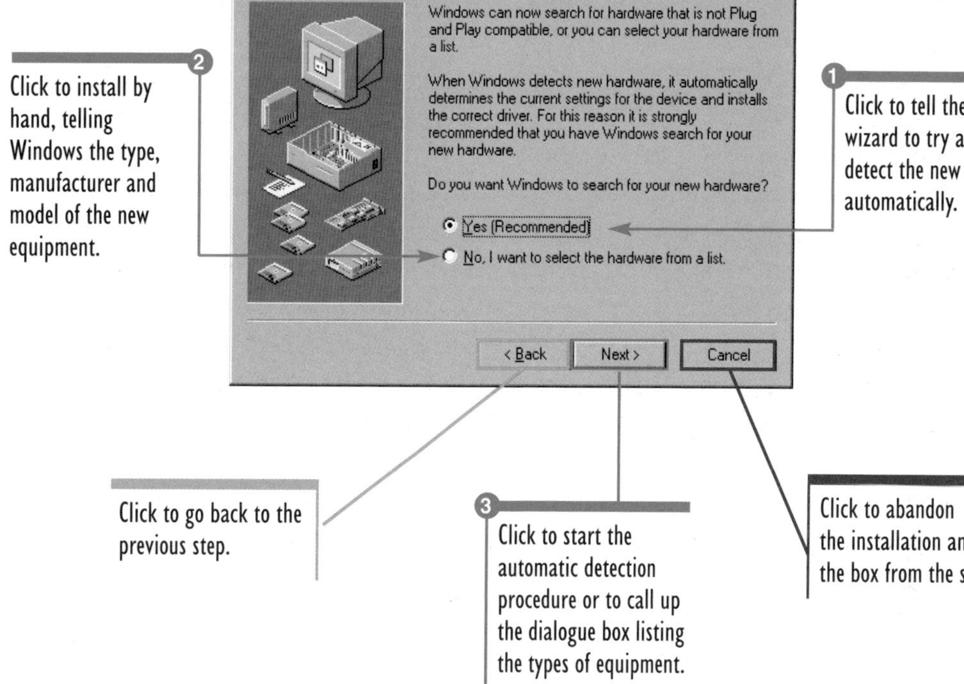

1 Click to tell the wizard to try and detect the new device automatically.

2 Click to install by hand, telling Windows the type, manufacturer and model of the new equipment.

Click to go back to the previous step.

3 Click to start the automatic detection procedure or to call up the dialogue box listing the types of equipment.

Click to abandon the installation and clear the box from the screen.

If installing a piece of equipment that is only just on the market, don't waste your time trying to get Windows to detect it. Choose the No option, select the type of equipment and click on the Have Disk button. Insert the disk containing the device drivers in the drive, and bingo...

Flow chart of automatic detection of hardware

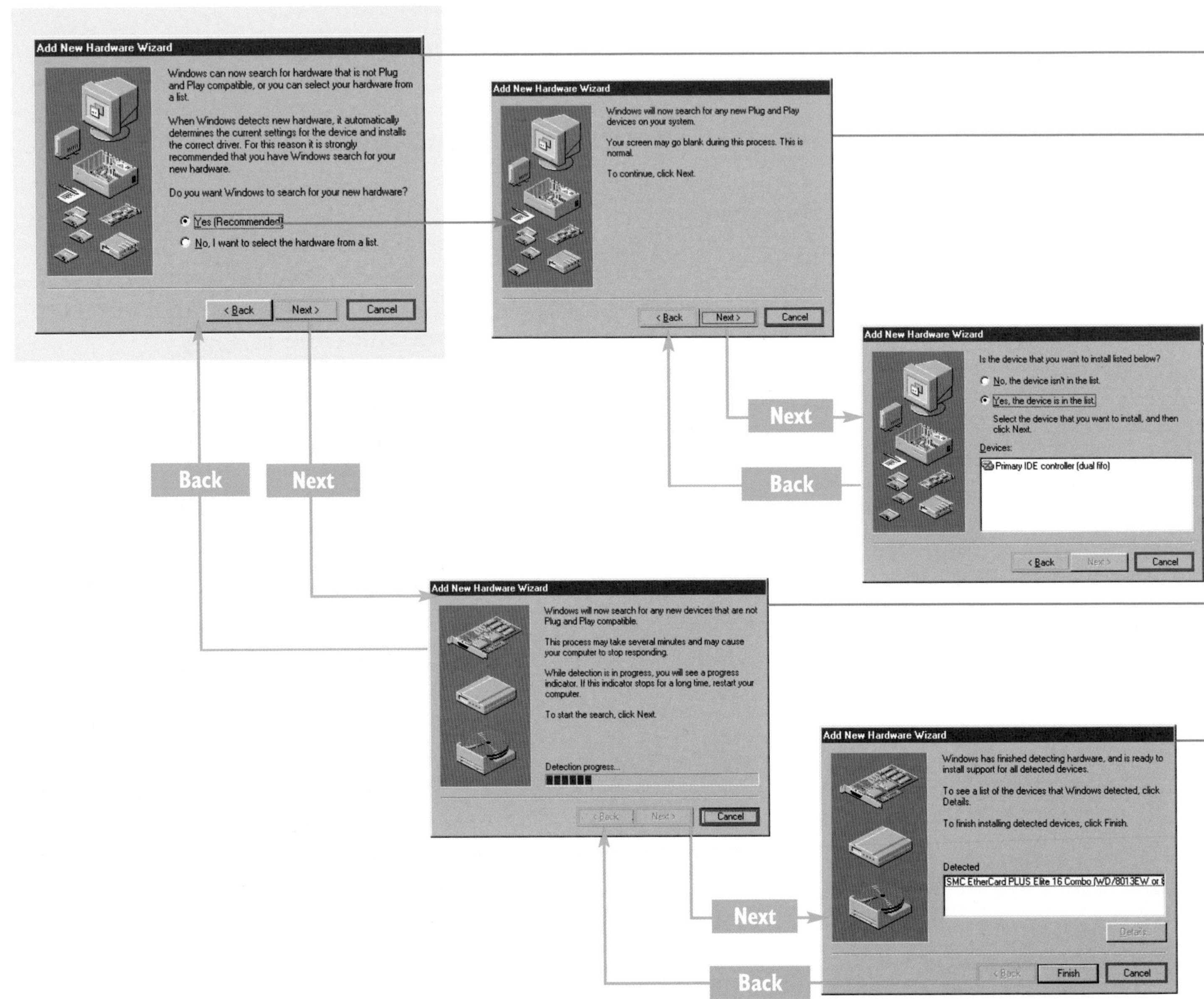

Tells Windows 98 to search for a new device which is *Plug and Play* compatible.

Windows 98 will search for a new device which is *Plug and Play* compatible.

Windows 98 has found the *Plug and Play* devices; all that remains is to copy the driver files to complete the installation.

Windows 98 is searching; this can take a few minutes.

Windows 98 has found the device; you can click on the *Finish* button to complete the installation; the drivers will be copied to your hard disk.

Cancel

Takes you back to the *Control Panel*.

In theory...

Adding new equipment to a system is now easier than ever with the new *Plug and Play* technology. Briefly, this means that the hardware device, your computer's BIOS and the Windows 98 operating system can 'talk' to each other. The first of these indicates what resources it needs to work properly, the second what system resources are available, whilst the third gets the other two to agree.

The *Add New Hardware Wizard* will first try to detect any *Plug and Play* components. If the new device uses the new technology, Windows 98 will display it in a list; all you need to do then is select it for Windows 98 to copy the drivers it needs to work properly.

If the device is not *Plug and Play*, Windows 98 will offer to search for cards newly installed in the computer. Choose this option first, because if Windows 98 finds them, the installation proper is finished. It will then copy the relevant drivers and you can restart the computer and start using the new hardware.

Flow chart for manual detection of hardware

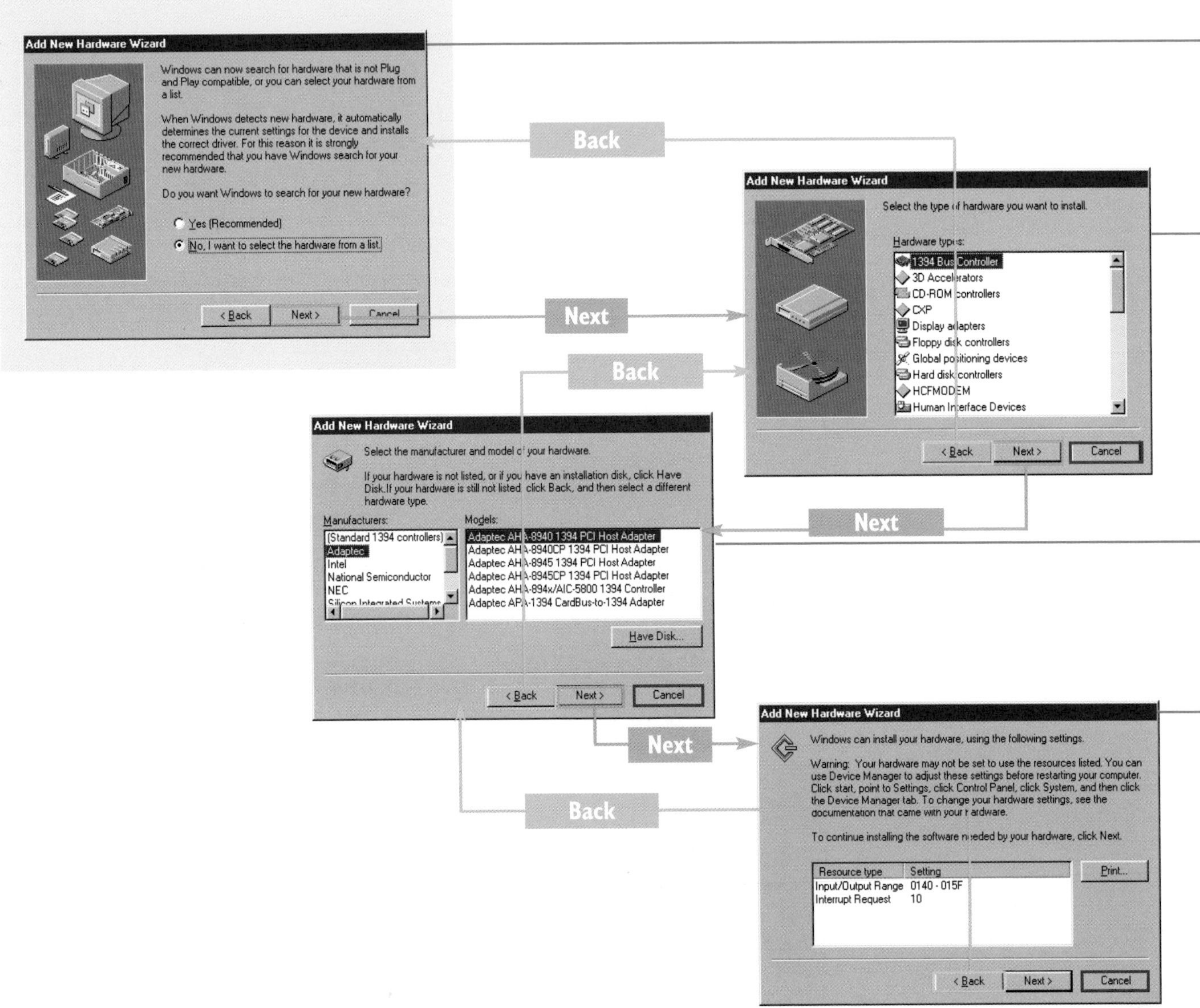

Tells Windows 98 that this is a manual installation: you have to supply the necessary information.

Lets you specify the type of equipment to install (here, an SCSI card).

Specifies the manufacturer (Adaptec) and model of the card (AHA-8940).

Windows 98 shows the resources assigned to the new device. If there is a conflict with another device, the system will call up the *System Properties* dialogue box to solve it.

Cancel

Takes you back to the *Control Panel*.

In theory...

If Windows 98 fails to detect the new hardware, you will have to install it by hand. This means you must supply all the particulars of the new equipment: type of component, manufacturer's name and model. When this is done, Windows 98 will display the resources used by the new device and then copy its drivers onto your computer's hard disk.

Managing your system

Control Panel / System

You make sure all the hardware equipment connected to your machine is working properly through the *System Properties* dialogue box, and especially the *Device Manager* tab. This shows you what cards and other components you have connected, and allows you to resolve any resource assignment conflicts you might get when adding new equipment. Windows 98 manages your devices by type or by connection. When viewing by type, just click the + sign to show all the devices installed. Double-clicking on a line shows you all the properties of the device: type, manufacturer, drivers used, resources assigned. This box is immensely helpful if you come up against a resource conflict. The *Device Manager* is also a quick way to see how much of your total system resources is being used; it's information that may be essential if you are about to buy a new piece of hardware. One final feature: the *Remove* button lets you delete a device from your system. You can also use the *System Properties* dialogue box to improve your computer's general performance by changing the way your drives work, the virtual memory and the video card acceleration settings. If you are using a laptop where the hardware configuration changes according to whether you are using it as a standalone or with its docking station, you can define hardware profiles with different numbers of devices.

HOW TO

There are three ways to get to the System Properties dialogue box:

Select the Start/Settings/Control Panel command, then double-click on the System icon.

Double-click in turn on the My Computer, Control Panel and System icons.

Right-click on the My Computer icon and select the Properties command from the context menu.

TIP

If a new piece of hardware causes your system to crash, you cannot get to the Device Manager to solve the problem. What you do then is restart the machine, and when you see the Starting Windows screen, press F8 and select Safe Mode. Windows 98 will always start in Safe Mode whatever the problem. Then go into Device Manager and try to resolve the conflict, or just delete the device from the list.

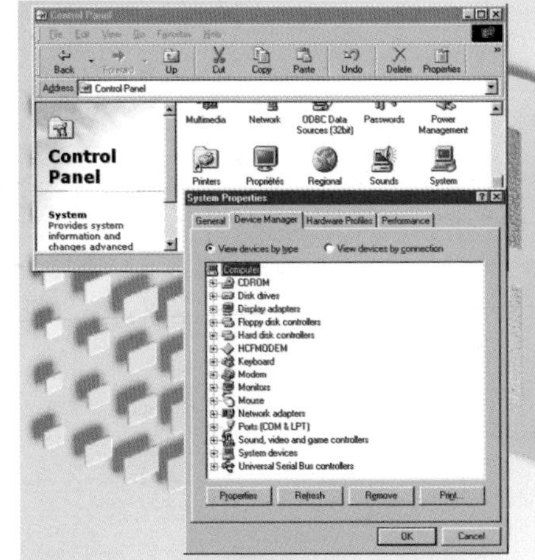

Checklist

1 The list shows all the devices connected to your system. You can find out what resources a device is using at any time by double-clicking on it or clicking the Properties button.

2 Double-click on the word *Computer* to show all the resources being used by the system (interrupt request, direct memory access (DMA) channel, memory and input/output addresses).

3 Click on the *Remove* button to delete a system device. Don't click on the type of device, but on the actual device shown under the type. And remember to physically disconnect it from your computer!

Managing the system

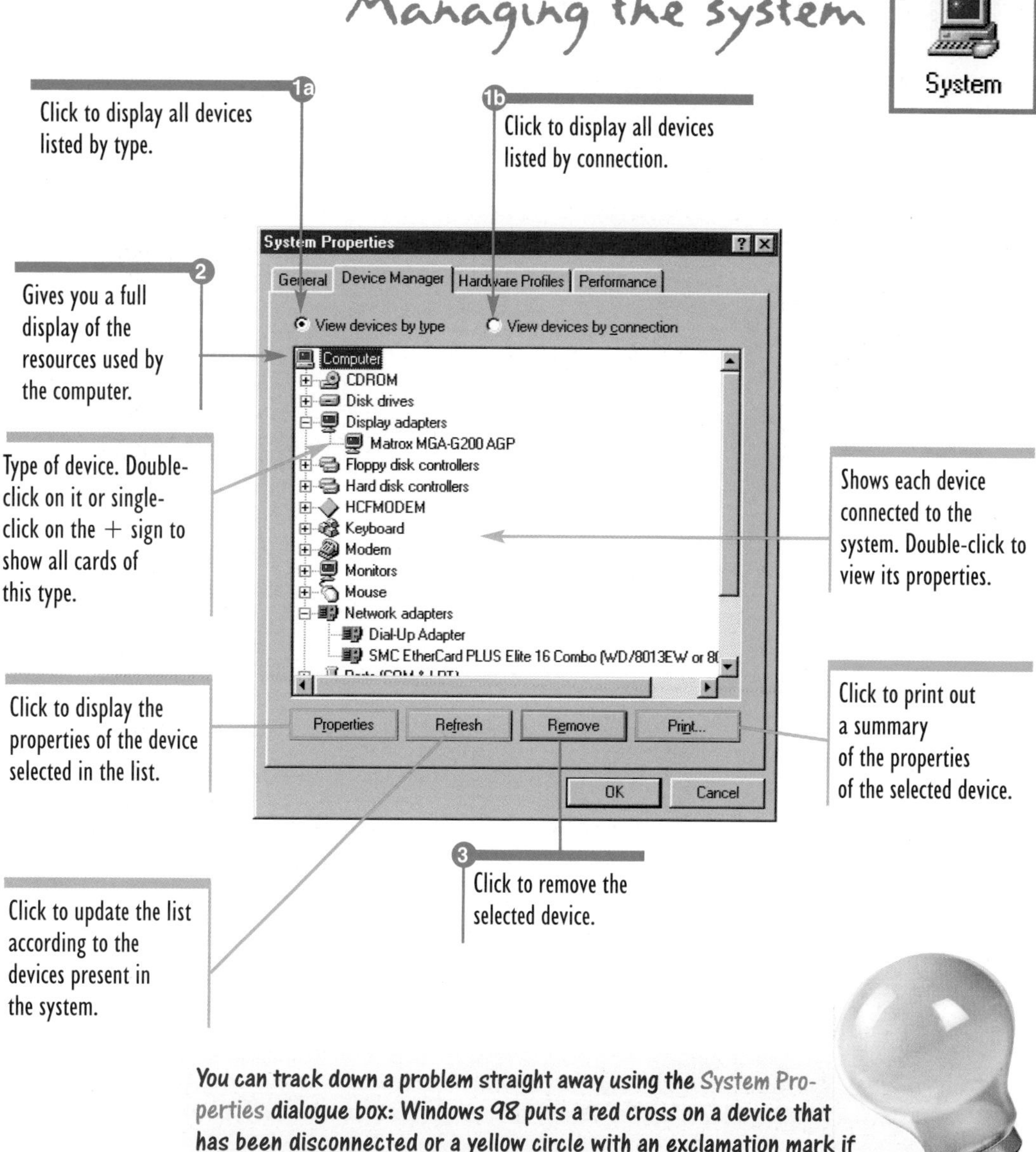

System
1a Click to display all devices listed by type.
1b Click to display all devices listed by connection.
2 Gives you a full display of the resources used by the computer.
Type of device. Double-click on it or single-click on the + sign to show all cards of this type.
Shows each device connected to the system. Double-click to view its properties.
Click to display the properties of the device selected in the list.
Click to print out a summary of the properties of the selected device.
3 Click to remove the selected device.
Click to update the list according to the devices present in the system.
System Properties
General
Device Manager
Hardware Profiles
Performance
View devices by type
View devices by connection
Computer
CDROM
Disk drives
Display adapters
Matrox MGA-G200 AGP
Floppy disk controllers
Hard disk controllers
HCFMODEM
Keyboard
Modem
Monitors
Mouse
Network adapters
Dial-Up Adapter
SMC EtherCard PLUS Elite 16 Combo (WD/8013EW or 8(
Properties
Refresh
Remove
Print...
OK
Cancel

You can track down a problem straight away using the System Properties dialogue box: Windows 98 puts a red cross on a device that has been disconnected or a yellow circle with an exclamation mark if there is some kind of conflict. The (device) Properties dialogue box will tell you more about the specific problem.

Defining different configurations

Hardware Profile tab

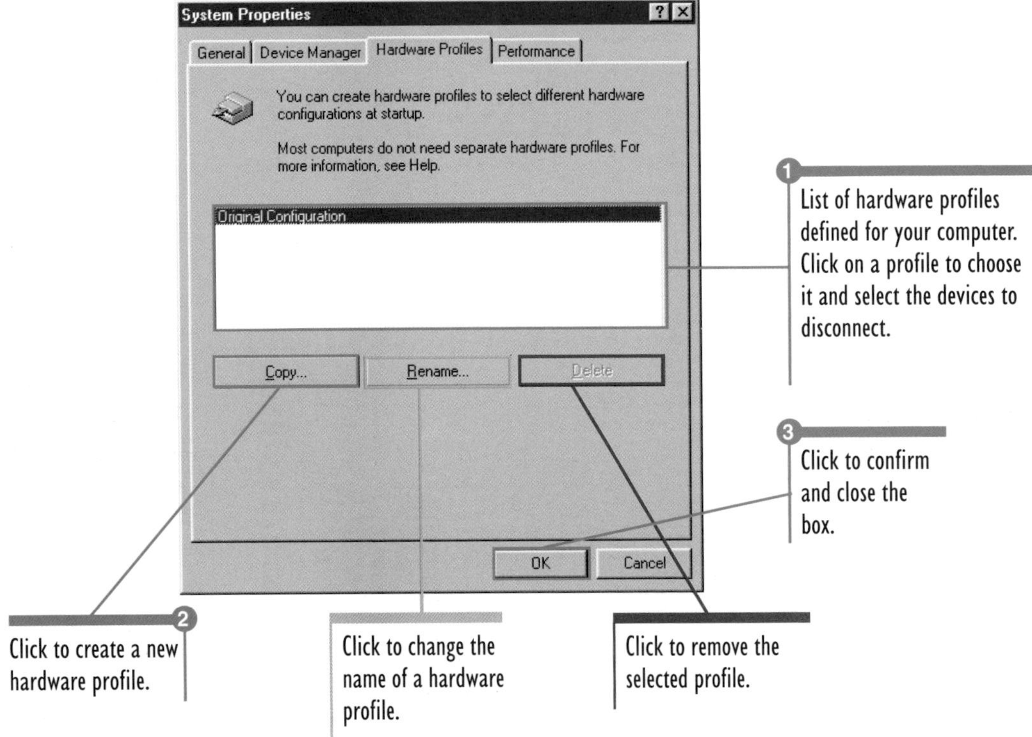

System Properties
General
Device Manager
Hardware Profiles
Performance
You can create hardware profiles to select different hardware configurations at startup.
Most computers do not need separate hardware profiles. For more information, see Help.
Original Configuration
Copy...
Rename...
Delete
OK
Cancel
1
List of hardware profiles defined for your computer. Click on a profile to choose it and select the devices to disconnect.
3
Click to confirm and close the box.
2
Click to create a new hardware profile.
Click to change the name of a hardware profile.
Click to remove the selected profile.

You don't need to manage hardware profiles yourself if you have a Plug and Play computer (BIOS, operating system and devices), because Windows 98 willl automatically recognise all the devices connected to the computer when you start it up.

A. Define different hardware profiles to disconnect some of your devices. This might apply if you have a laptop which uses different devices according to whether it is being used as a standalone machine or with its docking station.

B. To create a new profile, click on *Copy* and enter a new name. Select the devices via the *Device Manager* tab and deactivate them in the *Properties* dialogue box.

C. To remove a profile, select it in the list and click on the *Delete* button.

Checklist

1. The *Performance* tab gives you a bird's eye view of how your computer is performing. By clicking on the *File System* button, you can make it process information faster by choosing *Network server* from the drop-down list in the *Typical role of this machine* box.

2. You can also manage the virtual memory by clicking the *Virtual Memory* button and setting a minimum of more than 5% of your total hard disk capacity.

3. To speed up the display, click on the *Graphics* button and move the *Hardware acceleration* slider all the way to *Full*.

4. Click on *OK* to confirm any changed settings.

Managing system performance

Performance tab

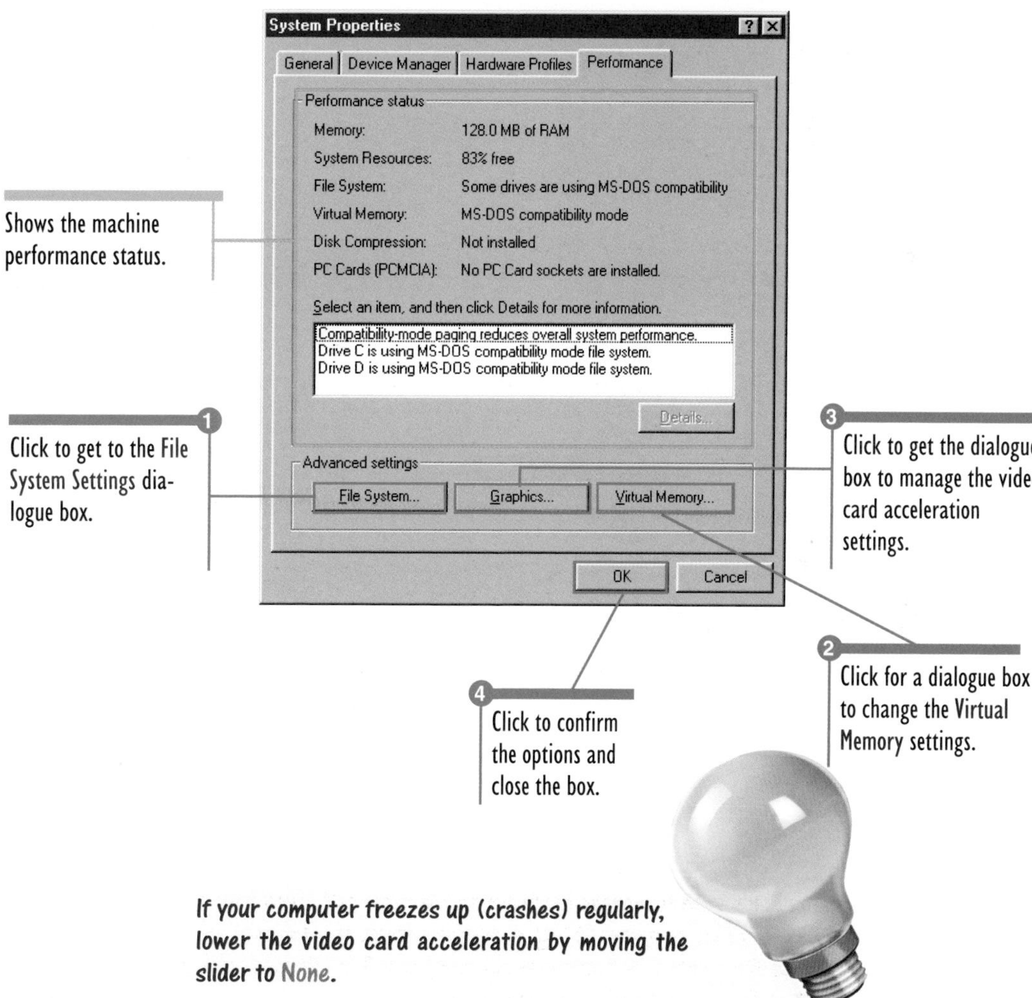

If your computer freezes up (crashes) regularly, lower the video card acceleration by moving the slider to None.

Flow chart of System Properties dialogue box (device manager tab)

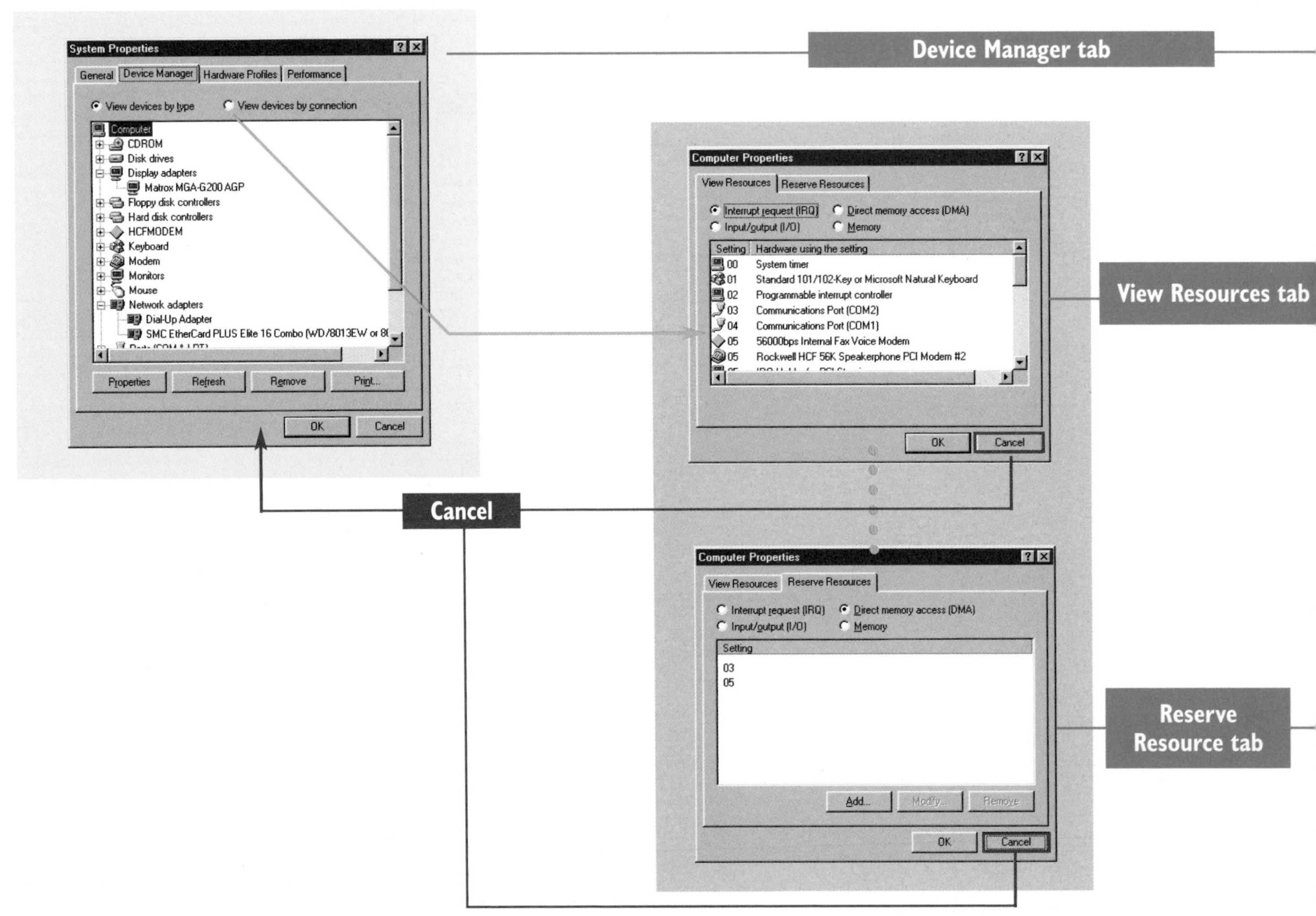

Lists all the devices installed on your computer. You can remove a component or modify a resource at any time by double-clicking on the device.

Shows the properties of a device. You can use this tab to disconnect the device for a particular predefined hardware profile.

Displays the list of resources used throughout the system. Windows 98 lists the interrupt requests, direct memory access (DMA) channels, memory and input/output addresses used by devices.

Shows the name and version of the driver files used by the device. You can also change the driver through this box (click on the *Update Driver* button).

Lets you reserve resources (IRQ, DMA, memory and I/O addresses). The screen shows the numbers already in use, which cannot be assigned to another device.

Shows all the resources used by the selected device (interruption, DMA channel, input/output range).

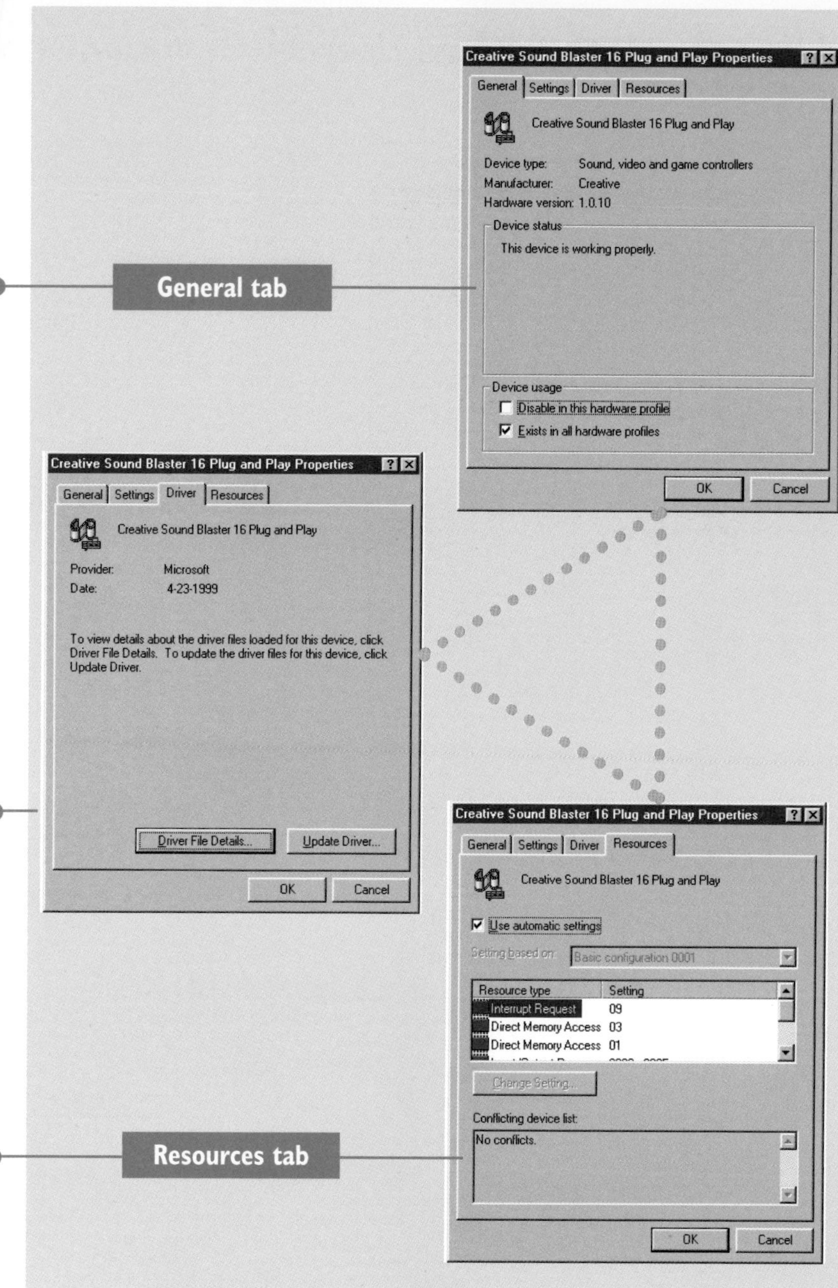

Flow chart of System Properties dialogue box (Performance tab 1)

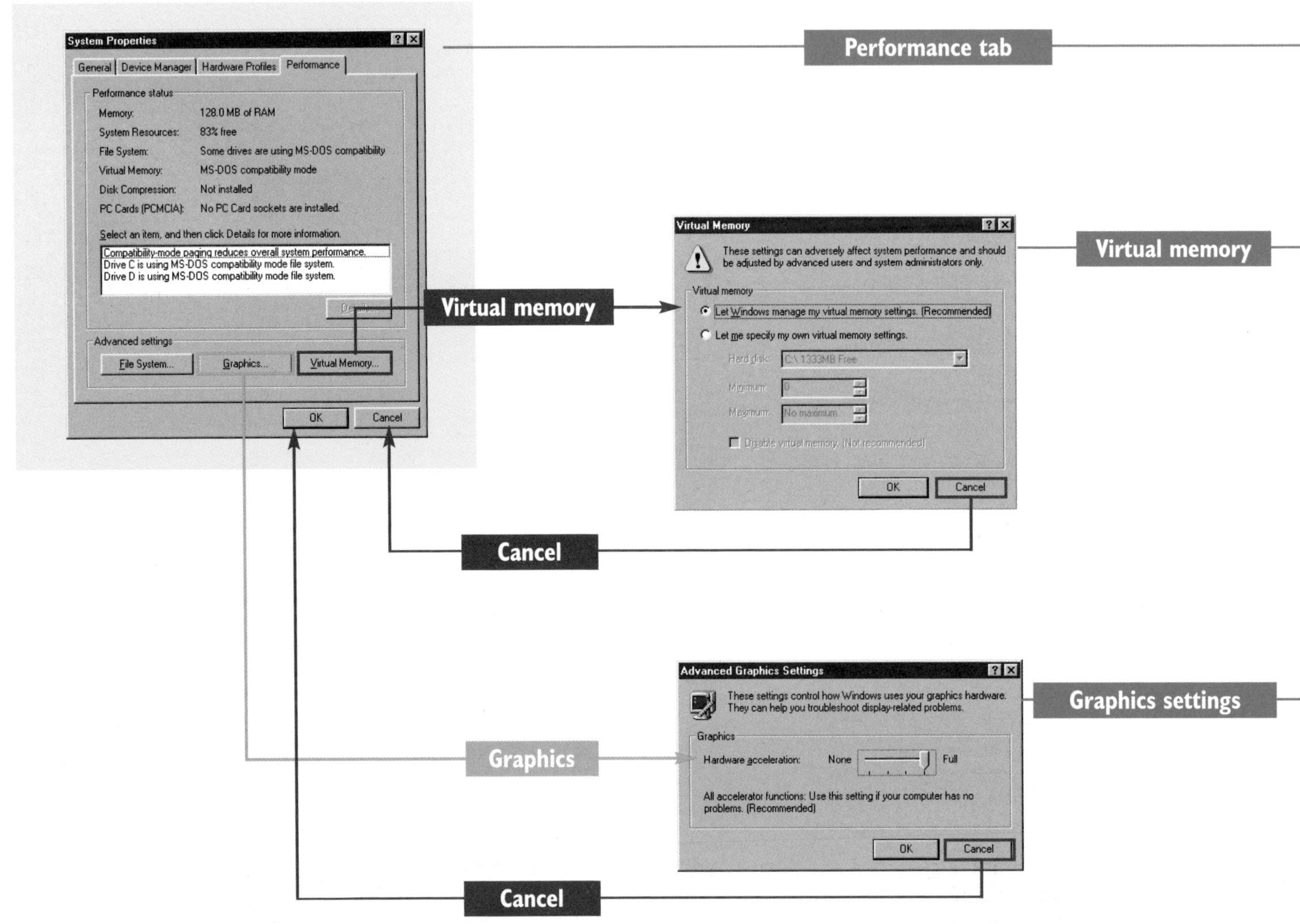

Gives a bird's eye view of the system performance.

Lets you define different hardware profiles to disconnect or reconnect different devices.

Lets you modify memory management to improve overall system performance.

Lets you create a new hardware profile. Just enter a different name in the text box and confirm by clicking *OK*.

Lets you run the graphics hardware faster to improve overall system performance.

Lets you change the name of the hardware profile.

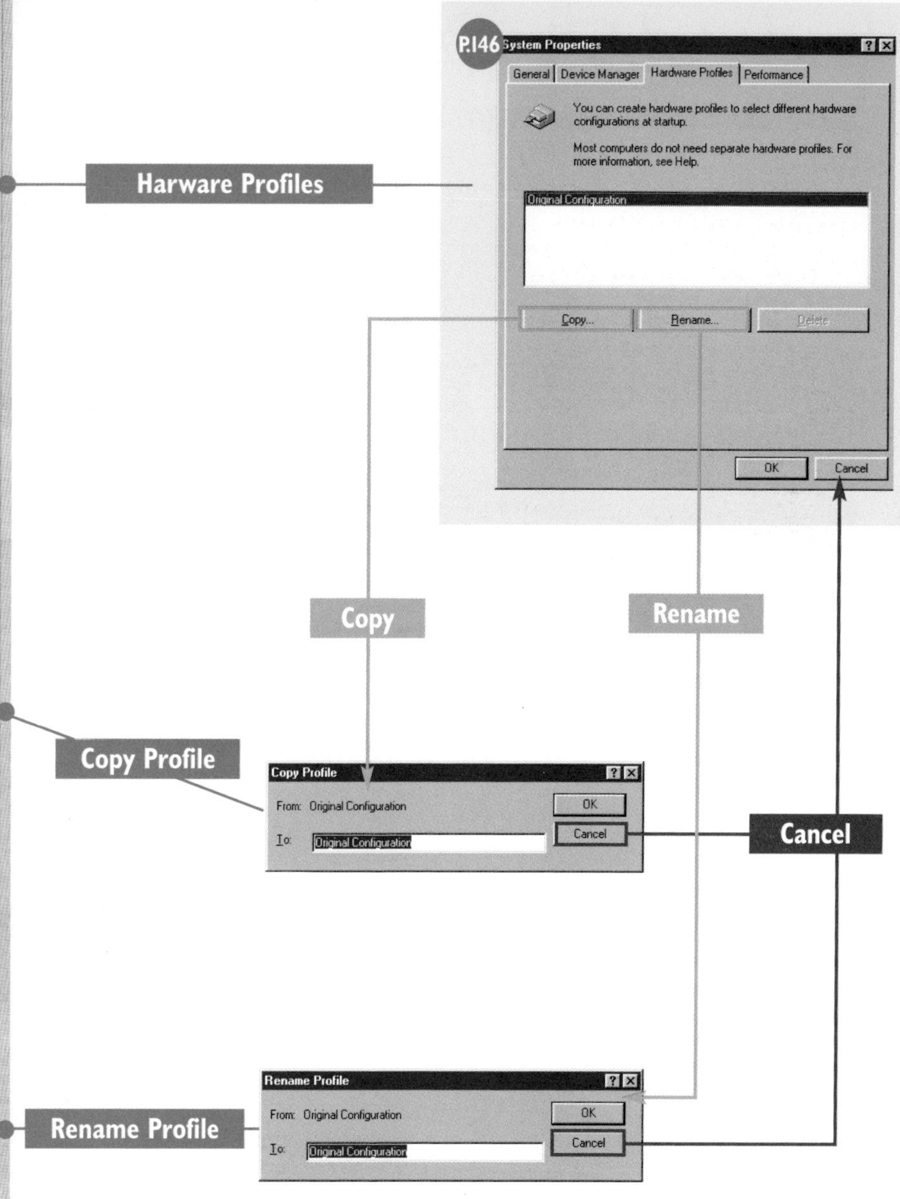

Flow chart of System Properties dialogue box (Performance tab 2)

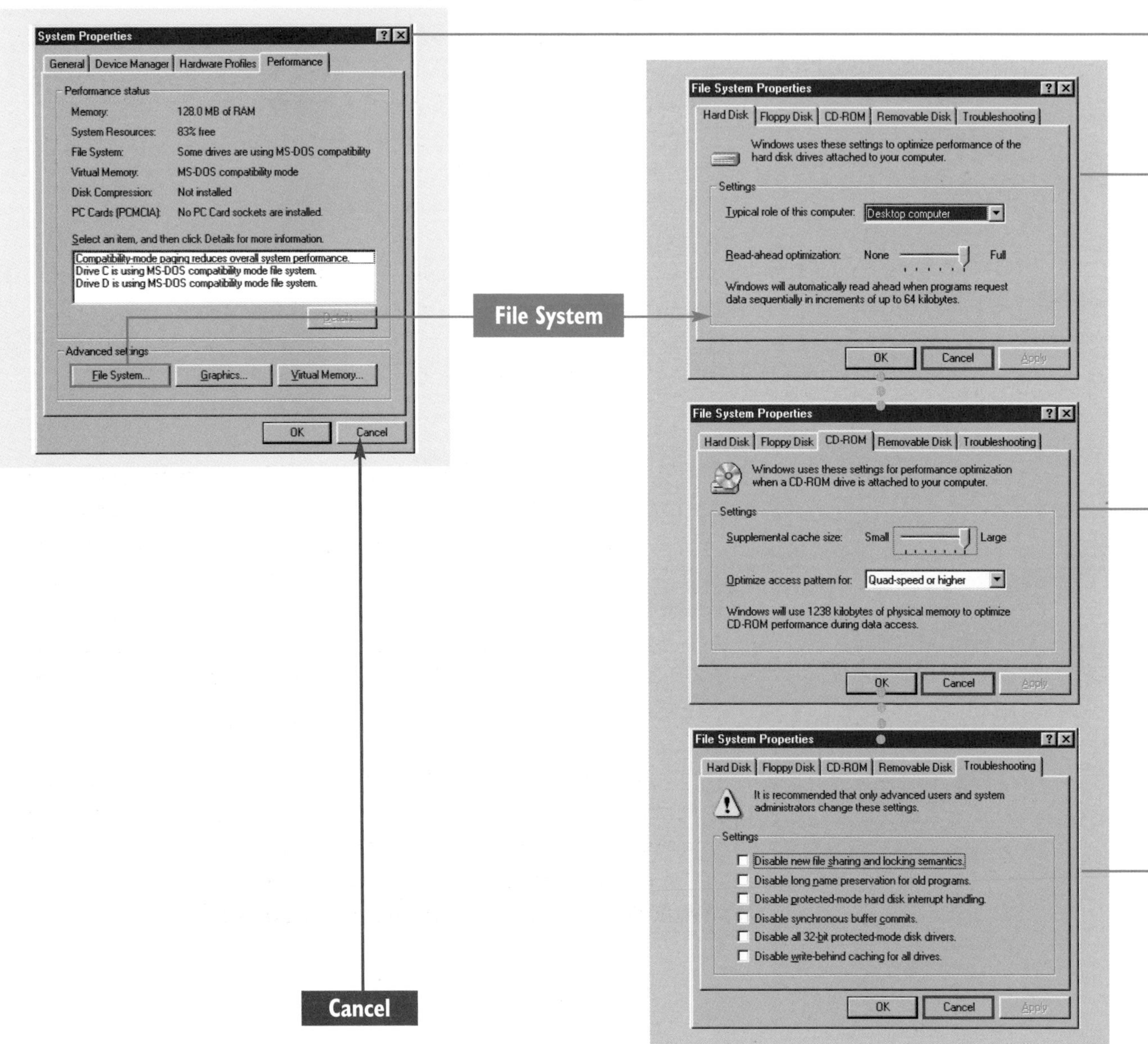

Hard disk tab

Gives a bird's eye view of the system performance.

Lets you set what the machine is used as, and optimise cache memory. Changing these settings can improve overall system performance.

CD-ROM tab

Sets the speed of the CD-ROM installed in the machine and the size of the supplemental cache. The larger this is, the better the CD-ROM is likely to perform.

Troubleshooting tab

Lets you set trouble-shooting options.

In theory...

If you add new hardware and it conflicts with equipment already installed, Windows 98 tells you by putting a yellow circle containing an exclamation mark on the relevant line in the *System Properties* dialogue box (*Device Manager* tab). The new device will not start working until you have resolved the conflict.

The only way to do this is to tinker with the resources assigned to the new card, and assign it one which is not already in use by another installed device. You can do this fairly easily through *Device Manager*.

First, double-click on the line which stands for the new device (where Windows 98 has put the exclamation mark) to call up the dialogue box containing its properties. Click on the *Resources* tab to show the resources assigned to the device. In the *Resource type* list, click on the resource for which there is a conflict. Observe the remarks which Windows 98 shows in the *Conflicting device* list box. If it says *No conflicts*, this is not the resource that is causing the problem. Once you've found the culprit, click on the *Change Setting* button; if it is greyed out, click the *Use automatic settings* box to remove the tick. When you click the button, Windows 98 will call up a new *Change Setting* dialogue box in which you can assign a new value to the resource. Be careful: choose a value that displays the message *No conflicting device* in the *Information on conflicts* box.

Chapter 5

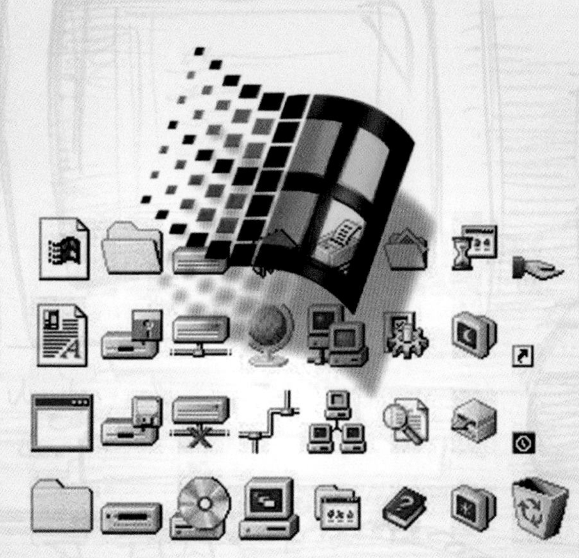

System tools

Maintaining the hard disk

System tools / ScanDisk

The *ScanDisk* tool can be used to detect errors on your computer's hard disk. These are usually caused by an untimely power failure, a crash and cold restart, or violent movement of the machine. The end result might be that the data on the disk is damaged, the system can no longer find certain sectors or the allocation table which controls the links between the different parts of a file contains errors. The job of *ScanDisk* is to scan the surface of the hard disc to detect the slightest logical error in the organisation of the stored data. *ScanDisk* starts by checking the file header and the startup sector. It then checks the file allocation table (FAT). Finally, it detects the loss of sectors or any disruption in the file chaining. The first step in launching the test is to select the drive and the type of test. A standard test will check files and folders for errors, while a thorough test will perform the standard test and check the disk surface for errors. The major asset of *ScanDisk* is that it can repair errors. Just tick the *Automatically fix errors* box, and *ScanDisk* will fix any errors detected.

HOW TO

To access ScanDisk:

Click Start / Programs / Accessories / System Tools and ScanDisk.

With MS Explorer: go to the Windows 98 installation folder (\Windows by default) and double-click Scandskw.exe.

Open My Computer and right-click on the drive you want to check. Click Properties in the context menu displayed. In the Hard Disk Properties dialogue box, click the Tools tab, then the Check Now button.

TIP

Avoid using the hard disk while ScanDisk is checking, and cancel the automatic screensaver option, because ScanDisk will stop immediately and will have to start checking the disk from the beginning again.

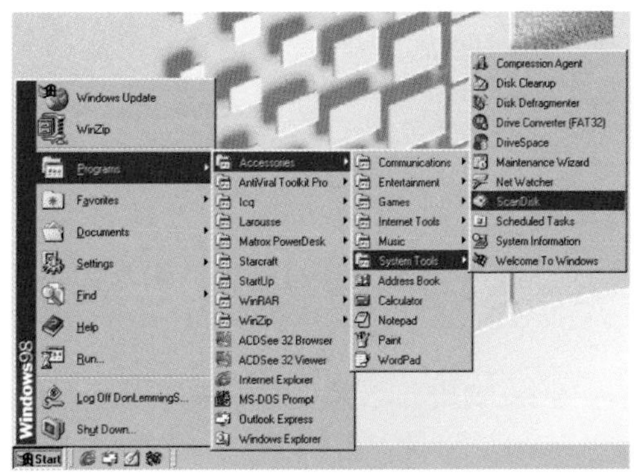

Checking disks

Start / Programs / Accessories / System Tools / ScanDisk

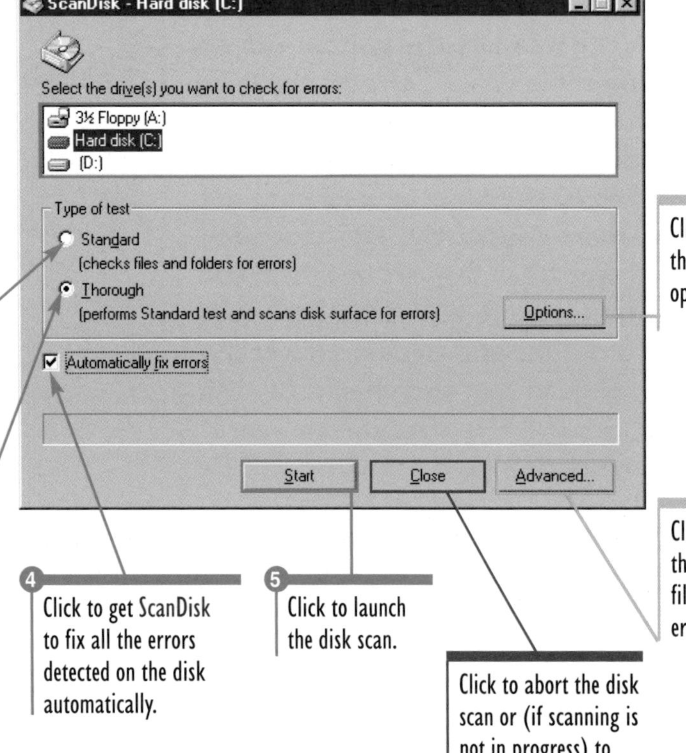

1. Start by selecting the drive to be checked.

3. Click to get ScanDisk to check for any errors in files and folders.

2. Click to get ScanDisk to perform the Standard test and also check the surface of the disk.

4. Click to get ScanDisk to fix all the errors detected on the disk automatically.

5. Click to launch the disk scan.

Click to abort the disk scan or (if scanning is not in progress) to close the dialogue box.

Click to change the surface scan options.

Click to change the settings for file and folder errors.

The default settings in the dialogue boxes for the Options and Advanced buttons are more than enough for repairing your disk. So it is not essential to change these settings. Do not forget to tick the Automatically fix errors box, however!

Checklist

1. Select the drive you want to check and chose the type of test (*Standard* or *Thorough*).
2. If you click *Thorough*, you can change the settings for this type of test by clicking the *Options* button.
3. If you click *Standard*, you can change the settings for this type of test by clicking the *Advanced* button.
4. Tick the *Automatically fix errors* box to have *ScanDisk* try to repair all the errors detected.
5. Click the *Start* button to begin.

Surface scan options

Options Button

A It's best to use the *System and data areas* option so that *ScanDisk* can scan the entire disk even if, in most cases, errors in the system area cannot be fixed.

B Leave the next two boxes unticked to make the test more complete.

C Click *OK* to confirm the options.

Note

ScanDisk repairs the data by putting it in a valid sector of the disk. Hidden and system files often remain in the same place on the disk because applications that refer to them would malfunction otherwise. That is the reason why the utility has an option for repairing bad sectors in hidden and system files.

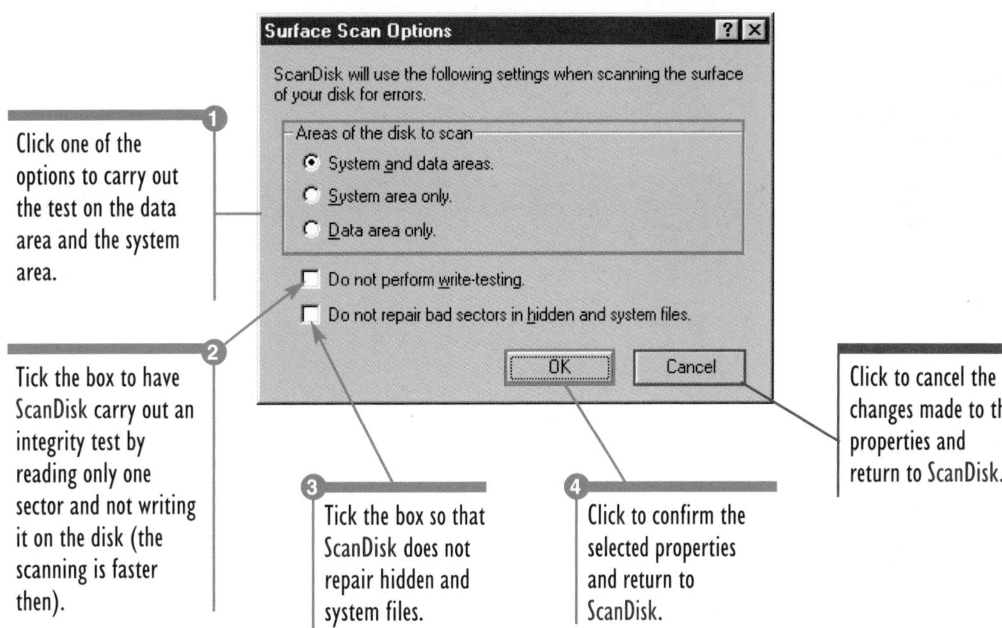

1 Click one of the options to carry out the test on the data area and the system area.

2 Tick the box to have ScanDisk carry out an integrity test by reading only one sector and not writing it on the disk (the scanning is faster then).

3 Tick the box so that ScanDisk does not repair hidden and system files.

4 Click to confirm the selected properties and return to ScanDisk.

Click to cancel the changes made to the properties and return to ScanDisk.

Advanced options

Advanced button

Click an option to tell ScanDisk to show a report that the disk scan has been carried out properly. This report may include the detection and repair of errors.

Select this option to get a file with a detailed sequence of the disk scan operation and the way any errors encountered were fixed. This file is stored in the root folder of the scanned drive under the name ScanDisk.log.

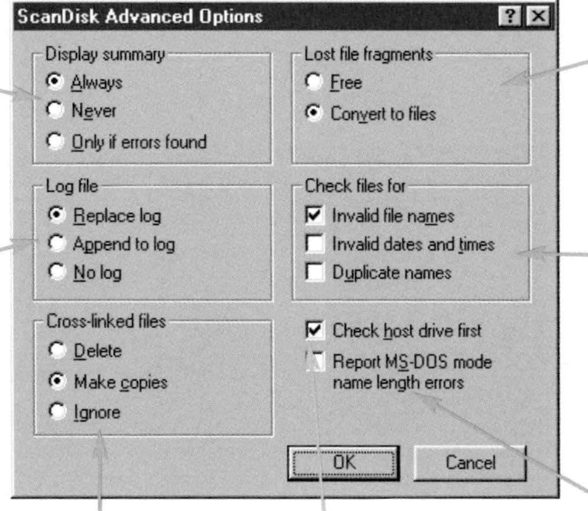

Select an option to treat lost file fragments (disk sectors containing data not referenced in the file allocation table (FAT)).

Click to select the type of errors to be detected by ScanDisk.

Click to select a method for repairing cross links (one or more files using the same disk sector). The best option is Make copies. ScanDisk recopies the common areas to restore at least one complete file.

Tick the box to tell ScanDisk to check the host drive of a compressed disk before continuing with the latter (errors on a disk can cause other errors on the compressed disk).

Tick the box to ask ScanDisk to display any errors that could occur with names with more than 8 characters (MS-DOS convention).

The default options are enough to detect and fix most of the errors that can occur on a disk. You can hone the settings by asking ScanDisk to provide a full report on any errors detected. In any event, click OK to confirm the changed settings.

A hard disk is composed of a set of groups of numbered sectors called clusters. All the files stored on a disk occupy one or more clusters. At the beginning of the disk or each partition, the system creates a startup sector, an allocation table, a copy of the table and a root directory. The rest of the partition is used to store files and folders.

The startup sector contains the number of sectors in each cluster and the size of the allocation table. For system disks, this area also contains a small program which helps the operating system to start. The allocation contains as many entries as there are clusters in the disk partition. The system uses this table to indicate whether a cluster is used by a file or a folder. If a file extends to several clusters, the table entry indicates a number corresponding to the next cluster in the file.

To repair errors in a bad sector, *ScanDisk* moves the data in it to another free and healthy sector on the disk.

Defragmenting your hard disk

System tools / Disk Defragmenter

Over time, as you add and remove files from your hard disk, Windows 98 leaves a growing number of blank spaces on it. When you write a file to disk, the system looks for the first free space and puts the data (or usually a few chunks of it) there. Eventually, you end up with bits of files scattered all over the disk. This fragmentation seriously slows down read–write times; simply put, access times get longer and longer. The *Disk Defragmenter* does two things: it puts the files in a single block, and puts them all at the beginning of the disk so as to leave the free space in a single block. The first thing you do is to tell it which disk to defragment. Then just click the *OK* button to start defragmenting. A dialogue box will pop-up on-screen showing you the program's progress. You can cancel or interrupt the process simply by clicking the *Stop* or *Pause* buttons.

HOW TO

To get to the Disk Defragmenter utility:

Click in turn on Start, Programs, Accessories, System Tools and Disk Defragmenter.

From Explorer: go to the Windows installation folder (default is \Windows) and double-click on the Defrag.exe file.

Open My Computer and right-click on the drive to defragment. Click on the Properties command in the pop-up context menu. In the (hard drive) Properties dialogue box, click on the Tools tab, then on the Defragment Now button.

TIP

Technically, you can continue working while defragmenting your disk (remember, Windows 98 is a multi-tasking system), but in fact the operation takes up so much of your resources that it's almost impossible to run other programs.

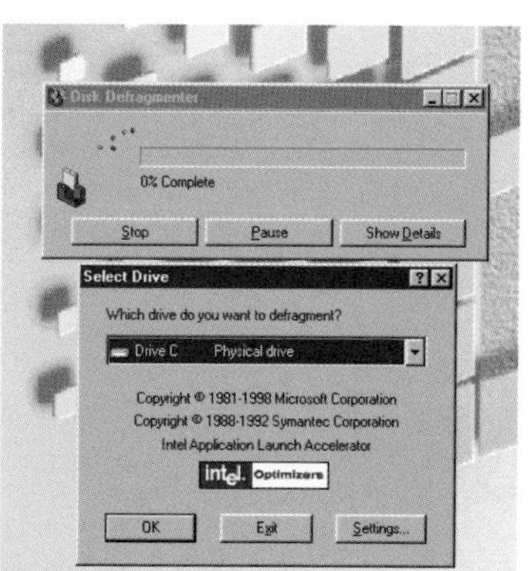

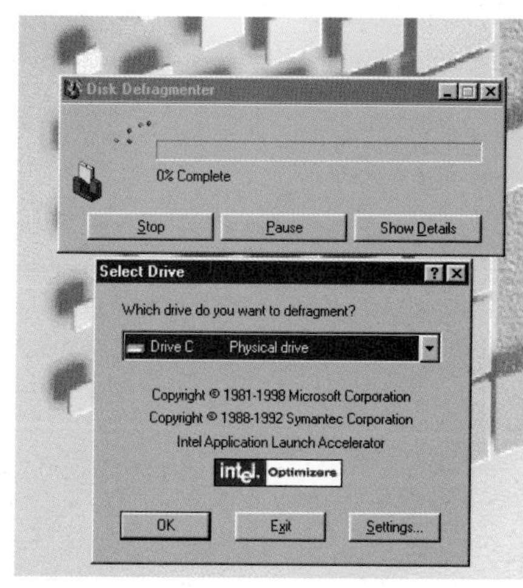

Defragmenting your hard disk

Start / Programs / Accessories / System Tools / Disk Defragmenter

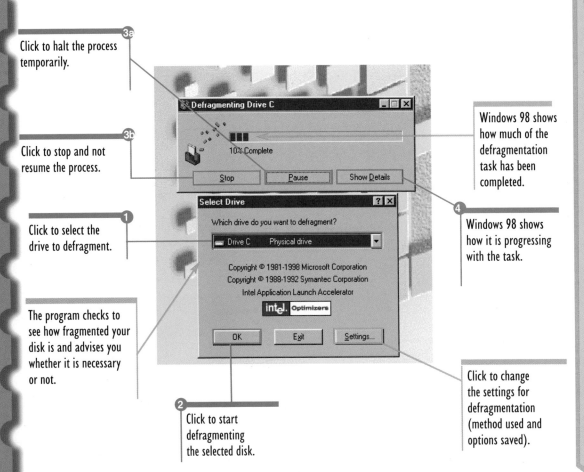

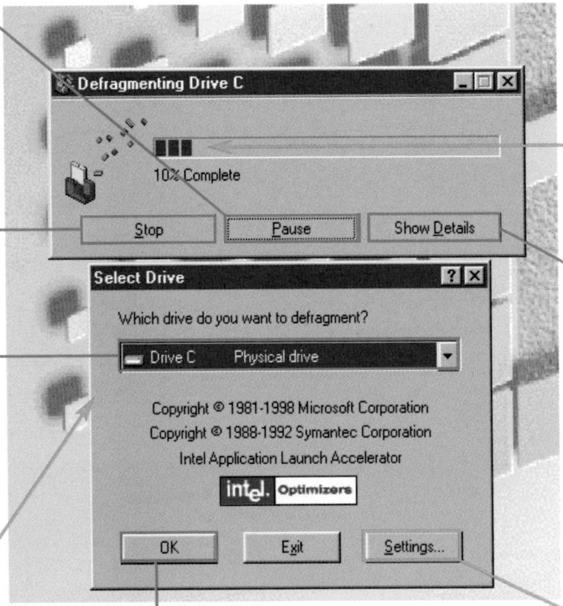

3a Click to halt the process temporarily.

3b Click to stop and not resume the process.

1 Click to select the drive to defragment.

The program checks to see how fragmented your disk is and advises you whether it is necessary or not.

2 Click to start defragmenting the selected disk.

Windows 98 shows how much of the defragmentation task has been completed.

4 Windows 98 shows how it is progressing with the task.

Click to change the settings for defragmentation (method used and options saved).

Checklist

1. First choose the drive you want to defragment.
2. Click *OK* to start the defragmentation process.
3. Click *Stop* or *Pause* to cancel or halt the defragmentation process.
4. You can see how the process is progressing by clicking the *Show Details* button.

Hint

Defragmentation is not something you do just once in your hard disk's life. You'll be amazed to see how much it can improve your hard drive's performance if you do it at regular intervals.

Checklist

1. For optimum performance, tick the *Rearrange program files so my programs start faster* box. This will make Windows 98 rearrange your most frequently used programs so that they load into memory more quickly. If the box is not ticked, Windows 98 will rearrange files into a single block.

2. Tick the *Check the drive for errors* box, because any error on the disk will start *ScanDisk* checking and running anyway.

3. Click on the *Every time I defragment my hard drive* button if you want *Disk Defragmenter* to save your options.

4. Click on the *OK* box to return to the *Select Drive* dialogue box.

Defragmentation Settings

Disk Defragmenter Settings

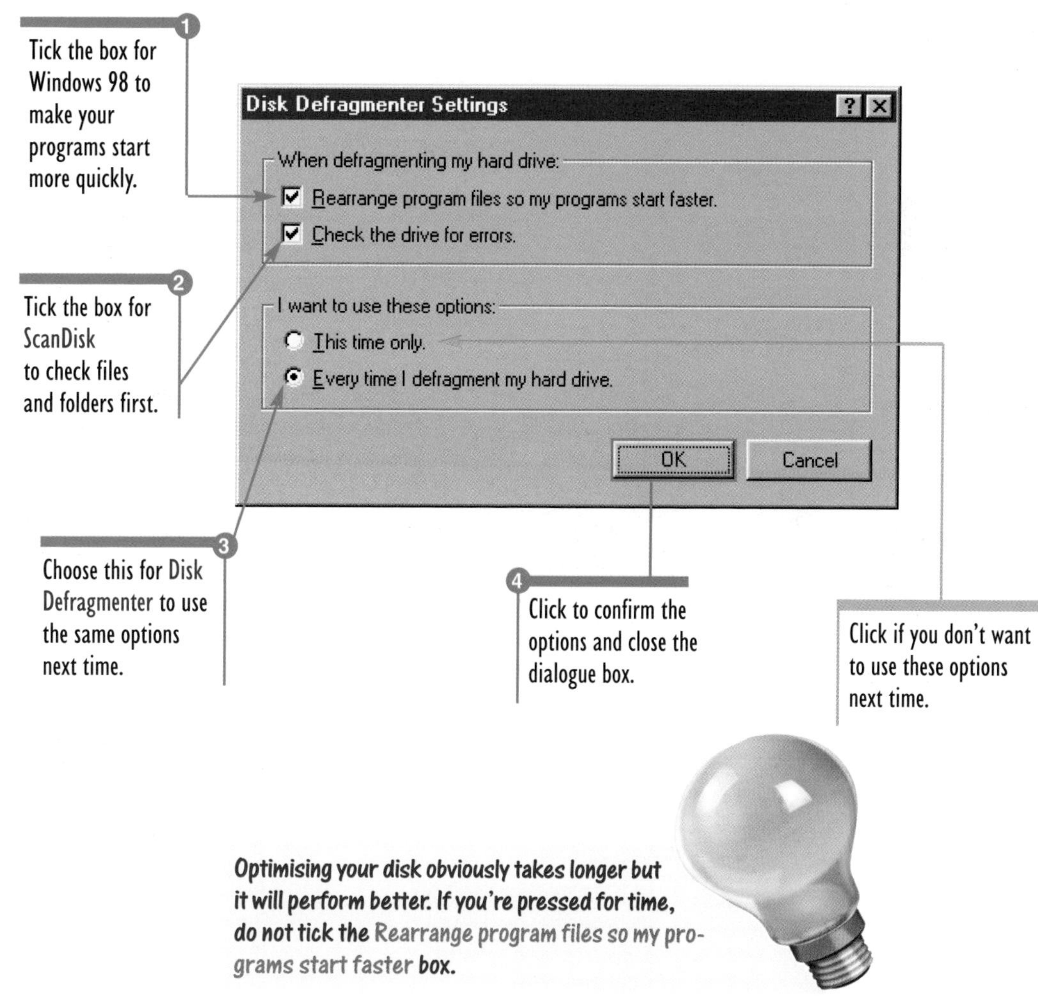

1 Tick the box for Windows 98 to make your programs start more quickly.
2 Tick the box for ScanDisk to check files and folders first.
3 Choose this for Disk Defragmenter to use the same options next time.
4 Click to confirm the options and close the dialogue box.
Click if you don't want to use these options next time.
Disk Defragmenter Settings
When defragmenting my hard drive:
Rearrange program files so my programs start faster.
Check the drive for errors.
I want to use these options:
This time only.
Every time I defragment my hard drive.
OK
Cancel

Optimising your disk obviously takes longer but it will perform better. If you're pressed for time, do not tick the Rearrange program files so my programs start faster **box.**

What's happening?

List of the different boxes representing clusters.

Each square stands for a chunk or cluster of data. You can watch your disk being defragmented.

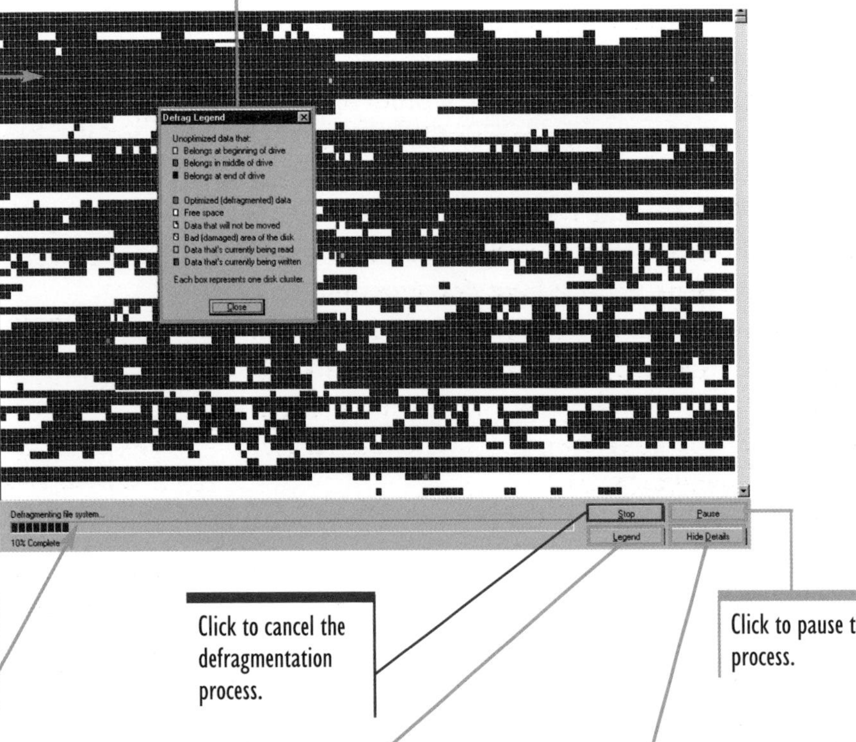

Defragmenter details the progress of the process.

Click to cancel the defragmentation process.

Click to pause the process.

Click to show the dialogue box which describes the different blocks representing clusters displayed on screen.

Click to return to a simpler dialogue box which does not display full details of the process.

The dialogue box which pops up on screen once you have started defragmenting does not show the details; different coloured squares represent clusters on the disk. You can use the *Details* button to display the dialog box as it is shown in the sample screen. By displaying all the clusters on the disk, you can see not only how the program is doing, but exactly how fragmented your disk is.

Note

It's a good idea not to display the details when defragmenting. It makes the process run much more quickly.

Finding files

Start / Find / Files or Folders

As you use your system, the programs you work with will start to fill up your hard disk with files. Before long, you will find it impossible to find a file quickly just by looking in folders and browsing through the names with Explorer. Happily, Windows 98 gives you a handy tool to help you locate files and folders across your computer's different hard drives. Just type in the name (or part of a name) of the file you wish to find in the text box, choose from the drop-down list the drive you wish to search, and Bob's your uncle! Within a matter of seconds, Windows 98 will locate the file, tell you which folder it is in and let you use it as if you were in Explorer. If the search turns up a folder, for example, you can double-click on its icon to view its contents. You can also search using the wildcard characters * and ? (which you'll remember from MS-DOS) to refine searches to find subsets of files. The *Find* command also offers other advanced options, such as searching by last modification date (*Date* tab), file type or size (*Advanced* tab).

HOW TO

Five ways to get to the Find utility:

Click in turn on Start, Find and Files or Folders.

From Explorer: choose the Tools/Find/Files or Folders command.

Open My Computer and click on the drive you want to search in. Choose the File/Find command.

Open My Computer and right-click on the drive you want to search in. Choose the Find command from the pop-up context menu.

Right-click on a closed folder to call up its context menu. Choose the Find command.

TIP

Where the Find utility looks for your file depends on how you launch it. If you click on the C: icon, Find will look on the C: drive. You can change this option directly in the Find dialogue box once you have called it up.

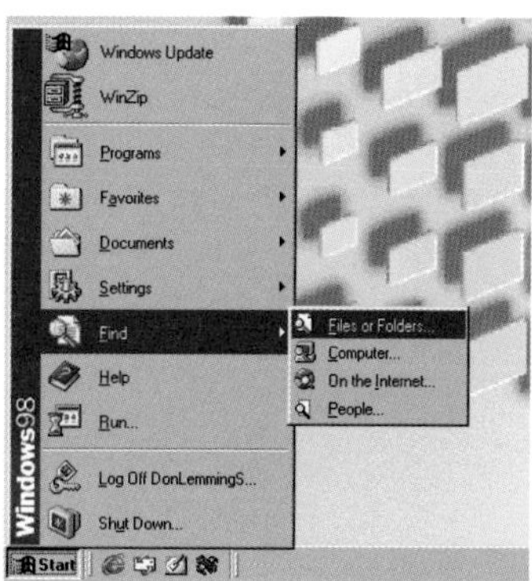

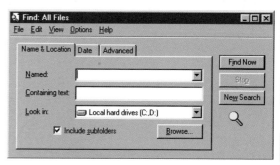

Finding a file

Enter a string of characters that the file should contain. If you can't remember the name of the file, but you know it was about fish, enter the word fish.

Click to cancel the search.

3 Click to start searching.

1 Enter the name of the file or folder you wish to look for.

2 Click to select the drive or folder you wish to start looking in.

Find: Files named readme.txt

File Edit View Options Help

Name & Location | Date | Advanced

Named: readme.txt

Containing text:

Look in: Local hard drives (C:,D:)

Include subfolders

Browse...

Find Now

Stop

New Search

Name	In Folder	S
Readme.txt	C:\WINDOWS\COMMAND\EBD	15
readme.txt	C:\WINDOWS\Desktop	1

2 file(s) found

Tick the box to search subfolders as well.

All the files or folders that match your search criteria are displayed.

Click to call up a dialogue box to choose the folder to look in.

Click to perform a new search. The list of files displayed in the Name box will be cleared.

Checklist

1. Enter the name of the file you wish to find: use the wildcards * and ? if you wish.
2. Tell *Find* where to search in the *Look in* box.
3. Click on the *Find Now* button to start searching. When the file you want is displayed in the window, you can click on the *Stop* button.

Hint

If you want to search across all the system's drives (including on remote networked computers), choose *My Computer* in the *Look in* box.

Date tab

Click on this button to search for files regardless of when they were created, last modified or last accessed.

Click on this button and enter two dates. All files modified between these two dates will be listed in the window.

Click on this button and specify the period during which you believe the files were created.

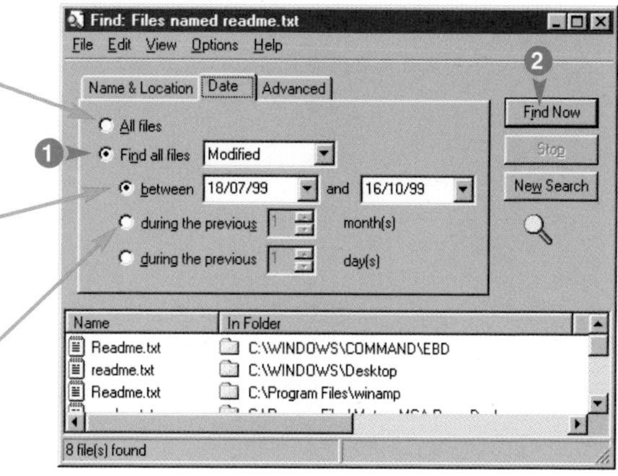

Checklist

1 Click on the *Find all* files button and choose a criterion for the search, based on the date when the file was created, last modified or last accessed.

2 Click the *Find Now* button to start searching. The *Date* criteria are used in conjunction with the criteria set in the other two buttons.

Checklist

1 Enter the type of file you wish to look for.

2 Enter the maximum or minimum size the file should be in order to be selected.

3 Enter a file size.

4 Click on *Find Now* to start the search.

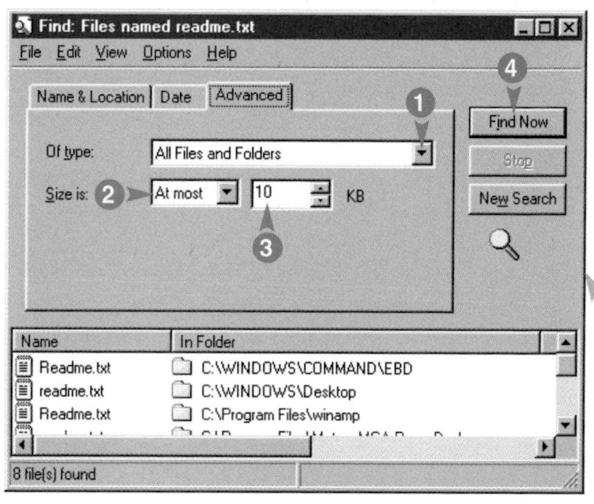

Advanced tab

The Advanced criteria act in conjunction with those specified in the Name & Location, and Date tabs when looking for files and folders.

Choose the At least option in the Size is box and enter a size (in KB) to look for all files with a size equal to or larger than that specified. Or choose At most to look for all files with a size equal to or smaller than that specified.

Tips for successful searching (1)

Enter...	To find
Test.doc	files with exactly this name
*.doc	all files with the extension .doc (whatever their name)
f*.*	all files starting with the letter f (with any extension)
???.doc	all files with a three-letter name and the extension .doc (any name as long as it has only three letters).

Choose *My Computer* to search across all drives in the system (A:, C:, D:, E:, etc.). It will also include all network drives.

Choose *Floppy (A:)* to look in just the A: drive.

Choose *(C:)* to look in the C: drive.

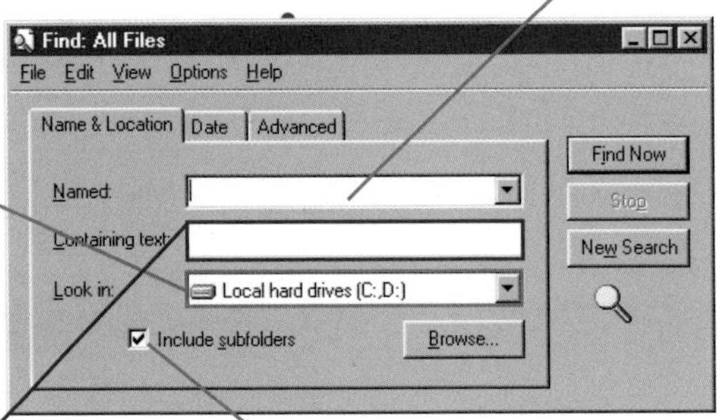

Enter *Report No. 1* in the text box to display a list of all documents (with any extension) in which this string of characters is found.

Clear this box to look only in the root directory or upper-level folder specified.

Tick the box to search subfolders as well.

Tips for successful searching (2)

Click to ignore the file creation or last-modification date. The only search criteria which Find will then use are Name & Location and any options relating to the file contents, type and size.

Enter 03/08/99 in the first text box and 01/11/99 in the second box to look for all files created or modified between 3 August 1999 and 1 November 1999.

Enter 03/08/99 in the second text box to look for all files created or modified before 3 August 1999.

Enter 31/10/99 in the first text box to look for all files created or modified after 31 October 1999.

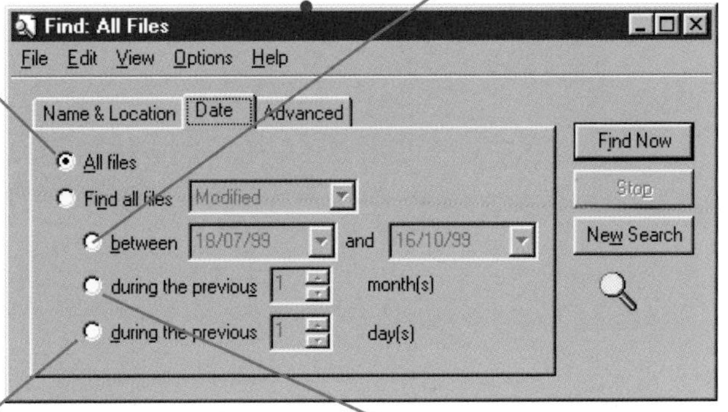

Enter 30 in the text box to look for all files created or modified during the previous 30 days. If today's date is 31/10/99, it will display all files created or modified between 1/10/99 and 31/10/99.

Enter 2 in the text box to look for all files created or modified during the previous 2 months. If today's date is 1/11/99, it will display all files created or modified between 1/9/99 and 1/11/99.

Tips for successful searching (3)

Select *All Files and Folders* to search through all file types.

Choose *Microsoft Word Document* to search for all files created with the Word wordprocessor.

Click on *Icon* to look for all file types containing icons (files with the *.ico* extension).

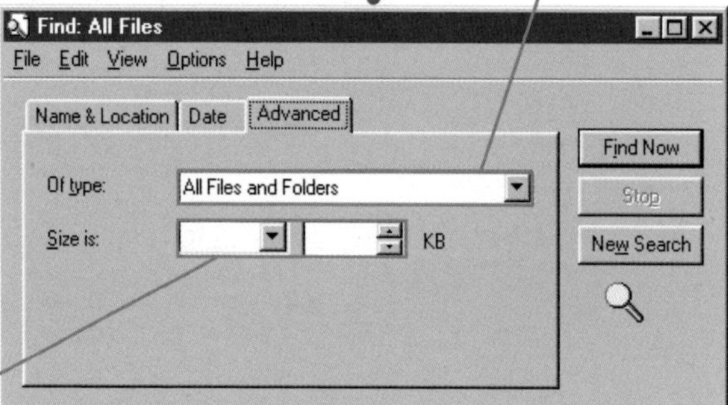

Select *At least* and enter *50* in the text box to list all files with a size of 50 kB or more.

Select *At most* and enter *100* in the text box to list all files under 100 kB in size.

Chapter 6

Windows 98 and the Internet

Connection to the Internet

Start / Programs / Accessories / Communications / Dial-Up Networking

Before you can start surfing the Internet, you will need a connection via an Internet Service Provider (ISP). The number of these is growing daily, and you can find a local one (almost) anywhere. When you sign the rental contract (ie when you pay), you will be given explanations and full details of the server through which you access the Internet.

The basic information you need to connect to the Internet is a user name (eg jsmith), a password (eg ijf89we) and an e-mail address (eg beta@imaginet.co.uk). Your ISP will also give you some technical information about the server itself: a telephone number to call, the type of network protocol used, how to assign an IP address, and DNS server addresses. You'll need all this information when you try to access the Internet for the first time.

Windows 98 supplies a wizard dialogue box to guide you through the process of entering these settings.

HOW TO

There are two ways to get to the Dial-Up Networking folder:

Click in turn on Start, Programs, Accessories, Communications and Dial-Up Networking.

Open My Computer and double-click on the Dial-Up Networking icon.

TIP

If you can't find the Dial-Up Networking folder in My Computer, you'll have to install it yourself from the Windows 98 CD-Rom. Open Control Panel and double-click on the Add/Remove Programs icon. In the Add/Remove Programs Properties box, click on the Windows Setup tab, then on Communications in the Components list. Click on the Details button, and then put a tick in the Dial-Up Networking box. Finish by clicking OK twice.

The first thing you do is to use the *Make New Connection* icon in the special *Dial-Up Networking* folder which Windows installs by default in *My Computer*. The Wizard will walk you step by step through identifying the modem through which you'll connect and the telephone number to dial to access the server. Then, you can specify the server's particular settings in the connection created by Windows.

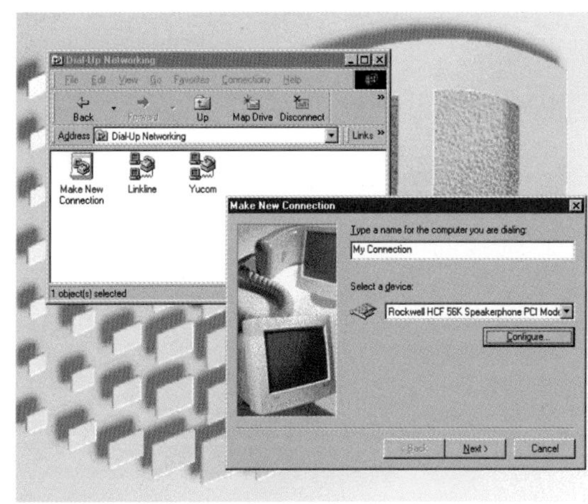

Make New Connection Wizard

Checklist

1. Enter a name in the *Type a name for the computer you are dialling* text box. When your connection is set up, Windows 98 will create a new icon in the *Dial-Up Networking* folder with this name. You will only be able to connect to the Internet by clicking on this icon.
2. Enter the modem you want to use to connect. Click on the arrow and select it from the scrolling list.
3. Click on Next to move to the next screen.

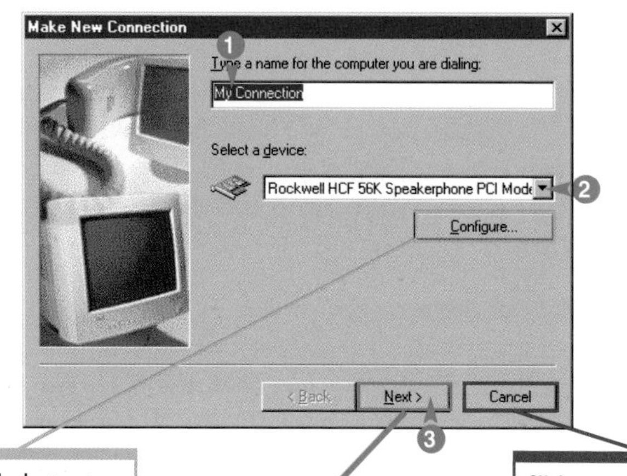

Click on the button to configure the modem.

Click to cancel the operation.

Clicking on the Configure button lets you enter specific settings for your modem to connect to the Internet. Windows 98 calls up a Properties dialogue box with General, Connection and Options tabs.

To identify the server, enter:

1. The area code for the server's telephone number.

2. The server's telephone number.

3. The country code.

Items 1 and 3 can be chosen from a drop-down menu.

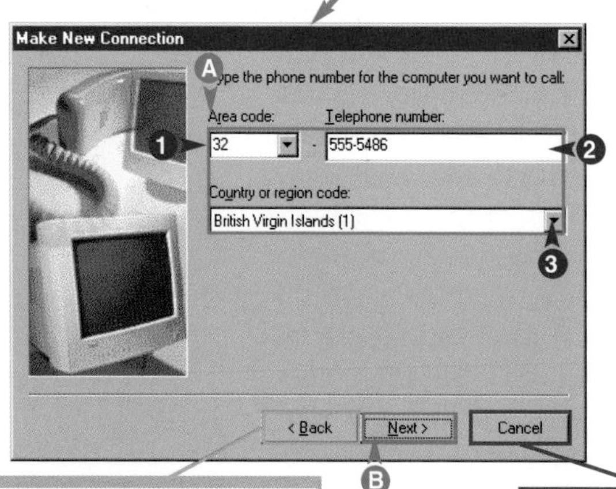

Click to go back to the previous Wizard dialogue box.

Click to cancel the operation.

- A. Enter the server's area code and telephone number. Your ISP will supply you with this information.
- B. Click on the *Next>* button to finish setting up the connection. Windows 98 will automatically add a new icon to the *Dial-Up Networking* folder with the name you entered in the first dialogue box.

Checklist

1. Right-click on the icon created by the *Make New Connection Wizard* in the *Dial-Up Networking* folder: a context menu pops up. Choose the *Properties* command to call up a dialogue box with the connection name. The *General* tab displays the information you entered through the *Make New Connection Wizard*.
2. Change the telephone number in the *Telephone number* box.
3. Change the modem used to connect in the *Connect using* drop-down list.
4. Click on the *Configure* button to change the modem's settings.
5. Click *OK* to confirm your choices.

Information about the server

Properties command / General tab

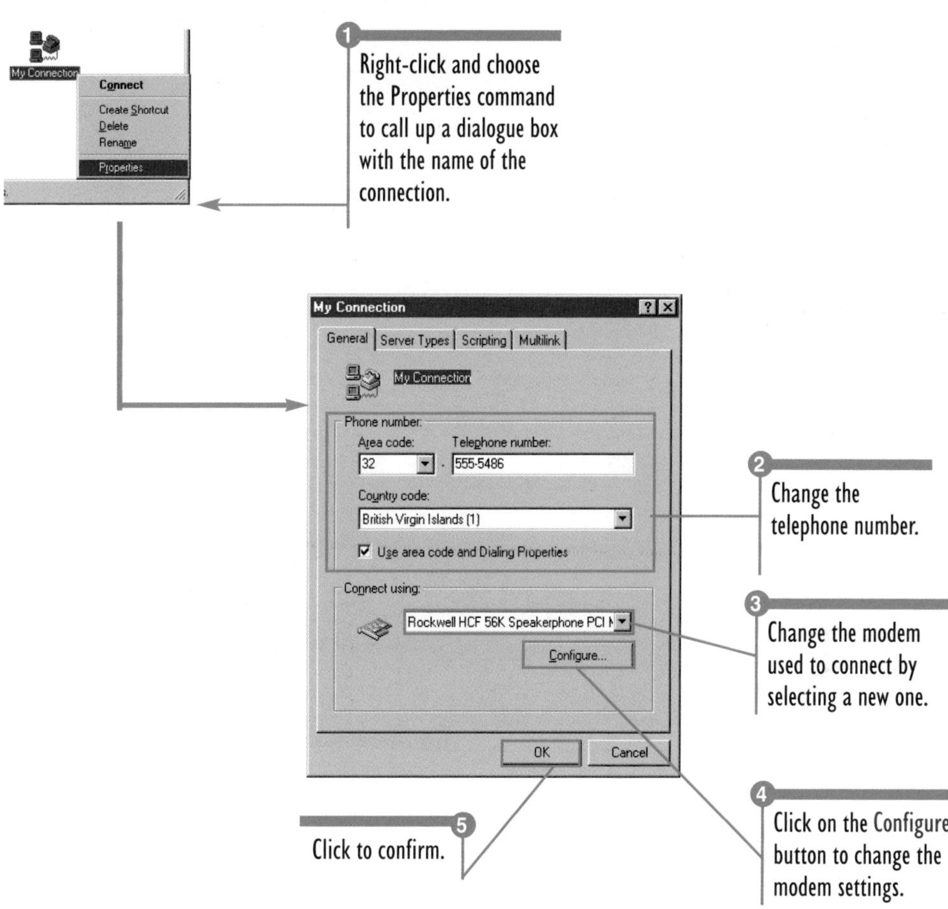

Specifying protocols and their settings

Properties command / Server Types tab

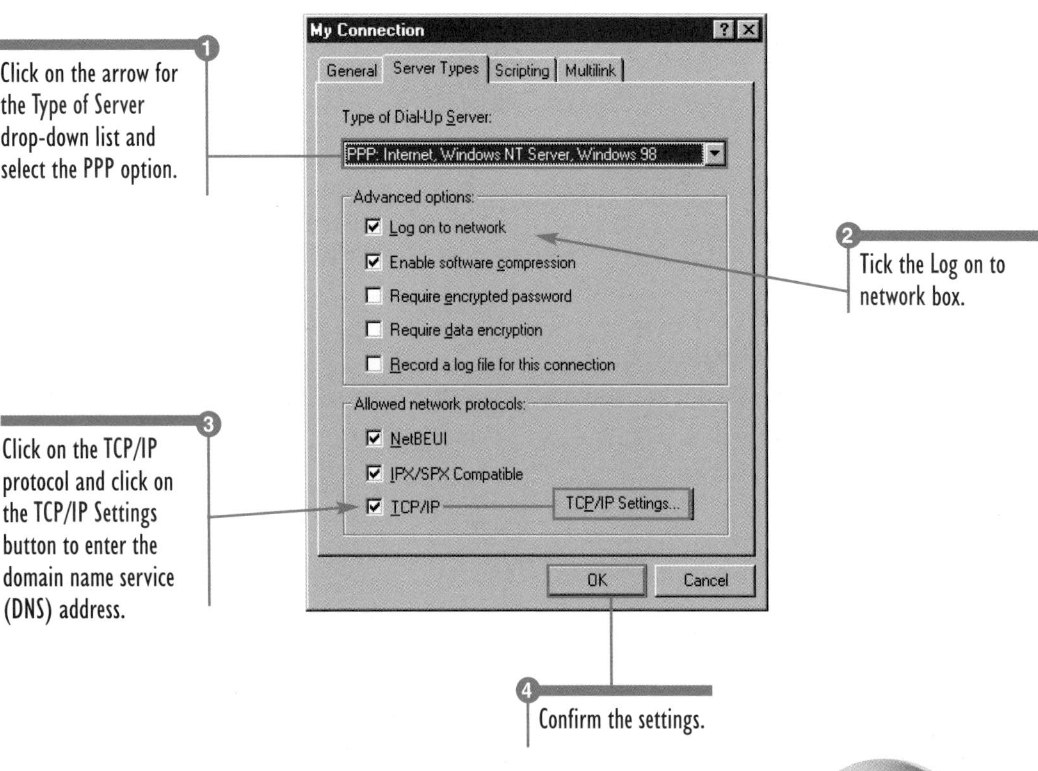

The settings described in this section are just to give you an idea. They will apply for some service providers, but you should always follow the information given by your own ISP. Most ISPs will also provide you with an installation program which will set up your connection for you.

Checklist

1. Click on the arrow for the *Type of Dial-Up Server* drop-down list and select the option *PPP: Internet, Windows NT Server, Windows 98;* this is the type of server you are accessing.

2. Tick the *Log on to network* box and clear the ticks from the other two option boxes shown in the illustration opposite.

3. Click on the *TCP/IP* protocol and click on the *TCP/IP Settings* button to enter the domain name service (DNS) server addresses (main and alternate) as four digits.

4. Click *OK* to confirm the settings.

How do I get to a site?

Once you have set up your dial-up networking connection, you can try to actually get onto the Internet. Double-click on the connection icon to call up a *Connect To* dialogue box. Enter your user name in the first text box, then your password and tick the *Save password* and *Connect automatically* boxes for Windows 98 to save your password (it won't ask for it again) and make the connection when you double-click.

To get to a site, you need to enter an address in the form *http://www.marabout.com* (for example). Windows 98 gives you an address bar to type it in. Press the *Enter* key to confirm, and the system will search for the site and display it on screen. You can display the address bar in any folder. But even better is to use a purpose-designed navigator (like *Netscape Communicator* or *Internet Explorer*).

As well as the address bar, you can also use the *Run* dialogue box that pops up when you click on *Start/Run*. Enter an address in the *Open* text box and confirm by clicking *OK*. Windows 98 will run the navigator and display the site's home page.

HOW TO

To display the address bar in a folder, select the View/Toolbars/Address bar command or right-click on the menu bar and select the Address bar command.

To call up the Run dialogue box, select the Start/Run command, or press the Windows + R keys.

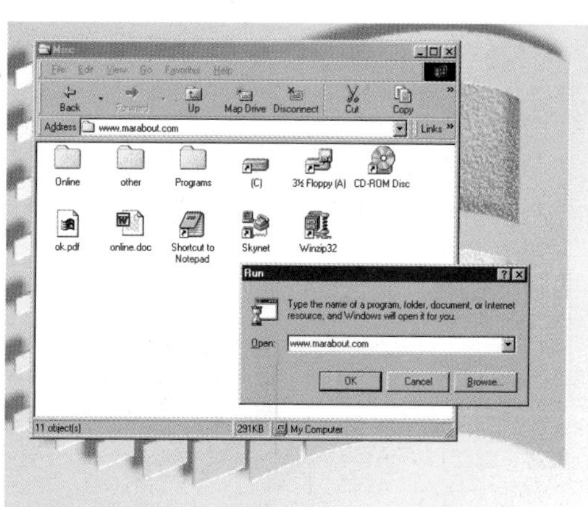

Getting to a site

Address bar and Run dialogue box

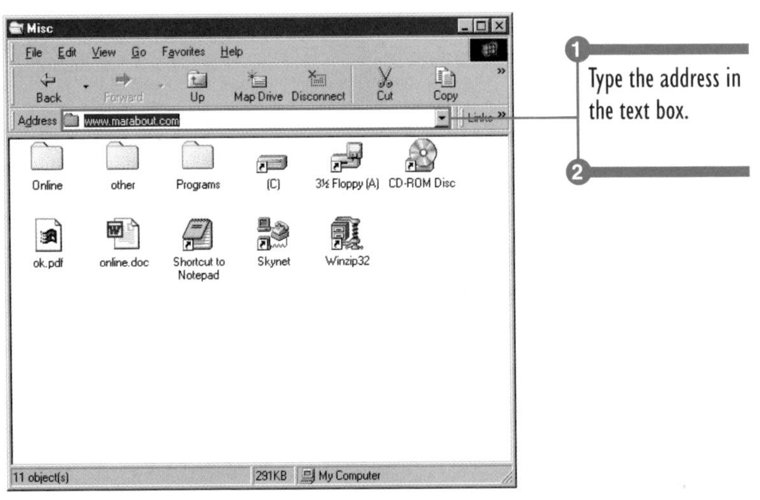

1 Type the address in the text box.

2

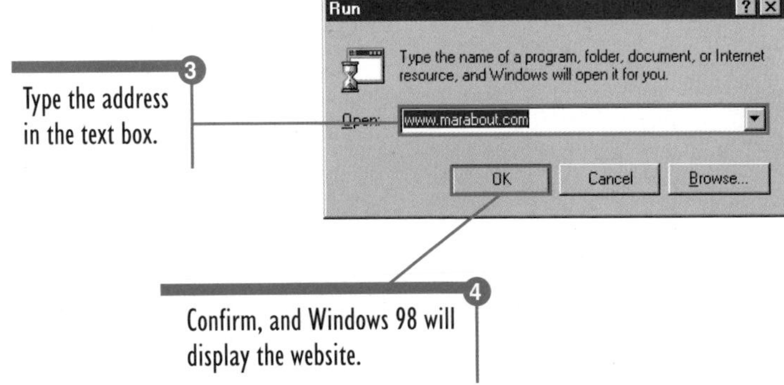

3 Type the address in the text box.

4 Confirm, and Windows 98 will display the website.

Checklist

Using the Address bar:

1. Type the address in the text box. You don't need to include the prefix *http://* because Windows 98 puts that in automatically. Windows 98 remembers all the addresses you enter in this box, and so the next time you enter the same address, Windows 98 will display the full address after you have typed in a few characters.

2. Press *Enter* to confirm; Windows 98 will display the site's home page if it finds it.

Or, using File/Run:

3. Type the address in the text box, but without the prefix *http://*. Remember, Windows 98 stores each new address you enter.

4. Click *OK* to confirm; Windows 98 will display the website.

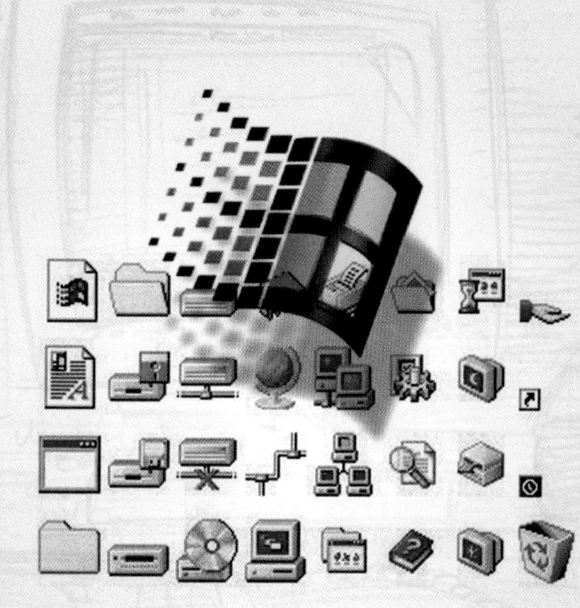

Glossary

ActiveX

Technology developed by Microsoft for Internet Explorer to run applets (Java applications) directly on the browser. ActiveX applications can be integrated in HTML and developed in Visual Basic. ActiveX thus occupies a strategic place in all applications created for the Web.

Autoexec.bat

One of the startup configuration files of MS-DOS. This file contains the commands which are activated automatically when the computer is started. It can be edited easily with any word processor that can save in ASCII.

BIOS

Basic Input/Output System

A basic program that acts as a buffer between the computer and the operating system. BIOS makes the link between the hardware, the operating system and the application. BIOS is started every time the computer is switched on, and loaded in ROM (Read Only Memory). For this reason it is often called ROM BIOS. Several companies today specialise in BIOS, and so updates are readily available on the Internet.

bps

Bits per second

Unit of measure for a data transfer rate, i.e. the number of bits transmitted on a transmission line per second. This measure indicates the baud rate (data transmission rate) of a modem.

DMA channel

Direct Memory Access channel

Channel for accessing memory directly without any intervention from the microprocessor, accelerating thus the interchanges between the computer's programs and peripherals.

Config.sys

One of the configuration files of MS-DOS containing the command lines for the drivers of peripherals. It is an ASCII file which can be edited with any word processor. A basic file for starting PCs, it is executed when a PC is started.

Driver

Specific program that controls a peripheral. Most drivers are supplied with Windows, but some manufacturers have specific drivers that have to be installed when the peripheral is connected.

FAT

File Allocation Table

Allocation table used by the operating system to locate files on the disk. A file is not stored all in one piece. It is first exploded into groups of sectors. Each of these groups is then stored independently and the whole is dispersed on the disk. This allocation table is managed in 16 or 32 bits (FAT 16 or FAT 32).

Hayes

Name of a set of modem commands developed by Hayes Microcomputer Products and now considered the de facto standard. These commands are also referred to as 'AT' commands, because they all start with the AT (Attention) signal. For example:

ATA Pick up the phone.
ATD! Redial last number.
ATZ Initialise modem.

HTTP

HyperText Transmission Protocol

Transfer protocol for hypertext pages on the Web. This is the code indicated to access a Web page from a browser. Example: http://www.microsoft.com

Interrupt number

The number of a sub-program run as a matter of priority at the request of a microprocessor, a peripheral or a program.

MIDI

Musical Instrument Digital Interface

Standard communication protocol for links between computers and electronic musical instruments. The **GENERAL MIDI** standard comprises a set of rules for managing sound cards.

MS-DOS

The first operating system for PCs, developed by Microsoft. Although Windows 98 is itself an operating system, **MS-DOS** is indispensable for starting the computer and for solving certain problems.

Plug and Play

Technology thanks to which every such add-in board inserted in or peripheral connected to a computer is immediately recognised and installed. In other words, under Windows 98, a Plug and Play peripheral will be operational immediately.

Plug-in

A small additional program installed on a software item to enhance its performance or add new features. This program is actually added to, and becomes an integral part of, the basic software.

Protocol

Rules governing the interchange of information in telecommunications. Some protocols are used for error correction, others for compression, transmission or communications. To operate in a network, the computers connected to that network must use the same protocols.

Proxy server

A computer that sits between a user's computer and the server computer. It carries out an operation on behalf of the user. In some systems, the proxy server saves loading time (it acts as a buffer) or protects the network by filtering incoming and outgoing requests (ie it acts as a filter).

Resolution

The number of pixels displayed on a screen. The larger the number of pixels, the higher the resolution. For monitors, this resolution is usually 640 x 480, 800 x 600 or 1024 x 768.

Resource

A resource (human, hardware or software) required to carry out a task. The resources of an IT system are the computer (and its components) and the peripherals connected to it. The software resources are the programs installed on the computer. The program resources are the elements of the program made available to the user: dialogue box, fonts, etc.

ROM

Read-Only Memory

Refers to memory that can be read but not modified. A program written in ROM cannot therefore be altered. Some ROMs can be modified by the user, but are then called EPROM.

TCP/IP

Transmission Control Protocol/Internet Protocol

Communication protocol on the Internet. The TCP/IP is a client/server protocol with the distinguishing feature of being both software- and hardware-independent. It is a set of programs for direct connections (Telnet), file transfers (FTP), e-mail (SMTP), newsgroups (NMTP), etc. TCP/IP is the only protocol used on the network. So every connection to the Internet requires a TCP/IP connection first. TCP/IP is delivered as standard in Windows 98.

Index

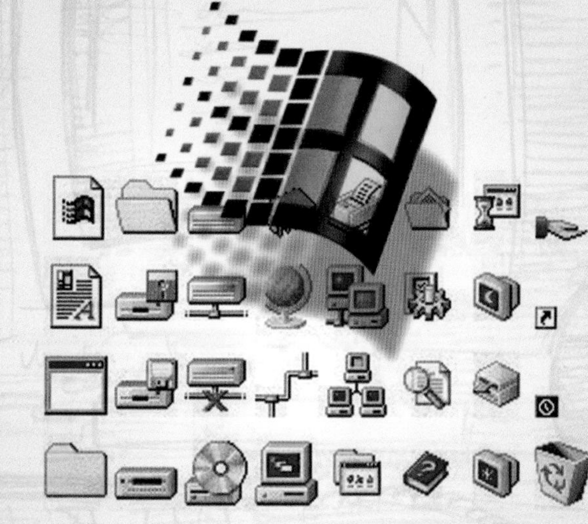

Index

D

E

F

G, H

I

J, K

L, M

N

O

P, Q

R

S

T

V, W